THE ETHICS OF KNOWLEDGE CREATION

Methodology and History in Anthropology

Series Editors:

David Parkin, Fellow of All Souls College, University of Oxford

David Gellner, Fellow of All Souls College, University of Oxford

THE ETHICS OF KNOWLEDGE CREATION

Transactions, Relations and Persons

Edited by
Lisette Josephides and Anne Sigfrid Grønseth

berghahn
NEW YORK · OXFORD
www.berghahnbooks.com

First published in 2017 by

Berghahn Books

www.berghahnbooks.com

Library of Congress Cataloging-in-Publication Data

A C.I.P. cataloging record is available from the Library of Congress

British Library Cataloguing in Publication Data

A catalogue record for this book is available from the British Library

Printed on acid-free paper

ISBN 978-1-78533-404-7 hardback
ISBN 978-1-78533-405-4 ebook

CONTENTS

**Part III: Bioethics, Bio-politics and Humanity beyond the
            Local**

ILLUSTRATIONS

Figures

Table

THE ETHICS OF KNOWLEDGE CREATION

TRANSACTIONS, RELATIONS AND PERSONS

Anne Sigfrid Grønseth and Lisette Josephides

Introduction

This volume is concerned with tackling questions of increasing complexity in today's society, as it deals with the foundations, the ethics, and the deployment of knowledge, all so crucial to human lives. In a sense, all human endeavour and striving involves ethical concerns. These concerns have always been implicitly, and in the last decade more explicitly, addressed in anthropological research. By focusing on the ethics of knowledge creation, relations of knowledge and knowledge deployment, the current volume employs and develops novel conceptions that contribute to the understanding of ethical concerns. As part of this process, the volume aims to demonstrate how studies of relations and transactions of knowledge can stimulate an ethical concern that may encourage respect for human individuality, diversity and reciprocity. Moreover, in emphasizing the relations and commitments through which people create knowledge, the volume also contributes to philosophical debates about common humanity. Thus the various chapters all offer insights into how the relations and transaction of knowledge unavoidably deal with ethics: the ways we live together and treat and see each other. From this perspective, we propose to explore knowledge as an extension and a product of human persons and relations, making this volume as much about the creation of knowledge as about ethics.

Our concern with human affinity, as it essentially includes difference, is reflected in how we explore the ethics of knowledge creation as always being embedded in a complex web of relations between people distinctly positioned within social and material structures, cultural values and meanings. How these relations affect and interact in the creation, communication, management and deployment of knowledge is necessarily always an ethical issue. These relations also continuously affect the recognition and decision of what is 'valuable knowledge' in a given context of interaction at different levels, scales and places at different times, and how 'value' may be affected by 'legitimacy'.

The call for respect and tolerance for human difference and individual direction for one's own life-course (as knowledge may offer substantial gains but also considerable losses) recognizes how transnational, global and nation state networks and institutions, guide, control and govern how and what kind of knowledge is valued, created, distributed and managed (see Rabinow 2003; Strathern 2005). As international and national state-regulated conventions, laws and agreements increasingly tend to reach into, define and shape people's and individuals' day-to-day lives, the issues of the kind and content of knowledge, how it is created, transacted and imparted, or kept back, is of crucial ethical concern and vital for people's and individuals' power to voice concerns of their own that affect important areas of their lives, such as material and social security, reproduction, identity, health and well-being.

Individually and in concert the chapters draw attention to a growing tendency for a more uniform and universalizing transnational regulation of knowledge creation and ethical approaches. Concurrently, an increasing movement between nation states of culturally and sociopolitically diverse people both supports and disputes the ethics and usefulness of such uniformity.[1] The chapters in Part I of the volume show how fieldworkers are governed in part by personal and cultural morality and institutional ethics, which they may challenge and attempt to transgress through their subjectivity and imagination (Grønseth, Bacchiddu and Kohn). This approach demonstrates how knowledge sometimes needs to be created in an open and unforeseen space between the negotiating parties (fieldworker and informants), which cannot be encapsulated by standardized regulations and guidelines.

Part II reaches beyond the self and other relations as they are discussed in Part I, focusing on how 'indirect' fieldwork or the fieldworker as a third party deals with data not only from within, but also (and even more so) beyond the interpersonal encounters. The two chapters here show that there is no easy way in which the fieldworkers can transfer or deploy knowledge from the field as conveyed by their informants or received by the audiences (Huttunen and Bradley). Part III, on the other hand, moves beyond both one-to-one and mediated relations, and places published reports, texts and statements and their interaction with a public audience population as a new set of relations to be analysed by the investigator. While demonstrating how an imagined community is guided by the state and commercial agents, the chapters in this section further discuss the ethics of knowledge itself, as they in different ways ponder the responsibilities and consequences that follow from acquiring the knowledge or cultivating the kinds of selves required for knowledge (Finkler, Melhuus and Josephides).

Following the flow from investigating one-to-one relations, mediated fieldwork, and public documentation and population, the volume demonstrates the need to recognize knowledge as inseparable from the persons involved in the creation and employment of it. Thus, globalization and the movement of people do not point in a uniform direction, but they underscore the humanity of knowledge, as it contains similarity and difference and universality and particularity all at the same time (Appadurai 1996, 2001; Beck 1992; Eriksen 2013).

In what follows we first discuss how we see ethical knowledge as appearing in lacunae between what we frame as 'state practices' and 'social practices', since we argue that it is attached to relations and persons. Following this view, and secondly, we tease out two kinds of management of knowledge; one of 'regard' and one of 'disregard'. Here we argue that an emphasis on the ethics of knowledge creation can resist the claim that the human condition bears the traits of 'bare life', and instead offer a juncture that can point towards freedom, equality and well-being. In the third section we discuss the creation of knowledge as an ethical practice in which one is willing to stretch one's capacities towards a practice where means and ends are the same. We then transgress somewhat against the usual moral stance of anthropology and ask what it means for ethics to be seen as an attribute of persons. Fourth, we examine the process of knowledge creation and discuss how the chapters display relations and transactions of knowledge that together offer a view of ethics as relations and practice. Fifth, we argue that the process of knowledge creation can transgress against the practice of fieldwork and writing anthropological texts as we underscore the ethnographer's continual engagement with the field, and stress how researchers engage in knowledge creation, seen as a process in understanding self and Other in a shared social human world. In conclusion, we highlight how the anthropological knowledge created is never fully complete or neutral, as it is always part of relations and persons with responsibilities and commitments.

In a Lacuna:
Knowledge as Attached to Relations and Persons

By focusing on the ethics of knowledge creation, we suggest in this volume that tensions between human similarities and differences appear in what we identify as 'state practices' and 'social practices' of knowledge creation. State practices are seen as the need to oversee ethical knowledge creation by governmental laws, regulations and programmes that define and direct what kind of knowledge is pursued, how it is pursued and by whom, who has access to it and is able to impart it, and from whom it is withheld. Social practices are seen as ethical knowledge created in transactions and engagements with communities and face-to-face relations, regulated and directed by human capacities for empathy, imagination, affinity and solidarity. In linking state and social practices of ethical knowledge creation, we find lacunae that we suggest result from state practices being insufficiently based in ethical relations in the community and a face-to-face level of social practices. In these lacunae we can detect the lack of appreciation of how knowledge is always (both in commission and omission) attached to individual persons and populations dealing with issues of life-course concern, such as their senses of agency, self, identity, belonging and well-being (see Grønseth 2013).

Within a variety of research disciplines and professional services, knowledge is created that is not always imparted to the actual persons who were involved in the relations and transactions that created the knowledge, or who might be seriously affected by the knowledge. Thus, the knowledge created remains as what we call a hidden 'substantial or technical knowledge' to be used in accordance with and as instructed by politically defined purposes, and not as 'social knowledge' open and available for everyone's use. This, we suggest, is a concern at all levels of knowledge creation: knowledge created within one-to-one relations and/or indirect and mediated fieldwork and professional practices, and, most prevalent, in policy documents and reports.

Recognizing how knowledge is often withheld from open access and use, it appears that when engaging in processes of creating substantial/technical knowledge we learn foremost about how to gain knowledge – as a kind of discipline – and not about the knowledge itself. Thus the process, we suggest, becomes knowledge about how to gain knowledge. But why do we create knowledge that is not used by or released to the larger public or the actual persons who are affected by the knowledge? What is the use of learning to know how to know, when the knowledge itself is not available and imparted? Such questions are problematic, as we acknowledge that some knowledge may be the by-product of other knowledge, or its very value may depend on its limited dissemination. Furthermore, the potentiality of knowledge to inspire certain kinds of action may make it dangerous in some people's hands, or it may simply open the way for action that goes against conventional or accepted morals. Considering such views, we underscore how we see the process of knowledge production to become ethical or unethical at the moment knowledge is withdrawn or upheld by people or institutions.

Locating itself within this burgeoning field, the current volume focuses on how knowledge is entangled in relations and engagements between people, including researchers and informants, and emphasizes how such relations and obligations are part of philosophical discussions about a common humanity (see Gaita 1998; Josephides 2008). While not addressing directly the question of how to live an ethical life, or asking about the place of the ethical in human life (Lambek 2010) or how to construct oneself through ethical practices (Rabinow 2003), the volume implicitly engages these debates from a different standpoint. This is a standpoint from which we see knowledge to be an attribute of persons, as Strathern highlights in the Afterword. Included in our approach is an acknowledgement of how knowledge is created, managed and used for specific purposes, though not necessarily always leading to the intended and desired results.

Face-to-Face Transactions, Mediating the Field, Humanity beyond the Local

Given our concern with the ethics of knowledge creation, we emphasize how ethics is part of the human condition. As humans we are always subject to ethics as displayed in the consequences of actions, evaluations, acknowledgements, caring, success and failures, both our own and those of others. Tacit, implicit ethics are concerned here, not related to any single religion or philosophical metaphysics but, as Lambek (2010) points out, the 'ordinary ethics' of everyday life. In turn, the ethics of ordinary life are closely linked to, and often coarsened, in the broader social forces such as professional conduct, human rights, refuge and citizenship, justice, reproduction and bio-technology. As our volume joins what appears to be an 'ethical turn' in theorizing and documenting ethics as central in human life, we push anthropology forward to recognize the ethics of knowledge creation, as it is central for the conditions in which human life is conducted, experienced and lived.[2]

In our focus on ethics as a human dimension, rather than a dis-tinct cognitive, social or cultural compartment of creating knowl-edge, we seek to contribute to and influence anthropological theory. This does not imply ignorance of how ethics in knowledge creation is also always part of history, as in the practices of priests and clerics, the philosophical or professional objectification of ethics, or ethical articulations in modern law and expertise management, as in bioethics. Rather than differentiate a distinct domain or practice of ethics of knowledge creation, we seek to deepen our under-standing of the vast range of steps and aspects that interact when examining the ethics of knowledge creation. Holding that the ethics of knowledge creation is relevant in various domains subject to technological, political and social reflections and interventions, we recognize that it is also articulated in globalized situations or 'global assemblages' (Ong and Collier 2005), which define new material in the form of collective and discursive relationships that reconstitute not only the classical concepts of society, culture and such, but also the reflections and regime of ethical concerns in anthropological and social research (Strathern 2003, 2005, 2006; Kenway and Fahey 2009).

Managing Knowledge:
'Ethics of Regard' and 'Ethics of Disregard'

Considering the vast layers of transacting participants, audiences, employers, interests and regulations that are at stake and interact in the creation of knowledge, we suggest that ethical knowledge creation is part of two different kinds of ethics: 'ethics of regard' and 'ethics of disregard'. An ethic of regard, we propose, is based on engagement in face-to-face relations of respect and equality in which knowledge is transacted and becomes the source for knowledge creation. We hasten to note that not all face-to-face relations are based on respect and equality, but may instead lead to discrimination and suppression. However, when knowledge is created without recognizing its source, or without entering ethically grounded relations of regard, it becomes necessary to make laws and regulations that advise on how to impart and deploy the knowledge. In this perspective, knowledge created outside an ethic of engaged face-to-face relations (which may or may not be based on respect) can be seen as created within an ethic of disregard that relies on controlling the knowledge by institutional or state regulations. Moreover, when applying regulations there is a need to employ judgement, which is not always factual, honest, or truthful to lived life. Thus we suggest that state practice, as it is seen to be founded on an ethic of disregard, might turn out to serve interests that groups and individuals feel do not respond to concerns of their everyday lives with their critical moments of misfortune, rupture or serious illness. However, we ask if judgement is not also in use in the ethics of regard. How to judge whether attachments are good or bad is complex (see Latour 2004).

Considering how ethics is meant to guide how we treat each other in face-to-face relations as well as in the politics of constituting the social structures we live within, we suggest that the distinction between an ethic of regard and an ethic of disregard is a fruitful one in responding to Agamben's concept of 'bare life' (1998). We understand bare life to be a human condition, which lies, as Ziarek (2008) points out, between the biological *zoe* and the political *bios* (Arendt 1998 [1958]), or between 'mere life' and 'good life' (Aristotle 1998, book I, chapter 2:10). Mere life, Agamben says, 'is not simply natural reproductive life, the *zoe* of Greeks, nor *bios*' but rather 'a zone of indistinction and continuous transition between man and beast' (1998: 109). Underlining the flexibility of the position of being in between, we suggest the ethics of regard and disregard afford an entry at various junctures along the continuum and serve as an avenue for an eventuality of freedom and equality.

Bare life is not *zoe*, it is life wounded, expendable, endangered, calling to mind Adorno's reference to the effects of sovereign violence, stripped of political significance and any specific form of life (Ziarek 2008: 90). Bare life is double, as it is excluded from the *polis*, while simultaneously it is included by way of exclusion and exposed to unlimited violation. Recognizing this hidden incorporation of bare life within *polis*, the human condition of modern democracies is, according to Agamben, characterized by being subject to sovereign power while at the same time claiming individual human rights and liberties. While not engaging further with the implications that follow, we declare for a need to resist the imposition of a human condition bearing the traits of bare life, and offer the ethics of knowledge creation as a fruitful alternative.

However, when we as scholars in qualitative research settings set up and engage in face-to-face relations that make knowledge apparent, or make new knowledge, how are these creations different from the state-regulated creation of knowledge? Cannot also a social practice of knowledge creation founded in ethics of regard serve interests that are not in tune with the informants' everyday life concerns? These quandaries are most apparent in Part I of the book in which an ethic of regard in terms of face-to-face interviews and participant observations make the starting point for acquiring knowledge. The chapters recognize a reflection on the social position and situatedness of the interviewer, which can affect motivations and serve as incentive for research interpretations and knowledge creation. They also reflect on the relation with the informants and on the informant herself or himself being an investigator on her or his own terms; a reflection of the informants as equal, fully social and moral persons. Thus, the chapters of Part I make an attempt to understand the lives of others as persons that are explorers in their own lives; a perspective we suggest offers the informant a chance to resist oppression and the structures of bare life.

In being loyal to Papushpa's exploration of her life within the strict control of her father and family, Grønseth reflects on how it challenged her own moral stand, thus offering a space for negotiating Papushpa's life concerns. Experiencing a different but similar control, Bacchiddu learnt about the Apiao and the adoptees only when her investigation became a practice of 'doing difference', while she entered the field attuned to equality and sameness. With reference to four different field sites, Kohn came to recognize that each field site required a distinct approach, as she realized that her ethically based preparations for the field needed adjustments. Kohn's chapter can be seen to sum up the three chapters when she argues that the ethics of fieldwork lie in the actual practice itself; a practice of relations between differently situated investigating persons (researcher and informants). Acknowledging the complexities in plural motivations, interests and powers lying within and between the informant and researcher, we argue for a need to stimulate a research practice – an ethic of regard – attuned to the concerns of the everyday life of the Other, and as such stimulate opposition against degradation, oppression and sovereign powers.

Considering the institutional and state-regulated knowledge creation within an ethic of disregard, the determination of ethics leads to regulations in which the state or institution declares that it is acting in the best interests of the society or institution. Even so, it remains

to be seen how and when it accords with particular groups' and individuals' interests. This issue is discussed in particular in Part III. First,
Finkler shows how the personalized genetic testing in the United States
is linked to developments in the medical field and the cultural values
of individual autonomy and self-knowledge, but 'passes over' how the
same knowledge interferes in and affects people's lives in ways they
are not consciously aware of, thus 'stripping' them in terms of political life. In a similar vein Melhuus teases out the ethical complexities
of how Norwegian cultural values are made into mandates for ethical
correctness, while she discusses how such ethics serve or do not serve
the interests of individual lives.

The chapters in Part II deal with issues 'in between', or rather
the overlaps of the ethics of regard and disregard, as the researcher
herself is highlighted as a kind of third party. Huttunen describes the
complicated layers of individual, professional and global relations she
is brought into when she is asked to act as an intermediary on behalf
of a Bosnian refugee in psychotherapy, and ponders the issue of how
to handle such complex and intermingled interests. Bradley's chapter
similarly offers a reflection on the unease of making use of local fieldworkers within the dictates of a larger research programme, running
the risk of endangering living life.

In this complex interrelation between ethics of knowledge creation
within engaged face-to-face relations, and state regulations carried
out with reference to judgement, we see a question of the viability of
the knowledge created. The question relates to the issue of the 'sound-
ness of the foetus', so to speak. In assessing viability, we see a need to
ask: What are the practical implications of the knowledge created,
and for whom? How does the new knowledge make everyone more
capable of dealing with their life concerns? What possibilities does the
new knowledge add to everyone's life-course and well-being?

As the distinct chapters and the volume as a whole demonstrate,
such questions are not easily answered, and we offer no check list to
tick off and be satisfied that 'ethics has been taken care of'. Rather, we
underline that it is in the query itself that the issue of ethics appears,
as it is in the process of transacting, managing and creating knowledge that ethics – of regard and disregard – becomes as animated and
complex as life itself. As the volume displays a variety of fields of relations, we become aware, as Strathern observes in the Afterword, how
we tend to see knowledge as a kind of information and data attained
or kept by others. Recognizing a need to reach beyond knowledge
as such a Europe-American kind of objectified object we call for not
only contextualization in terms of history, culture and politics, but

an awareness of the person, as we realize that 'Knowing and knower may be more or less distinctive or convergent, but exist for each other' (Strathern in Afterword). Thus, the ethics of knowledge creation is flexible and contextual, not to be defined or placed once and for all but following the flow of relations between persons within distinct cultural and social systems and structures and resisting the production of bare life.

Creation of Knowledge as Ethical Practice

Stretching One's Capacities

This volume takes a position in which we see ethics as telling us about knowledge as it is negotiated, managed, distributed and challenged by judgements, ideologies and genealogies in shifting social and cultural contexts. Our contemporary world is characterized by an increasing degree of formalized ethical considerations, boards, standards and guidelines, shaping not only global and local trade, business, and political agendas and activities, but also social and anthropological research. In addition, there are strong political demands on research to contribute with concrete social impact and interventions. Together, these are forces that set frames for the kind of knowledge researchers create and the lives we live both globally and locally.

When referring to the terms 'ethical' or 'ethics' these are not easily disentangled from 'moral' or 'moralities'. Rather than deciding for a priori assumptions about what is moral in terms of conventional norms or principle values considered as 'good', 'right' or 'generous', social scientists commonly explore how what is said and done by people in everyday life is made sense of a posteriori (Das 2010; Fassin 2012), thus an inductive approach. Traditionally, philosophers tend to confirm morality as culturally bound values, while ethics is seen as an overarching and philosophical theme. However, more recent anthropologists are inclined to use the terms interchangeably (Fassin 2012: 6). Among anthropologists, there is no common trend. While some anthropologists establish a difference, others do not attach any importance to such a possible difference.

However, which stand one takes reflects different understandings of subjectivities and subjectivation as social processes. During the last decades of the twentieth century, anthropologists have focused on subjectivities as traditional, based on the assumption that moral norms and values govern collective and individual behaviour (Edel

1962; Pocock 1986). More recently, anthropologists have called for a focus on how ethical practices result from social agency (Fassin 2012). As Didier Fassin notes (2012: 6), this implies on the one hand an understanding of moral norms as dominating and not leaving initiative to individuals (Laidlaw 2002), and on the other hand an ethical subjectivation engaged by social agents through technologies of the self (Faubion 2011). Even though the two views share the same call for an ethical stance (rather than moral), they differ in that the one sees individuals as free ethical agents, and the other sees a genealogy of ethics. Thus, depending on the view taken, morals and ethics, or morality and ethic, can be regarded as indistinctive or distinctive.

Our volume does not primarily engage with morals or ethics 'of the Other' as being the interlocutors in the research process. Rather, it grapples with ethics in the relations of knowledge creation. However, it still engages a critical debate of ethics. It does so as the chapters across the three parts underline a need for not taking for granted our common sense of 'good' and 'bad', 'right' and 'wrong'. Together the chapters highlight how ethics are usually not given a priori but rather interpreted a posteriori by the interlocutors and the anthropologist. In particular, Josephides engages the relationship between knowledge and ethics in four figures of knowers, as she examines the cultivation of the kind of selves required for knowledge in a historical, philosophical and anthropological enquiry. As a whole, the volume addresses the debate of anthropologists as subjects engaged in moral commitment and ethical positions, although not always consciously. Furthermore, the chapters scrutinize the ethical justifications, reasoning and consequences of knowledge as containing descriptions, interpretations and actions in our contemporary world. Thus, we hold that by exploring the relations and creation of knowledge, we always deal with ethical concerns of how we treat each other.

The ethics of knowledge creation are also importantly present in academic exchanges. A recent volume (Josephides 2015a), whose impetus was to recognize the inspirational work of Marilyn Strathern in anthropology and beyond, explored knowledge exchange and the different ways in which knowledge is produced through chapters that developed insights by re-contextualizing aspects of Strathern's work from several perspectives: vis-à-vis the studied people in the field, in relation to knowledge production and academia and in relationships with fellow anthropologists. These investigations brought into focus the requirements and obligations of knowledge in a general way, at the same time as they advanced these themes into new territories. Such theorizations of ethnographic writing, as a form of knowledge grounded in relationships, is well-documented in anthropology. Strathern herself participated in a concluding dialogue that evaluated the research directions inspired by her scholarship, thus taking forward a joint project to a synthesis that suggested new paths and new questions for research (Josephides 2015b).

How we treat each other lies at the very heart of our well-being and everyday life, individually as well as collectively, and speaks directly to the anthropological quest for knowledge about the lives of humans; the human condition. Exploring knowledge creation within the frames of the mundane everyday life reveals ethics that are relatively tacit, as this creation takes place within social relations and practices, which are also inherently emotional and imaginative. When ethical questions become explicit it is generally as a result of ruptures, disputes or renewals (Lambek 2010). In the creation of knowledge, as in research, there are many explicit and formal ethical rules and standards that regulate the researcher's conduct and approach towards her or his field of interest and the relation to the interlocutors or informants. However, during the enquiry and ethnographic fieldwork many ethical concerns may transgress, challenge and dispute such standardized guidelines, while not always offering a certain answer. This is related to how we understand what is 'ethical' in a broad sense, referring to a field of action or practical judgement, rather than to what is good or right (Lambek 2010: 9). Furthermore, we understand 'ethics' in line with Michael Lambek's (2010) comment that it recognizes a complexity and inconsistency in human action and intention, which mostly appears in philosophy and some linguistic or phenomenological oriented ethnography. This approach to ethics is far from moral codes and instructions; rather, it suggests that we have limited self-understanding (Lambek 2010; Nehamas 1998: 67).

Seeing knowledge creation as a kind of practice, it is ethical (as are other practices) as long as the goal is not instrumental but reaching for the best within its practice – and for human good or well-being. The ethical practice implies the willingness to stretch one's capacities, in a sense in which means and ends are one and the same. This is in line with how Hannah Arendt employs 'actuality' as activity that does not pursue an external end, but utilizes the full meaning in the performance itself (1998 [1958]: 206). In a sense, this is the practice of living life for life itself. Thus, ethical knowledge creation is not governed by reaching an instrumental goal, but creating knowledge for the human good. Taking this stand, we recognize that the ethics of knowledge creation are not possible to decide beforehand, as it takes place in the actuality; in the practice of the here and now, as it entails a complex web of power- and social relations, emotions, sensations and imaginations.

The Anthropologist's Ethical Stance

As Wiktor Stoczkowski (2008) points out, anthropology has traditionally sought to ensure social progress (in the West) by means of knowledge. This, Stoczkowski observes, appears for instance in how Edward Burnett Tylor saw studies of our savage past as helping to purify and set new moral codes that would enable social reforms (see Tylor 1871: II, 410). Furthermore, it emerges in how Durkheim (1994 [1912]) believed studies of primitive people contribute to a renovation of our Western culture, and how Lévi-Strauss (2003 [1971]) understood ethnology as transmitting a wisdom to the West that would contribute to a new moral order reconciling us with nature (see Stoczkowski 2008: 347). Together, such understandings imply that the creation of knowledge and social reform were seen as harmonious tasks. This interwoven ambition was present in the 'colonial anthropology' of the 1920s, in the 'applied anthropology' of the 1940s and 1950, and later in the 'critical anthropology' from the 1970s and onwards in terms of reflectively taking on blame and responsibility for Western traditions of imperialism, colonialism, capitalism, racism, nationalism and more, again moving towards a moral purification of the West (Stoczkowski 2008: 348).

In a similar vein, some anthropologists call for moral commitment by empathizing and defending the rights of the oppressed (see for instance Scheper-Hughes 1995), whereas others term such a call as 'moral anxiety' (Faubion 2003). Common to all these approaches is a belief that the fundamentals for knowledge creation match the fundamentals of ethics.

However, this volume focuses on knowledge as an attribute of the (knowing) person, rather than going further into the discussions of knowledge as a means for doing good. In line with this, we propose that knowledge creation takes place in the linkage between not only the local and the non-local, but also (and more fundamentally) in the process of the knowledge seeker becoming a knower (see Josephides this volume; Daston and Galison 2010). Our stress on the linkage between knowledge and person relates to an ethical view of virtue or care for self and humanity.

This approach is in line with the Foucauldian and Aristotelian view in which an action is assessed by the virtuous disposition that underlies the agent's psychology (Fassin 2012: 7) or, as 'the manner

in which one ought to form oneself as an ethical subject acting in reference to the prescriptive elements that make up the code' (Foucault
1990 [1984]: 25–26). In accordance with such a view, this volume
proposes to understand ethics as a process of inner states encouraged
by virtue and care, while also encouraging action. This view has the
additional merit of allowing differentiated ethnographic approaches
that look for general moral codes, or ethical debates understood
through particular situations and contexts.

This understanding differs from the deontological ethics deriving
from Durkheim and Kant in which 'morality is duty plus desire' (Fassin
2012: 7), meaning we are both obliged and inclined to do good. As
Fassin (2012) points out, it is a view in which an action is judged
by respect to the rules or principles that govern the agents, imposed
upon them as a superego. Our understanding also differs from the
ethics of consequence, which assess actions and conducts by their
consequences more than their conformity with existing rules (deontological) or as a result of a particular disposition of the agent (virtue
and care). However, in the lived everyday life that anthropologists
study, the three moral paradigms are often inextricably entangled. The
blurring between political and moral arguments also appears in our
volume, such as in Melhuus' discussion of reproductive technologies,
Finkler's genetic make-up, and less overtly in other chapters.

The Process of Knowledge Creation: Relations, Morals and Ethics

Ethics is part of the human condition, as we are predisposed to feel,
experience, reason, judge and create knowledge within a moral sen-
sibility. Moralities of the general human striving and endeavours on
the one hand, and the obligations or duties and sense of 'ought' on the
other hand, may be seen as a useful distinction (Edel and Edel 1959)
though it may become both too narrow and too wide. However, the
distinction is useful in identifying vital and dynamic interrelationships between values deriving from cosmologies and metaphysics on
the one hand, and the behaviours and practices of everyday life on the
other. This dynamic can be seen as the centrepiece of Howell's collection *The Ethnography of Moralities* (1997), which further addressed
problems of 'doing fieldwork' and 'writing anthropology' as the twin
anthropological methodologies (see also Carrithers 2005). Sharing an
interest in ethnographic methodology, our exploration of the ethics of
face-to-face fieldwork relations stresses the need to recognize, beyond

the verbal and factual, also the tacit, intuitive, intimate, imaginative, emotional and empathic aspects as crucial to the creation of knowledge (see also Grønseth and Davis 2010; Josephides 2008).

Such relational, intersubjective, personal and imaginative capacities involved in the creation of knowledge appear in particular in the chapters of Part I. Reaching out to the Tamil/Norwegian socially isolated teenager Papushpa, Grønseth recognizes how knowledge fundamentally is generated in relations and the imagination. From this perspective, the chapter focuses on how embodiment, engagement and empathic relations attend to the human experience. Thus, Grønseth comes to realize how the subject always holds both a personal and social history, which cannot be fully grasped by symbols or language.

Advancing a field of dangerous knowledge, or the protection of knowledge, Bacchiddu similarly enters the borderlands between self and Other. Taking an approach of silence, Bacchiddu learns by 'doing' among the Apiao people, and attends to the life stories of her informants, the adoptees. From such engaged interpersonal relations, Bacchiddu realizes how she is in a similar position as her informants in terms of seeking 'sameness', while managing a compulsory difference.

Kohn's chapter links to Grønseth's and Bacchiddu's chapters, as she discusses the need to appreciate the researcher's sensitivity and response to the field. Drawing on three distinct fieldwork settings, Kohn argues for the need to reflect on their differences and relations. She becomes aware how each small change in context and relation invokes new questions, methods, transactions and creations of knowledge, which can be overlooked or obstructed by the requirements of institutional ethics review bodies.

Emphasizing ethnographic and anthropological explorations, the volume as a whole is concerned with how knowledge can no longer be restricted to face-to-face relations but must include the effects of technology, global consumption patterns and changing geopolitical configurations (Moore 1996). However, our focus is on the acknowledgement that human beings can access a particularly intense form of intersubjective understanding, and have a rich potential for social forms that are created by the capacity to influence, convince, teach or coax each other, always leading to results that are not given or known in advance (Carrithers 1992, 2009).

Following such an approach, Part II elaborates the unforeseen and unexpected consequences and quandaries of knowledge production. Here, the focus is on how indirect or mediated fieldwork deals with reference not only to interpersonal encounters, but also beyond them. Part II discusses how the fieldworker is captured in the web of her or his relations and social position. In Huttunen's chapter a Bosnian refugee and psychotherapeutic patient invites Huttunen into the therapeutic room and wants his story told to the world as a witness statement to historical events. Reflecting on this encounter, Huttunen discusses how she came to act as a 'hinge' between the confidential stories created in the therapy setting and the social and political stories, and in this move transforms the personal stories into knowledge of collective significance. Similarly, Bradley's chapter discusses how she became the central axis for creating knowledge in a large-scale, multisited and policy-driven project in four different countries (India, Pakistan, Tanzania and Nigeria). While reflecting on the challenges in teaching ethnographic methods to local fieldworkers, she came to a realization of how ethnographic methods create data from differently situated views. The data furthermore offered complexities and contradictions, which did not easily respond to the research programme. Thus while both Huttunen and Bradley discuss the lack of a predictable or straightforward way in which ethnographers can transfer or deploy knowledge from the field, as conveyed by their informants or received by the audiences, they also point towards a complex task of renegotiating moral worlds.

In the large-scale analysis offered in Finkler's chapter, what is questioned is the significance of personalized genetics for individual humans' relations to self, family, kin and society. The knowledge retrieved by the new genetics, Finkler argues, affects our understanding and dealings with privacy and confidentiality, in particular in the field of medicine, as well as in fields that evoke ethical concerns related to property and ownership. Such ethical dilemmas arise when new knowledge about ourselves, our personhoods or our possible future – especially concerning health and sickness – is gained by personal genetic information. In the small-scale analysis given in her chapter, Grønseth highlights how personal moral challenges raise ethical issues of judgement and responsibility. Confronted with her informant's suffering and quest for well-being by complying to her Tamil family's and her father's social control, and being held captive by her promise not to interfere, Grønseth argues for a need to recognize a space for the empathic and imaginative creation of knowledge, acknowledging that one can never completely know oneself or the Other.

However, this volume reaches beyond the research process as such and grapples with ethics of knowledge creation in social and cultural processes at different times, places and scales. We share

Harris's concern in *Ways to Knowledge* (2007) when attending to how knowledge links to practices, skills, experiences, tacit knowledge and meaning, though our interest additionally addresses the significance of the research set-up when engaging in the relations and transactions of knowledge creation. These issues make up the core of Huttunen's and Bradley's chapters. Huttunen discusses how the therapeutic relationship can be a space or 'global form' (Ong and Collier 2005) similar to the truth commissions, in which anthropological enquiry can take place, while she points to the continuous need for contextualization and audience. Bradley examines the difficulties in using untrained local research assistants, in particular when asking them to record informal conversations with people from their own community, in which many were personally well known. While reflecting on ethical concerns in transacting and presenting the view of 'the Other', the chapter also considers how, among some local research assistants, there emerged an increased self-awareness of their own knowledge guiding their everyday life and world view. This is in line with how we seek to discuss the ethics and relations of knowledge creation, as it highlights an appreciation of an equal and conjoined humanity, while also recognizing human ambivalence and sometimes failure in identifying with an exclusive collective, which is freely or forcefully chosen (see also Herzfeld 1995).

From Fieldwork to Ethnographic Writing and Anthropology

In his book on 'Making', Tim Ingold (2013: 4, 5) talks about anthropology and ethnography as antithetical ways of knowing, with the first being 'a transformational space for generous, open-ended comparative and critical enquiry into the conditions and potentials of human life' and the second turning participant observation into qualitative data 'to be analysed in terms of an exogenous body of theory'. While we would argue that ethnography helped create that body of theory, we are drawn to his formulation that knowing is 'understanding in practice', enmeshed with 'making' as an active engagement with the material world (2013: 5). Participant observation, Ingold argues, is a way of knowing 'from the inside', 'because we are already *of* the world' (2013: 5; see also Faubion and Marcus 2009). When we extract 'data' from this existential mode of knowing and present them as knowledge reconstructed from the outside, we set up participant observation as a paradox when it is simply part of dwelling in the world. Arguing otherwise removes us from the world in which we dwell and 'leaves us strangers to ourselves' (Ingold 2013: 5). Understanding fieldwork and ethnography as part of world-dwelling liberates us from 'descriptive fidelity' and opens up 'transformational engagements' with people beyond the settings of fieldwork. This openness acknowledges that the theorist 'makes through thinking' and thus that fieldwork is just part of that process (Ingold 2013: 6).[3]

In the process of the creation of knowledge, then, we recognize how the relations and interface between self and Other are the moment and place in which the researcher transforms field-site experiences into ethnographic writing (Halstead, Hirsch and Okely 2008; Strathern 1991). Other processes of knowledge creation also take place between self and Other, although at different levels. Halstead, Hirsch and Okely (2008) point out how the ethnographer's reflections and scrutiny in the research process are agents that facilitate a certain kind of 'crisis' or transformative process. Grønseth and Davis (2010) argue that the ethnographer's own embodied experiences in the field can attune the ethnographer to an empathic and tacit mode of knowledge that speaks of imparted experiences of everyday life close to how it is felt and lived by the Other.

Acknowledging such a transformative process captures the writing of the 'ethnographic present' in constant change rather than as fixed and unchanging. Thus the discussion of the ethnographic present is addressed here less as writing against or disturbing culture (Abu-Lughod 1991; Gupta and Ferguson 1992; Brightman 1995; Kuper 1999) and more as escaping ordinary historical categories while being informed by the anthropologist's continual involvement with the field. This view is in line with the volume's appreciation of the researchers' continual engagement as part of the anthropological practice of fieldwork and writing, although we underscore the need for an explicit discussion of ethical involvement that recognizes a responsible and solitary engagement when entering relations, setting up research design, transacting knowledge, and managing the knowledge created.

Representation: Knowledge for Whom or for What?

As can be seen from the discussion in the previous section, ethics of knowledge creation is closely linked to representation. For whom is the knowledge created and to what end? Issues of representation, audience and purpose are part of this volume's concern and are discussed from different approaches, particularly in Part III of the book. In 'Robust Knowledge' Marilyn Strathern (2005) discusses two modes of knowledge production, one in which 'traditional' science is seen as 'external' with the task of reconstituting society, and another in which 'contemporary' science is 'internal', no longer an authoritative project but instead adding uncertainty and instability with control exercised indirectly from the inside (Strathern 2005: 466). Once 'robust through its own validation procedures', science now needs society to confer acceptability (Strathern 2005: 476).[4] But it is institutionalized forms of audit, rather than society or the public, that must confer acceptability.[5] The new 'primitive', in Edwards' ironic reflection, 'is the scientifically illiterate' (Edwards, Harvey and Wade 2007: 9). We need to be literate to understand how science 'abdicates responsibility for the application of its findings to "society"' (Edwards, Harvey and Wade 2007: 9).

In Melhuus's chapter this abdication is not vis-à-vis society but in relation to the individual. Melhuus discusses the effects of managing 'who is entitled to know', and whether knowing is necessary when assessing questions of reproductive medicine and sperm donation in the context of the state's institutionalization of ethics, which according to politicians speak to social core values. Yet as Melhuus demonstrates, there is no consensus among legislators or the public at large about the regulations and legislation, though there is a general agreement about the need for regulation as a precaution against potential social harm. The legislation, Melhuus argues, is not only about managing risk but is also a political strategy for protecting what is deemed to be Norwegian sociocultural values, while also articulating tensions between knowing, not knowing and who is 'the knower/non-knower'.

In a similar vein, Finkler's chapter adumbrates the propensity of knowledge of personalized genetics to convince us that we can control risk, and in Beck's words, 'colonise the future' as we make the 'unforeseeable foreseeable' (1998: 12). Failure to avoid risk, Finkler argues, easily results in the individual person being blamed for his or her sickness, overlooking how choice and decision are not only individual but are also anchored in culturally constructed notions of probability and statistics that constantly create new realities.

Josephides's chapter steps all the way back to discuss knowledge creation as a kind of methodology of understanding, in an enquiry into the cultivation of the kind of selves required for knowledge. It identifies three key terms: relations, knowledge and persons, and discusses four figures of knowers in historical context: the pure observer, the thinking man/woman defending the virtues of knowledge, the knower shaped simultaneously by the content and the context of

knowing, and the researcher placed between obligations and requirements, enmeshed in conditions of knowing that are shared by all
knowers and at all times. The discussion draws on materials from
anthropology, philosophy and philosophy of science, especially the
history of objectivity, where three types of epistemic virtue are identified (truth to nature, objectivity and trained judgement), onto which
the four figures of knowers can be mapped.

As this volume, and Part III in particular, grapples with the
issues of ethics and representation it also raises a vast array of
dilemmas that have been thoroughly debated in other publications
(Amit 2000; Caplan 2003; Fluehr-Lobban 2002; Pels 1999, 2000;
Scheper-Hughes 1995; Strathern 2000). Knowledge is created for a
number of different audiences, which for anthropology and social
sciences in general include the subjects themselves. However, some
researchers find their writing (and thus the knowledge it creates
and presents) contested by their subjects (see for instance Caplan
2003), which raises the question of 'who has the right to represent
others'.

When considering the wider public as the audience there are intri-
cate questions of how to (re)present and explain knowledge to often
sceptical audiences (for instance, in courts of law or political debates),
which can include a need to challenge stereotypes and preconceptions.
In such cases the researcher's empathy and engagement can often
become temporarily secondary and undermined by contexts for the
presentation and deployment of knowledge that require an authoritative, objective and factual form (Caplan 2003; Strathern 2005).
Furthermore, the ethics of knowledge creation are complicated by the
researcher's positioning, as we acknowledge how researchers themselves affect the relations, interpretations and creation of knowledge
by their own personal, social and cultural background and position in
the field. While we see threads of the anthropological classical debates
on morality, rationality and ethics, we engage in and highlight a
methodological discussion of the ethics of knowledge creation seen
as a process of understanding the self and Other as sharing a social
human world.

Concluding Remarks

This volume takes us through some of the complexities of the ethics
and relations in the process of knowledge creation. While the volume
concentrates on the ethics of knowledge creation, it also demonstrates

how anthropologists create knowledge, which can never be fully neutral or complete. We recognize how 'an impartial social inquiry is impossible' (Barnes 1967: 203), as the knowledge we create is always inferred by relations of responsibility and commitment. However, we appreciate the stand that anthropology does not give a rationale for advocacy or speaking for a particular cause, even though it may become a 'moral imperative' (see Hastrup and Elsass 1990: 301), as there is no way for the anthropologist to avoid involvement. Since the discipline recognizes that the ethnographers themselves are part of the encounter, they are also part of the material and knowledge created (among many others, see Caplan 2003; Grønseth and Davis 2010). Furthermore, taking it as given that there is no clear-cut distinction between self and Other – in that they only exist for each other – the anthropologist cannot fully speak for the Other. Rather, it is in the interplay between self and Other, between knowing and not knowing, that the ethics appear.

From such a view, we highlight how the volume's concern with the creation of knowledge as part of relations and transactions further-more calls for ethics that encourage respect for human individuality, diversity and reciprocity. This call responds to today's global and trou-blesome standardization and polarization of similarity and difference, though also to the anthropological community in terms of appreci-ating and reflecting on the contextual, reciprocal and interpersonal relations that create knowledge.

Anne Sigfrid Grønseth is Professor of Anthropology at Lillehammer University College, and head of Unite of Health, Culture and Identity. She has also held a position at the Norwegian Centre for Minority Health Research. Recent publications are *Lost Selves and Lonely Persons: Experiences of Illness and Well-Being among Tamil Refugees in Norway* (2010), *Mutuality and Empathy: Self and Other in the Ethnographic Encounter* (eds) (2010), and *Being Human, Being Migrant: Senses of Self and Well-Being* (ed.) (2013).

Lisette Josephides is Professor of Anthropology at Queen's University Belfast. Previously she has taught at the University of Papua New Guinea, the London School of Economics and the University of Minnesota. She trained in anthropology and philosophy and con-ducted lengthy fieldwork in Papua New Guinea. Major books include *The Production of Inequality* (1984), *Melanesian Odysseys* (2008), *We* *the Cosmopolitans: Moral and Existential Conditions of Being Human* (2014, co-editor A. Hall) and *Knowledge and Ethics in Anthropology: Obligations and Requirements* (2015).

Notes

1. One way uniformity is achieved is through audit – see Strathern 2005 discussed below.
2. Though here we are concerned with the 'extraordinary' ethics of knowledge exchange and do not engage the distinction between anthropological knowledge and local knowledge, the concept of 'ordinary ethics' is germane to our enquiry. Jarrett Zigon (2014: 746) has mounted an extensive critique of 'everyday ethics'. In his phenomenological hermeneutics of 'embodied morality' ethics is 'tacit, grounded in agreement rather than rule, practice rather than knowledge or belief' (2014: 748). Zigon argues that if we see moralities and ethics not as aspects of primary cultural and social practices (such as politics or religion) but as distinct and significant factors in shaping these, then we are at risk of occupying a 'transcendental moral position' (2014: 747) that dissolves ethics into the social (2014: 749); in effect, it gives us the beast with two heads: Aristotelian Kantianism that combines the ordinary with the transcendental (2014: 750).
3. Jarrett Zigon (2014: 754) understands Ingold's paradigm of 'dwelling' as allowing people to become 'something that previously would not have been possible'. While the building of new 'subjective worlds' is an activity that we see happening in many of the chapters, we leave it to the reader to determine whether the vocabulary of dwelling adds understandings beyond definitions of 'dignity' and Aristotelian 'grounding experiences'.
4. Some of these ideas originate in Nowotny et al. (2001), where they identify 'a shift from attempts to place science more firmly *in* society towards the idea that science should be more accountable to society, and that this is best achieved by bringing *society* into science' (Edwards, Harvey and Wade 2007: 9). For them, this communicative arena is 'the public space of the agora where ideas can be debated, negotiated, and science and publics are mutually informed' (Edwards, Harvey and Wade 2007: 14).
5. Commenting on Strathern's work, Alberto Corsin Jimenez (2007: 39) argues that today 'society decides what makes good science'. Specifically, the first 'management model of knowledge' thrives on critique, while the second is damaged by it. Thus, 'making knowledge flow' requires different management and organizational skills in the two models. The audit, according to Jimenez, 'is administration gone paranoid rather than public' (cited in Edwards 2011: 11).

References

Abu-Lughod, L. 1991. 'Writing against Culture', in Richard G. Fox (ed.), *Recapturing Anthropology: Working in the Present*. New Mexico: School of American Research Press, pp. 137–62.

Agamben, G. 1998. *Homo Sacer: Sovereign Power and Bare Life*, trans. D. Heller-Raozen. California: Stanford University Press.

Amit, V. 2000. 'The University as Panopticon: Moral Claims and Attacks on Academic Freedom', in M. Strathern (ed.), *Audit Cultures: Anthropological Studies in Accountability, Ethics and the Academy*. London and New York: Routledge.

Appadurai, A. 1996. *Modernity at Large: Cultural Dimensions in Globalization*. Minnesota: University of Minnesota Press.

———. 2001. *Globalization*. London and Durham: Duke University Press.

Arendt, H. 1998 [1958]. *The Human Condition*, 2nd ed. Chicago: University of Chicago Press.

Aristotle. 1998. *Politics*. Translated with Introduction and Notes by C.D.C. Reeve. Indianapolis/Cambridge: Hackett Publishing Company, Inc.

Barnes, J. 1967. 'Some Ethical Problems in Fieldwork', in D.G. Jongmans and P.C. Gutkind (eds), *Anthropologists in the Field*. Netherlands: Van Gurcum and Co. (Originally published in the *British Journal of Sociology*. 1963 14(2): 11–134.)

Beck, U. 1992. *The Risk Society*. London: Sage.

———. 1998. 'Politics of Risk Society', in J. Franklin (ed.), *The Politics of Risk Society*. Cambridge: Polity Press.

Brightman, R. 1995. 'Forget Culture: Replacement, Transcendence, Relexification', *Cultural Anthropology* 10(4): 509–46.

Caplan, P. (ed.). 2003. *The Ethics of Anthropology: Debates and Dilemmas*. London: Routledge.

Carrithers, M. 1992. *Why Humans Have Cultures*. Oxford: Oxford University Press.

———. 2005. 'Anthropology as a Moral Science of Possibilities', *Current Anthropology* 46(3): 433–56.

Carrithers, M. (ed.). 2009. *Culture, Rhetoric and the Vicissitudes of Life*, volume 2, Studies in Rhetoric and Culture. New York and Oxford: Berghahn.

Das, V. 2010. 'Engaging the Life of the Other: Love and Everyday Life', in M. Lambek (ed.), *Ordinary Ethics: Anthropology, Language, and Action*. New York: Fordham University Press, pp. 35–62.

Daston, L. and P. Galison. 2010. *Objectivity*. Brooklyn: Zone Books.

Durkheim, E. 1994 [1912]. *The Elementary Forms of Religious Life*, trans. K.E. Fields. New York: The Free Press.

Edel, A. 1962. 'Anthropology and Ethics in Common Focus', *Journal of the Royal Anthropological Institute of Great Britain and Ireland* 92(1): 55–72.

Edel, M. and A. Edel. 1959. *Anthropology and Ethics*. Springfield, IL: Chares C. Thomas.

Edwards, J., P. Harvey and P. Wade (eds). 2007. *Anthropology and Science: Epistemologies in Practice.* Oxford: Berg.

Eriksen, Th. H. 2013. *Globalisation: Studies in Anthropology.* London: Pluto Press.

Fassin, D. 2012. *A Companion to Moral Anthropology.* Oxford: Wiley-Blackwell.

Faubion, J.D. 2003. 'Toward an Anthropology of Ethics: Foucault and the Pedagogies of Autopoiesis', in: E. Wyschogrod and G. McKenny (eds), *The Ethical.* Malden, MA: Blackwell Publishing, pp. 146–65.

———. 2011. *An Anthropology of Ethics.* Cambridge: Cambridge University Press.

Faubion, J.D. and G. Marcus (eds). 2009. *Fieldwork is Not What It Used To Be: Learning Anthropology's Method in a Time of Transition.* London: Cornell University Press.

Fluehr-Lobban, C. 2002. 'The Dialogue Continues: Ethics and Anthropology in the 21st Century: Towards a new Professional Ethics', in *Ethics and the Profession of Anthropology: Dialogue for a New Era.* Philadelphia: University for Pennsylvania Press.

Foucault, M. 1990 [1984]. *The Use of Pleasure.* New York: Vintage Books.

Gaita, R. 1998. *A Common Humanity: Thinking about Love and Truth and Justice.* London: Routledge.

Grønseth, A.S. (ed.) 2013. *Being Human, Being Migrant: Senses of Self and Wellbeing.* New York and Oxford: Berghahn.

Grønseth, A.S. and D.L. Davis (eds). 2010. *Mutuality and Empathy: Self and Other in the Ethnographic Encounter.* London: Kingston Press.

Gupta, A. and J. Ferguson. 1992. 'Beyond "Culture": Space, Identity, and the Politics of Difference', *Cultural Anthropology* 7(1): 6–23.

Halstead, N., E. Hirsch and J. Okely (eds). 2008. *Knowing How to Know: Fieldwork and the Ethnographic Present.* New York and Oxford: Berghahn.

Harris, M. (ed.). 2007. *Ways of Knowing: New Approaches in the Anthropology of Experience and Learning.* New York and Oxford: Berghahn.

Hastrup, K. and P. Elsass (eds). 1990. 'Anthropological Advocacy: A Contradiction in Terms?', *Current Anthropology* 31(3): 301–11.

Herzfeld, M. 1995. 'It Takes One to Know One: Collective Resentment and Mutual Recognition Among Greeks in Local and Global contexts', in R. Fardon (ed.), *Counterworks: Managing the Diversity of Knowledge.* London: Routledge, pp. 124–42.

Howell, S. (ed.). 1997. *The Ethnography of Moralities.* London: Routledge.

Ingold, T. 2013. *Making: Anthropology, Archaeology, Art and Architecture.* London: Routledge.

Jimenez, A.C. 2007. 'Industry Going Public: Rethinking Knowledge and Administration', in J. Edwards, P. Harvey and P. Wade (eds), *Anthropology and Science: Epistemologies in Practice.* Oxford: Berg, pp. 39–57.

Josephides, L. 2008. *Melanesian Odysseys: Negotiating the Self, Narrative and Modernity.* New York and Oxford: Berghahn.

Josephides, L. (ed.) 2015a. *Knowledge and Ethics in Anthropology: Obligations and Requirements*. London, New Delhi, New York, Sydney: Bloomsbury Academic.

Josephides, L. 2015b. 'Obligations and Requirements: the Contexts of Knowledge', in *Knowledge and Ethics in Anthropology: Obligations and Requirements*, L. Josephides (ed.). London, New Delhi, New York, Sydney: Bloomsbury Academic, pp. 1–27.

Kenway, J. and J. Fahey (eds). 2009. *Globalizing the Research Imagination*. London: Routledge.

Kuper, A. 1999. *Culture: The Anthropologists' Account*. Harvard: Harvard University Press.

Laidlaw, J. 2002. 'For an Anthropology of Ethics and Freedom', *Journal of the Royal Anthropological Institute* 8(2): 311–32.

Lambek, M. (ed.). 2010. *Ordinary Ethics: Anthropology, Language and Action*. New York: Fordham University Press.

Latour, B. 2004. 'Whose Cosmos, Which Politics? Comments on the Peace Terms of Ulrich Beck', *Common Knowledge* 10(3): 450–62.

Lévi-Strauss, C. 2003 [1971]. 'Ramener la pensée à la vie: An Interview with Georges Kutukdjian', *Magazine Littéraire*, hors-série 5: 53–59.

Moore, H.L. (ed.). 1996. *The Future of Anthropological Knowledge*. London: Routledge.

Nehamas, A. 1998. *The Art of Living*. Berkeley: University of California Press.

Ong, A. and S.J. Collier (eds). 2005. *Global Assemblages: Technology, Politics, and Ethics as Anthropological Problems*. Malden, MA: Blackwell.

Pels, P. 1999. 'Professions of Duplexity: A Prehistory of Ethical Codes in Anthropology', *Current Anthropology* 40(2): 101–36.

———. 2000. 'The Trickster's Dilemma: Ethics and the Technologies of the Anthropological Self', in M. Strathern (ed.), *Audit Cultures: Anthropological Studies in Accountability, Ethics and the Academy*. London and New York: Routledge.

Pocock, D.F. 1986. 'The Ethnography of Morals', *International Journal of Moral and Social Studies* 1(1): 3–20.

Rabinow, P. 2003. *Anthropos Today*. Princeton: Princeton University Press.

Scheper-Hughes, N. 1995. 'The Primacy of the Ethical: Propositions for a Militant Anthropology', *Current Anthropology* 36(3): 409–40.

Stoczkowski, W. 2008. 'The "Fourth Aim" of Anthropology: Between Knowledge and Ethics', *Anthropological Theory* 8(4): 345–56.

Strathern, M. 1991. *Partial Connections*. Savage, MD: Rowman & Littlefield.

———. 2003. *Commons and Borderlands: Working Papers on Interdisciplinarity, Accountability and the Flow of Knowledge*. Herefordshire: Sean Kingston Publishing.

———. 2005. 'Robust Knowledge and Fragile Futures', in A. Ong and S.J. Collier (eds), *Global Assemblages: Technology, Politics, and Ethics as Anthropological Problems*, Malden, MA: Blackwell Publishing, pp. 464–81.

———. 2006. 'A Community of Critics? Thoughts on New Knowledge', *Journal of the Royal Anthropological Institute* 12(1): 191–209.

Strathern, M. (ed.). 2000. *Audit Cultures: Anthropological Studies in Accountability, Ethics and the Academy*. London and New York: Routledge.

Tylor, E.B. 1871. *Primitive Culture: Researches into the Development of Mythology, Philosophy, Religion, Art and Custom*. London: John Murray.

Ziarek. E.P. 2008. 'Bare Life on Strike. Notes on the Biopolitics of Race and Gender', *South Atlantic Quarterly* 107(1): 89–105.

Zigon, J. 2014. 'An Ethics of Dwelling and a Politics of World-Building: A Critical Response to Ordinary Ethics', *Journal of the Royal Anthropological Institute* 20(4): 746–76.

Negotiating and Transacting Knowledge in the Field

The opening chapters (by Anne Sigfrid Grønseth, Giovanna Bacchiddu and Tamara Kohn) investigate the relations and contexts – with their accompanying ethical implications – in which researchers acquire knowledge about the individuals and groups whose lives they study. They demonstrate that ethnographic and face-to-face encounters are saturated with ethical concerns. They set up an interactive structure (a relationship) with an 'Other' in a context of submerged or unstated interests and epistemological foundations, but at the same time they are ruled by subjectivity and imagination. While the chapters highlight various techniques in the transaction of knowledge, they also illustrate the personal investments and transformations and concomitant epistemological, methodological and ethical shifts in the process of understanding and representing others. Given these negotiations and transformations, to what extent does the knowledge thus created be said to belong exclusively to one group? Moreover, in classical ethnographic encounters the researcher appears in two negative guises: as having more to gain from the interaction, and as wielding the upper hand in determining the perimeters of the exchange and the knowledge to be transacted. But face-to-face encounters as interactions imparting information escape the ethnographer's control. Thus, this section also highlights how the anthropological quest for understanding human social life must encompass not only the creation but also the positioning and managing of knowledge, which includes questions of how knowledge is viewed in the societies concerned. The ethical question in writing an ethnography is not only one of accurate representation and due respect to the people studied, but also of how to transmute local knowledge into 'universal knowledge' while remaining true to the relations of its origin.

Chapter 1

EMPATHIC RELATIONS WITH TAMIL REFUGEES

CHALLENGING MORALITY AND CALLING FOR ETHICS OF KNOWLEDGE CREATION

Anne Sigfrid Grønseth

Introduction

This chapter explores the ethics of knowledge creation as it takes place in empathic and imaginative relations between self and Other. The exploration sets off from my own experiences while conducting ethnographic fieldwork among Tamil refugees in a small fishing village in the far north of Norway, with a concern for experiences of illness and well-being. During my fieldwork, I was not only challenged by social and cultural distinctions between 'us' and 'them', but confronted with moral dilemmas and quandaries. In dealing with such difficulties, I came to recognize how creation of knowledge is fundamentally generated in imaginations, and relations and engagements with the Other. While engaging with the Tamils, I encountered both similar and opposing values, meanings and practices to those that are part of my own culture and morality, and which I generally felt comfortable with on a day-to-day basis. However, when managing the moral challenges and dilemmas that emerged during fieldwork, I faced some troublesome ethical issues related to judgement and responsibility. In this chapter I will examine a case study of such a moral dilemma and argue the need for an ethical approach to knowledge creation based on an acknowledgement of its relational and imaginative quality, together with a hopeful aspiration to demonstrate solidary equality and common humanity.

When highlighting the relational quality of ethics and morals, it is necessary to recognize how morality is linked to cultural and/or

religious beliefs in terms of what constitutes a good life: success, prosperity and a sense of well-being, satisfaction and happiness. The route
to achieve well-being and happiness varies, as morality is universal
but is not absolute. Morality regulates complex interactions within
social groups by individuals' capacity to experience, perform and act
on empathy, reciprocity, altruism, cooperation and a sense of fairness.
Individual persons tend to conceive accepted codes of conduct as fundamentally moral and ethical while these often derive from general
social principles. As such, morality and ethics can be seen at the same
time as coercive and part of the human creation of meaning, politics
and power relations. In this view, a community's continuous existence
can be conceived to depend on a widespread conformity to particular
moral codes paired with a fear that adjusting morals in response to
new challenges will lead to the demise of the community. A threat to
one's own community and morals is often experienced as a threat and
challenge to self-identity and moral integrity. Thus, it appears that
ethics and morality are constituted in the encounter between self and
Other, as 'Other' can be an individual human being, a community, an
institution, a social principal, a structure, value or meaning. While
understanding ethics and morality as closely intertwined, the chapter
will grapple with the complex distinctions, as one can see ethics to
be more in line with a general human aspiration and attempt, and
morality as more closely linked to commitments and liabilities, or a
sense of 'ought to' in everyday practical life.

In what follows I will briefly introduce a theoretical approach to ethics
and knowledge, as it is further discussed in this chapter. Then, I will
present a wider context of the study on Tamil refugees in Norway – the
field site and methods – before I present a case study of a teenage Tamil
girl, who lived her daily life with strong restrictions on her freedom to
engage with other people. This is followed by an analysis of the case, as
it illuminates moral quandaries, judgement and actions in the encounter between self and Other in the creation of knowledge. By way of conclusion I highlight that my analysis cannot only focus on conscious
meanings and intentions, as we need to recognize an active space for the
embodied, empathic and imaginative creation of knowledge.

Theoretical View:
Knowledge as Embodied Relations

Considering that the aim of my research was to learn about Tamils'
experiences of illness and well-being (see Grønseth 2001, 2006a,

2006b, 2007, 2010a, 2010b), I was challenged to extend myself beyond culturally, socially and morally structured positions and to reach towards the Other with an approach that recognizes the Other as an equal human being. With such an aim and approach, the research methods expanded on interviews and participant observation to focus on being with, sharing experiences with and engaging in Tamils' everyday life (Grønseth 2010b; Ingold 1993). Aiming to learn about sensitive areas of Tamil life concerning emotional and sensorial experiences expressed in bodily aches and pains, I engaged in the Tamils' everyday life with an effort to empathize and embody similar social experiences. This did not imply an effort of socialization so as to 'become a Tamil' (see Lutz 1988),[1] but to enter a borderland between self and Other in which we could share intersubjective experiences (Grønseth 2013; Grønseth and Davis 2010; Jackson 1998; Moore 2011). Entering into and staying with such relations, I suggest, provides an opportunity to explore a kind of knowledge that challenges often habituated (Bourdieu 1989) and one's own taken for granted moralities, while calling for an ethics of humanity.

From this understanding, I suggest that encounters between 'us and them' and 'self and Other' offer an opportunity for exploring the ethics of creating knowledge. Furthermore, I argue, it is a kind of knowledge that comes from attending to our 'being in the world' (Merleau-Ponty 1962 [1945]), as it is motivated, perceived and experienced by our bodily senses, passions and capacities. It is an embodied ethic in which being in the face of the Other offers not just ethical rules and answers, but an ethical perspective or source (Levinas 2003 [1972]). It is an ethic that offers potentiality and hope, or wishful thinking; it is not about being, but about should-being. Appreciating the relational quality of ethics, it is seen to come from intersubjective moments in which the self arises and is shaped by continuously changing modes of embodied social practices, from the interplay between object and subject, self and Other (Foucault 1998; Jackson 1998; Moore 2011). Both Otherness and selfhood are outcomes not only of intersubjective engagement as conceptual intention, but are lived, embodied and sensed as introceptivity (Merleau-Ponty 1964: 114–15, 121). From such a perspective, I suggest that approaching and being in the face of the Other, in this case Tamil individuals, challenges one's own standards of morality and gives access to a sense of responsibility for the Other as a mutual human being.

Exploring the embodied encounter between self and Other, a space of intersubjectivity, I suggest, creates a kind of knowledge that is not only or fully about self or Other. Focus is not foremost on what I learn about 'the Other' as representing 'Tamil knowledge and traditions', or about what Papushpa, a Tamil teenage girl, transmits about such. Nor is focus alone on what I learn about (my) self and 'Norwegian knowledge and traditions'. Rather I focus on knowledge as it is created in the face-to-face and embodied encounter between us; as knowledge is experienced, imagined, managed, transacted, negotiated and conducted in our encounter, and thus always partial and not complete. The knowledge created in the embodied encounter I propose to reach beyond self and Other (as this includes particular practices, values and moralities) and moreover engage with ethical concerns of being human. Thus, I suggest the exploration of the embodied encounter is of concern for the ethics of knowledge creation.

Tamil Refugees in Norway

Though the Sri Lankan conflict is beyond the scope of this chapter, I will outline briefly the civil war context for the Tamil refugees in Norway. The Tamil minority situation has been a political issue since Sri Lanka's independence in 1948. Political tensions and discrimination increased when, in 1956, Sinhalese was declared the official language. In June 1983 there were upheavals in which many were killed and others had to flee their homes. Among different political and guerrilla movements, the LTTE (Liberation Tigers of Tamil Eelam) were the most aggressive and led the opposition fighting for an independent state of Tamil Eelam. The traditional Tamil majority areas of Jaffna in the north and eastern Sri Lanka were declared war zones, and most Tamil people live in exile or as refugees in their own country. Following the end of the war in May 2009, the LTTE dropped its demands for a separate state in favour of a federal solution. Since the civil war ended, the Tamil diaspora has continued protesting against the war by urging governments to undertake war-crimes inspections in Sri Lanka.

While acknowledging the tensions and complexities of the civil war and ultimate declaration of peace, the focus of the present chapter is on Tamils from Sri Lanka who are living in Norway as refugees in diaspora. According to Statistics Norway, by 1 January 2011, 13.1 per cent of Norway's total population consisted of around 460,000 immigrants and their descendants from 219 different countries and self-governed regions (for more on Norway's immigrant populations, see Henriksen et al. 2010). At that date, 157,692 immigrants had refugee backgrounds, of whom 114,760 were refugees themselves and a further 42,932 had arrived to be reunited with family members. This total represents about 3.2 per cent of Norway's total population. Of this population, 14,293 have a Sri Lankan background. According to figures from 1 January 2012, a year later, 8,816 individuals were first-generation immigrants and 5,477 had been born in Norway of parents who came from Sri Lanka. Virtually all the Sri Lankans are Tamils.

Being a refugee implies a deep sense of being forced to escape from life-threatening circumstances like political persecution and war, often implying sudden departures and a need to travel at great risk, together with great uncertainty about one's destination and future prospects (Daniel and Knudsen 1995; Hammond 2004; Jenkins 1996; Malkki 1995; Migliorino 2008; Sideris 2003; Zmegac 2007). While Tamils are generally identified as refugees, they also share features with overlapping categories of diasporic or transnational populations. Many Tamils tend to maintain a myth about their homeland: they see their ancestral home as a place of eventual return, they are committed to the restoration of this homeland, and they display a continuous relationship with it (see e.g., Bicharat 1997; Clifford 1994; Safran 1991; Slymovics 1998). Simultaneously, Tamils engage in transnational relations and practices by circulating people, money, goods and information, thus keeping in touch, participating in family events and taking part in decision-making with significant others spread throughout the world (see also Schiller et al. 1992; Rouse 1991).

Although the Tamil parental generation seeks to pass on a Tamil cultural identity to the younger generation, many Tamil parents realize the complex expectations and demands that their children must deal with. Many of the parents exert enormous pressure and social control to ensure that their children become 'good Tamils', which includes success in education and work. Trying to fulfil often mismatched and high expectations, many young Tamils experience an existential struggle to retain a minimum of self-esteem and a sense of living a worthwhile life (see also Engebrigtsen and Fuglerud 2007). One of the most precarious issues relates to social behaviour and control, which in particular includes partial social isolation for many girls. Such control is, from many Tamils' viewpoint, meant to secure Tamil respectability and prospects of marriage, as respectability and marriage are enforced and challenged by living in diaspora and in the new social and cultural context of Norway.

Field Site and Methods:
Sharing Experiences with Tamils in Arctic Harbour

After three years of shorter field visits to Finnmark, the northernmost county of Norway along the arctic coast, I was enabled to do a one year period of extensive fieldwork (1999–2000) living among the Tamils in one of the fishing villages, here called Arctic Harbour. The Tamils made up about 10 per cent of the total 2,500 population in the village. They all worked in the fishing industry and held the low status of 'cutters', meaning they cut and sliced fish filets along a running conveyor belt. The Tamil population consisted mostly of young families with small children, a few teenagers and some single young men. Generally, they were not fluent in Norwegian and had little social contact with Norwegians at work or in the community. They were well integrated economically but socially segregated from the local community. Living among the Tamils, I came to feel embedded in a similar segregation from Norwegian relations.

Interviews were initially conducted with a local interpreter, who himself was a Tamil refugee. As time passed, I recognized a limitation in the conversation and kind of knowledge I could access while working with formal interviews and an interpreter. When I sometimes visited Tamils on my own without the interpreter, I experienced another kind of communication, carrying meanings and knowledges of another mode and depth (Grønseth 2010b). Thus, I turned towards a methodology that transcended words and visual observations and reached towards a sense of sharing experiences, similarly 'attending to' (Ingold 1993: 220), or what I suggest was a process of 'embodying the Other' (see also Merleau-Ponty 1962 [1945]; Jackson 1998). I sought for meanings and knowledges by doing things together and sharing experiences with the Tamils. I engaged in looking at photographs and watching videos of ritual ceremonies with family members, cooking and sharing meals of curries and ritual foods, sharing moments of puja and devotion, walking the streets, buying groceries, working on the cutting line with them, picking up children from kindergarten, visiting the doctor and so on. Such an approach of emotionally, empathically and physically engaging with the Other I suggest can provide a bridge between the intrapersonal and the interpersonal and open the way for knowledge created from the borderlands between self and Other. It can be, I suggest, in these tensions of living in-between, in the encounter between self and Other's experiences of being in the world, that one can find an ethical approach and source that may transgress one's own morality, and create a heartfelt mode of knowledge about the Other.

In the following I present a case study of a young girl.

Case Study: Papushpa:
'How Can I be Free if I am Alone?'

One bright and freezing cold Saturday I went to visit Papushpa, a girl of about thirteen years of age. She had let me know that she was not allowed out of doors except for school and appreciated some company. As Papushpa was no longer a child and had turned into a young woman, her family had celebrated the puberty ritual of *Ritu Kala Samskara* in which she was gifted her first sari and jewellery. Following her entrance into young womanhood, Papushpa was under strict observation by her father and family so as to safeguard the family's reputation, and secure the best prospects for Papushpa's future marriage. Of particular concern was to ensure proper conduct, which according to her parents included practice and knowledge of the Tamil language, traditions and culture, obedience to family interests, assisting her mother with household chores, success at school, and not engaging in relations with young men or families and persons not deemed to be 'proper'.

When I arrived, Papushpa and her younger sister sat on the sofa in a rather dimly lit living room watching a cartoon show on TV. Her father was out doing some errands, her elder brother was with a friend and her mother was in the kitchen preparing curries. Papushpa smiled at me and patted a space on the sofa, inviting me to sit down. Her mother served us Tamil spicy snacks and soft drinks and joined us for a while. Papushpa said she was to look after her younger sister and could not go out. Only her elder brother was allowed to go out. Papushpa had asked him to buy her some sweets, and she was eager to see if he would remember. She told me about how she had once disobeyed her parents and went out to the shop herself. Her brother had seen her and made her return. When her father heard, he became angry and slapped her.

Sitting on the sofa in the dim light, hearing the cartoons and catching their rapid movements across the TV screen, I felt locked up in a tiny world in which I had little space and access to freedom. I felt encompassed by an atmosphere of accepting what was dictated as a necessity and giving into an ascribed destiny. I thought about asking Papushpa to accompany me outside, but felt it would be more of a relief and comfort to me than her, and decided instead to join Papushpa in her own ways of dealing with the situation. Papushpa's little sister sat on the floor trying to fix a broken toy and wanted Papushpa to help. After a short while the toy was repaired and Papushpa started to talk about the few other Tamil girls she used to be with at school. They were not in the same class, but met in the breaks. Papushpa said they used to meet in the schoolyard and wait together for the next class to begin. The girls used to walk together on their way home after school. It was a long time since they had played or spent time together outside school hours. Papushpa explained that the Tamil girls were expected to help their mothers in the house. Moreover, I was told, as the children grew older they were instructed to pay more attention to which families they should socialize with. As was often explained to me by many Tamils, 'Not all families are appropriate to visit and make friends with'. However, Papushpa looked forward to Sundays when the family went on visits. Most of all, she enjoyed visiting a family in which there was another boy of about her age.

Papushpa said she sometimes felt like a prisoner. She was afraid of the punishments if she was caught going out. She said she felt she was going mad. She had often found herself shivering and felt feverish and dizzy. She kept her hopes up by the prospect of her family moving to Oslo, where they had family, including several aunts who she could be with. In Arctic Harbour she felt isolated and lonely. One of her friends in Arctic Harbour had disobeyed her father by falling in love with a Norwegian boy and walking with him in the streets. Papushpa lost contact with this friend, who came to school only rarely and kept to herself. After some time Papushpa was told that her friend had moved, while her parents and siblings remained in Arctic Harbour. Rumour had it that her friend was at a psychiatric hospital. One year later Papushpa and her family moved to Oslo and still Papushpa did not know what had happened to her friend. Papushpa felt worried and scared about what might possibly happen to herself. She said:

> I look out of the window and the bright shiny snow hurts my eyes. It is like looking on my self. It hurts not only my eyes, but my heart and soul. I am imprisoned. See what happened to my friend. When we move to Oslo, there will be aunts and cousins with me. They can help. I can start making a life of my own. Here, I am stuck all alone in this living room. My head aches, my body shivers, my heart cries. Nobody knows my pain. I cannot tell anyone. I shall endure. My power will come from my suffering. I have made a vow to Saraswati.[2] If I obey, I will be strong and free.

Being close to Papushpa's imprisonment and hearing of her profound worries for her sanity and possible punishments, I was struggling with an intense wish to somehow bring her out of this situation. Upon leaving her house I wiped away tears, in empathy with Papushpa's loneliness and fear, but also tears for the deep challenge to my own moral integrity. Each time I passed the house, I looked to see if I could catch a glimpse of Papushpa in the window. I struggled with a sense of guilty conscience for not somehow interfering and pursuing what I felt was right; she should be free to go out, and by doing so oppose Tamil-Hindu traditions and religion, as well as her father and family. In my view it was morally right to let teenagers challenge authority, be it that of their parents and/or religiously defined restrictions. There should be the opportunity to explore different and unfamiliar aspects of life, and craft an identity and way of life for oneself. Based on such moral values, I felt obligated to help Papushpa onto such a path – a path that fitted with my Western, modern and Norwegian individualism and idea of the (largely) autonomous self. I felt that Papushpa was deprived of an existential part of what it is to be young and human; her freedom and right to choose a life for herself. I thought I ought to help her.

Simultaneously, when being with Papushpa (as was also the case in a few similar situations with other Tamils), I was told, and I also sensed, how what I thought was best for her, from her perspective, was very wrong. In engaging with Papushpa in her everyday life it became evident that she did not seek or want a life in which she needed to make choices of her own regardless of Hindu-Tamil traditions, religion, kin and family. She often spoke about how Norwegian youth behaved immorally and did not respect their parents and the elders. Sometimes she could envy their courage to speak their mind, but more often she dreaded what she conceived of as 'egoism' and 'individualism'. Rather than seeking strength from a desire to make her own decisions and freedom in the present, Papushpa sought power from 'doing the right thing', which in this case appeared to involve obedience and enduring the accompanying loneliness and sense of imprisonment.

Papushpa was convinced that her present obedience and suffering would bring a future in which she was powerful and free but also securely attached to her kin. As she said: 'How can I be free if I am alone?' By doing what she felt and believed to be morally right she hoped to find the strength to achieve a future in which she would be happy and in charge of her own destiny and able to develop herself.

More than ten years have passed since I first met Papushpa in her 'prison' in Arctic Harbour. When I met her again at a café in Oslo in

2007, I was happy to learn that Papushpa at this point in her life felt to a large extent free and happy. She was now in her early twenties and lived with her parents and extended family. She told me about her several friends from different countries whom she met up with in downtown Oslo for various talks, movies and just having fun. She had completed her higher education in biotechnology and held a respected job within her field. When I visited her at work, I saw a respected woman who was greeted warmly and with high esteem among her colleagues. Of course, the issue of marriage was lurking in her mind. However, she was convinced her parents would appropriate a good match in due course. As she said last time I met her:

> Suffering in my imprisonment made me strong. No one can get to me. I know what I want. I have obliged to my family and they cannot fault me. They recognize my strength and morality. I can do what I want now. I can speak my mind.

Situated Relations, Multiple Knowledges

Exploring the case study above, I take the approach of understanding ethics and knowledge to be about the relation between self and Others as it is created and displayed in ordinary everyday life (see also Moore 2011; Lambek 2010). However, I recognize that it is impossible to know self or Other completely (Derrida 1974: 139–40; Moore 2011). This is reflected in how I was often pondering the ethics of my relations with the Tamils. Should I have actively interfered when I became aware of what I at first glance considered wrong? Not doing so, was I motivated by taking the position of the 'neutral observing and not interfering researcher'? Was I motivated by an 'easy approach' of not taking responsibility and leaving it to them? Was I motivated by a wish to strive towards what I believed to be (rightly or not) a cultural relativistic concern for the social life of the Other? Or, was I motivated by an empathic imagination of the Other?

These questions are meant to bring forth how, when encountering Papushpa's situation, I was challenged by my own moral sense of right and wrong, while also experiencing what I believed to be an empathic and imaginative relation. On the one hand, I was struggling with a wish to act so as to arrange things as my embodied morality spontaneously thought right. On the other hand, I sought to act in accordance with what I believed to be more in tune with the Tamils, and thus reach beyond my own views and self, so as to enter an intersubjective space between self and Other. By being with and engaging with Papushpa, I hesitated to interfere. By staying with Papushpa within her restricted environment, I believe I gained knowledge about her sense of meaning and ability to attain power and freedom. In spite of her pain, Papushpa commented on her situation by saying: 'My power will come from my suffering. I have made a vow to Saraswati. If I obey, I will be strong and free'.

Being with Papushpa, I came to understand that her suffering and obedience was in complex ways related to both religious and social realms, which in Hinduism are closely interwoven and inseparable. This appears in different ways. The often-mentioned phrase 'Not all families are appropriate to visit and make friends with' can be understood within Tamil-Hindu practices of 'who to be with' and 'who not to be with', regulated by caste-belonging. Different families did not want to relate to or be associated with specific other families, as they belonged to different caste groups. I will elaborate briefly.

According to caste-belonging or *jajamini*, distinct groups perform land work, fishing, laundry, blacksmithery, carpentry and butchery. Likewise, there are specific groups that serve the higher castes of landowners and priests. However, in Sri Lanka's northern province of Jaffna (the province that many of the Tamils in Arctic Harbour came from), villages had no standard spatial organization (David 1977). Space within an agricultural, fishing or artisan village was organized variously in accordance with how the inhabitants were differently oriented concerning principles of purity and impurity, commanding and being commanded, as well as mercantile enterprise (David 1977; see also David 1974). The hierarchical social differentiation was coded by a symbolism of sharing, in which each caste shared natural substances (such as blood and spirit), traditional occupation, cattle brands and origin myths. From this, one can see how different caste groups might spatially live together, but be separated by rules of conduct and interaction.

Although during my fieldwork in Arctic Harbour many of the Tamils would not volunteer information about what caste group they belonged to, differences were brought into conversation when elaborating on social relationships among themselves. If we view caste as a matter of avoidance and association, then the pattern of being with neighbours becomes a plausible framework for how Tamils socialize in Arctic Harbour. Thus, even without addressing caste explicitly, it was a commonly shared knowledge that contained subtle difficulties that came into play in social interaction (see Grønseth 2010a; also Frøystad 2003).

Furthermore, by keeping her promise to Saraswati, Papushpa was convinced she would be rewarded by the goddess with great knowledge and power. More so, through her suffering, Papushpa expected to gain moral and social power. Papushpa's approach, I suggest, is fruitfully understood when linked to how Hindu life-philosophy includes the concepts of dharma and shakti. Let me expand briefly. Dharma may variously be understood as '"moral duty", "law", "right action" or "conformity with the truth of things"' (Kakar 1997: 37). Each pattern for action may be seen as the principle underlying social relation in which dharma is the means by which one reaches the goal of human life, moksha. If a person is able to stay true to what is understood as the ground plan of his or her life and fulfil his or her particular life task,[3] he or she is walking on the path to moksha. Acquiring knowledge of one's life task, and of the 'right actions', is a complicated matter though, and a relative one.[4] In this way it seems as though right action and the individual life task come to mean traditional action and jati (caste) dharma, and thus stresses the importance of community and dependence rather than individuality and autonomy. This implies that an individual's occupation and social acts are 'right' or 'good' if they conform to the traditional pattern prevalent in his or her kinship and caste group.

For Tamils in exile, such as Papushpa and her family, the possibilities of living in dharma are strongly challenged, as crucial elements of social and cultural life are missing. Within such a context, the power of shakti appears to come into play. Shakti brings attention to a spiritual force or power that one can attain as an individual person (Wadley 1977).[5] It is a term that addresses how individuals by conduct, actions, consumption and engagement can acquire moral qualities and power, not given by birth. While Papushpa herself did not mention dharma or shakti as such, I suggest that her understanding and actions can partly be understood as non-consciously inspired and embodied by such perspectives, as they are embedded in Tamil social life (see also Grønseth 2011). However, Papushpa was convinced that her present 'right actions', because they included obedience and suffering, would bring a future in which she was powerful and free but also securely attached to her kin. As she said: 'How can I be free if I am alone?' By doing what she felt and believed to be morally right and in accordance to dharma, she hoped to gain (shakti-) power and strength, enabling her to look into a future in which she pictured herself as happy and self-determined.

Engaging with Papushpa and the Tamils in the wider context of everyday life, as it includes Tamil-Hindu concepts and perspectives (see also Grønseth 2010a), I suggest opens up a relational and imaginative approach to ethics and knowledge. In the ponderings of my own subjective judgement and morality, it becomes apparent that knowledge about self and Other is only partial, relational and imaginative. As I admit to not knowing completely my own motivations, I cannot fully know Papushpa's. But it is the incompleteness, I suggest, that opens a space in which I can sense, empathize and imagine (myself and/or) the Other.

Furthermore, recognizing that our knowledge of the Other is always only partial is related to how the self does not exist without the Other (Jacques 1982), and that the self-Other relation is always situated (Simmel 1950: 308). Thus, it is in the interplay between knowing and not knowing, in the imagination of the Other, in the management of self in relation to Others as it is related to a practice of judgement or moral subjectivity that the ethics appear. Accepting that the relations of ethics and knowledge are always situated, I further suggest that ethics and knowledge themselves will always be multiple and flexible, and open to other versions, truths and interpretations.

Subjectivity: Creative Imagination of the World

Taking the view that self and Other require mutual dependence to exist, it also appears that the creation of knowledge is relational and part of a process of subjectification, which precedes and continuously constructs the self (Foucault 1989 [1969], 1998; Deleuze and Guattari 1987; see also Moore 2011). Within this view, I see subjectivity as including consciousness, feelings, agency and personhood, interacting in a fluid and flexible self that embodies perceptions, experiences and cognitions, together constituting a conceived reality or truth about the world of lived life. Moreover, I suggest that subjectification connects ethics, judgement and knowledge to the embodied, sensory and emotional aspects of subjectification and self, as it creates a grounded reflection of the reality of lived life and an often unspoken truth of social circumstances (see Nussbaum 1986; Lacan 1992; see also Grønseth 2010a and 2014). Considering this view, it appears that heartfelt, sensory and tacit knowledge about the Other is created when entering and engaging in face-to-face relations with the Other, and often (knowingly or unknowingly) challenges taken for granted moralities and senses of self. Rather than conforming to given structures, rules and answers, the embodied relation of living in the face of the Other (Levinas 2003 [1972]) can open the way for an ethical approach in which an empathic and imaginative force can push towards hope, wishfulness and satisfaction for the Other.

However, I argue that there is a need to recognize how in encountering the Other ethics are not only free individual inventions but are proposed or imposed upon the individual by her or his culture, society and community (Foucault 1985, 1998 [1969]) – though neither culture or society or any rules determine absolutely the shape or limits to the encounter and relation (see Faubion 2001; Moore 2011). Thus, I suggest that the case study displays both Papushpa's and my own struggle with tensions between imposed rules and moralities, and individual freedom in dealing with each of our individual situations and our mutual encounter.

Such tension, I suggest, is further linked to an acknowledgement that the self and the process of subjectification are more than local. The tensions between imposed principles and individual freedom also demonstrate a human form of agency and disposition to connect, as the individuals extend their self and their community to others, as well as to history and meaning (see also Moore 2011). The Tamils, such as Papushpa and her family, are not solely trying to be or act the same as the Tamil images, values and moralities that are presented in current surroundings and partly embodied as part of their habituated and 'longue durée' (Braudel 1972) history and traditions. More so, Papushpa and the other Tamils explore affective dispositions, consider potentialities offered, and seek to extend self and community into the local Tamil and Norwegian community, Tamil diasporic global community, and the wider world. The re-creation or imitation of what is left (the Tamil communities in Sri Lanka) is not purely imitative, it is improvised and created anew (see Argenti 2007; Grønseth 2013; Ingold and Hallam 2007). This is an understanding that reaches beyond (often presupposed) dominance, exclusion and suffering (while not ignoring these), within the Tamil community as well as in the encounter with the Norwegian community, an understanding that easily renders many individuals and communities as passive victims. Rather, the appreciation of ethics and knowledge as relationally constituted is meant as a complementary approach that engages with how people creatively imagine their world across time and space, and enhances their moral capacities, while also often maintaining versions of moral communities (see also Moore 2011; Karlström 2004).

Thus, I argue that human beings and knowledge about them are constituted by a relational character between self and Other (see also Grønseth 2014), as this is always communicated in social imaginaries and relations of power. As such, the relation self-Other as also subject-intersubjectivity is always historically specific and takes distinct forms at different times. Acknowledging the relational human – though not as transcendental or universal – the relations of knowledge creation are a matter for investigation calling for ethical commitment and concern.

Concluding Remarks: Ethics of Incomplete Knowledge

Considering my overall aim of exploring Tamil experiences of illness and well-being, I turned towards an approach of being with and sharing everyday experiences with the Tamils. In engaging with the Tamils I stretched myself towards the Other, and came to appreciate a creation of knowledge about the Other as it emerged in intersubjective moments on the borderlands between self and Other. From this position, it appears that knowledge can never be complete, and thus not singular. Furthermore, it is a position that challenges often taken for granted morals and ethics, as in the case of Papushpa. Considering this case, the multiplicity of ethics and knowledge appears in how I accompanied Papushpa in her isolation and suffering, rather than actively intervening. However, I sought to keep an eye on her and hoped that my visits, in a modest manner, could lighten her misery. My visits were thus motivated by a wish to keep her from crossing a line in her suffering, whilst also continue my academic effort to gain insight and create knowledge about Tamil everyday experiences of illness and well-being. More than utilizing the case study to judge my own or Papushpa's actions as such, it is meant to point towards an approach to knowledge creation that recognizes how ethics must be distinguished from sheer compliance or wrongdoing. By appreciating this distinction, I follow Henrietta Moore when she points out how such a distinction allows us to expand on how we understand social change and how it occurs (2011:15). Thus, I understand the ethics of creating knowledge as fundamentally related to how we deal with each other and comprehend the complexity in relations that characterize it.

Exploring illness, suffering and well-being can show how these experiences contain tensions in relations between dominance and freedom. In these relations there is often an emphasis on 'inner processes' shaped amid 'violence and social suffering' (Biehl, Good and Kleinman 2007:1). However, within such an approach, focus is here turned towards the human experience, and the intersections between the subjective and the intersubjective. Appreciating that the subject always has both a personal and social history, and that the intersubjective relations are formative, though not always explicit, I argue that our analysis cannot solely focus on conscious meanings and intentions. When further recognizing the subject as always embodied, it appears that individuals have experiences and stories that cannot be fully grasped by language and symbols. Thus, I suggest, an ethical approach is needed that recognizes a dynamic space for the embodied, empathic and imaginative creation of knowledge, as one can never completely know oneself or the Other.

Anne Sigfrid Grønseth is Professor of Anthropology at Lillehammer University College, and head of Unite of Health, Culture and Identity. She has also held a position at the Norwegian Centre for Minority Health Research. Recent publications are *Lost Selves and Lonely Persons: Experiences of Illness and Well-Being among Tamil Refugees in Norway* (2010), *Mutuality and Empathy: Self and Other in the Ethnographic Encounter* (eds) (2010), and *Being Human, Being Migrant: Senses of Self and Well-Being* (ed.) (2013).

Notes

1. Catherine Lutz (1988) argues that she undertakes a process of socialization that makes her like her informants, the Ilongot.
2. In Hinduism, Saraswati is the goddess of knowledge, music, arts and science. She is the companion of Brahma and is also revered as his shakti (a sacred force or empowerment, a primordial cosmic energy, and divine feminine creative power). It was with Saraswati's knowledge that Brahma created the universe.
3. Individual life task is in Hindu terminology referred to as *svadharma.*
4. Hindu philosophy and ethics teach that 'right action' for a person depends both on the cultural context in which he or she is born, the historical time in which he or she lives, the efforts required of him or her at different stages in life and on his or her psychobiological traits, which are the heritage of previous lives. Right and wrong is thus relative and only emerge out of the total configuration. A person can never know in an absolute sense, or significantly influence the configuration of svadharma, as it is given. A psychosocial consequence of this ethical relativism, or uncertainty, is that a Hindu person may find it difficult to take the cultural as well as the personal risk to make an individual judgement in a situation and then act upon it (Kakar 1997: 37). When

certainty proves impossible, one may at least increase psychological certainty by acting as one's ancestors did in the past and as one's social group does at present.

6. The religious term shakti holds the qualities of strength, energy and vigour, and one should note that its strength is based on a spiritual embodied force (Wadley 1977). This may be seen to fit with how Marriot and Inden (1977) refer to a non-duality between action and substance. Shakti is neither a physical nor moral power, but both. '*Shakti* is a result of morality or right action, which is transformed into an embodied *shakti*, which results in a transformed physical state (bodily substance)' (Wadley 1977: 139, parenthesis in original). From such ideas, one may see that religion has no separate realm, but it is part of everyday life.

References

Argenti, N. 2007. *The Intestines of the State: Youth, Violence and Belated Histories in the Cameroon Grassfields.* Chicago: Chicago University Press.

Bicharat, G. 1997. *Exile to Campatriate: Transformations in the Social Identity of Palestinian Refugees on the West Bank*, in Akhil Gupta, James Fergerson (eds). Durham, NC: Duke University Press, pp. 203–33.

Biehl, J., B. Good and A. Kleinman. 2007. *Subjectivity: Ethnographic Investigations.* Berkeley: University of California Press.

Bourdieu, P. 1989. *Outline of a Theory of Practice.* Cambridge: Cambridge University Press.

Braudel, F. 1972. *The Mediterranean and the Mediterranean World in the Age of Philip II*, 2 vols, trans. S. Reynolds. London: Fontana.

Clifford, J. 1994. 'Diasporas', *Cultural Anthropology* 9: 302–338.

Daniel, V. and J. Chr. Knudsen (eds). 1995. *Mistrusting Refugees.* California: University of California Press.

David, K. 1974. 'Spatial Organization and Normative Schemes in Jaffna, North Ceylon', *Modern Ceylon Studies* 3(1).

———. 1977. 'Hierarchy and Equivalence in Jaffna, North Sri Lanka: Normative Codes as Mediator', in K. David (ed.), *The New Wind: Changing Identities in South Asia.* Hague and Paris: Mouton Publishers.

Deleuze, G. and F. Guattari. 1987. *A Thousand Plateaus*, trans. B. Massumi. Minneapolis, MN: University of Minnesota Press. Vol. 2 of *Capitalism and Schizophrenia*, 2 vols, 1972–1980, trans. M. Plateaux. Paris: Les Editions de Minuit.

Derrida, J. 1974. *Of Grammatology.* Baltimore, MD: Johns Hopkins University Press.

Engebrigtsen, A. and Ø. Fuglerud. 2007. *Youth in Refugee-Families: Family and Friendship – Security or Freedom? [Ungdom i flyktningefamilier: Familie og vennskap – trygghet eller frihet?].* NOVA-rapport 3/07. Oslo: NOVA.

Faubion, J. 2001. 'Toward an Anthropology of Ethics: Foucault and the Pedagogies of Autopoiesis', *Representations* 74: 83–104.

Foucault, M. 1985. *The History of Sexuality. Vol. II: The Use of Pleasure.* New York: Pantheon.

———. 1989 [1969]. *The Archeology of Knowledge,* trans. A.M. Sheridan Smith. London: Routledge.

———.1998. *Ethics: Subjectivity and Truth (Essential Works of Michel Foucault, 1954-1984).* New York: New Press.

Frøystad, K. 2003. 'Master-Servant Relations and the Domestic Reproduction of Caste in Northern India', *Ethnos* 68(1): 73–94.

Grønseth, A.S. 2001. 'In Search of Community: A Quest for Well-Being among Tamil Refugees in Northern Norway', *Medical Anthropology Quarterly* 15(4): 493–514.

———. 2006a. 'Experiences of Illness: Tamil Refugees in Norway Seeking Medical Advice', in H. Johannessen and I. Làzàr (eds), *Multiple Medical Realities: Patients and Healers in Biomedical, Alternative and Traditional Medicine.* New York and Oxford: Berghahn, Chapter 10, pp. 148–62.

———. 2006b. 'Experiences of Tensions in Re-orienting Selves: Tamil Refugees in Northern Norway Seeking Medical Advice', *Anthropology and Medicine* 13(1).

———. 2007. 'Introduction: Ethnographic Humanism: Migrant Experiences in the Quest for Well-Being', *Anthropology in Action* 14(1&2): 1–11.

———. 2010a. *Lost Selves and Lonely Persons: Experiences of Illness and Well-Being among Tamil Refugees in Norway.* Durham, NC: Carolina Academic Press.

———. 2010b. 'Sharing Experiences with Tamil Refugees in Northern Norway: Body and Emotion as Methodological Tools', in A.S. Grønseth and D.L. Davis (eds), *Mutuality and Empathy: Self and Other in the Ethnographic Encounter.* Herefordshire: Sean Kingston Publishing.

———. 2011. 'Being Tamil in Norway: Negotiations of Well-Being and Identity', in R. Cheran, D. Singh, C. Kanaganayakam, S. Durayappah (eds). *World Without Walls: Being Human, Being Tamil.* Toronto: TSAR Publications.

———. 2013. (ed.) *Being Human, Being Migrant: Senses of Self and Well-Being.* New York and Oxford: Berghahn Books.

———. 2014. 'Experiences of Pain: A Gateway to Cosmopolitan Subjectivity', in L. Josephides and A. Hall (eds), *We the Cosmopolitans: Moral and Existential Conditions of Being Human.* New York and Oxford: Berghahn Books.

Grønseth, A.S. and D.L. Davis (eds). 2010. *Mutuality and Empathy: Self and Other in the Ethnographic Encounter.* Herefordshire: Sean Kingston Publishing.

Hammond, L. 2004. *This Place Will Become Home: Refugee Repatriation To Ethiopia.* Cornell: Cornell University Press.

Henriksen, K., L. Østby and D. Ellingsen (eds.) 2010. *Immigration and Immigrants 2010*. [Innvandring og innvandrere 2010]. Oslo: Statistics Norway [Statistisk sentralbyrå].

Ingold, T. 1993. 'The Art of Translation in a Continuous world', in G. Pàlsson (ed.), *Beyond Boundaries: Understanding, Translation and Anthropological Discourse*. Oxford: Berg.

Ingold, T. and E. Hallam (eds). 2007. 'Creativity and Cultural Improvisation: An Introduction', in *Creativity and Cultural Improvisation*. Oxford: Berg, pp. 1–24.

Jackson, M. 1998. *Minima Ethnographica: Intersubjectivity and the Anthropological Project*. Chicago: University for Chicago Press.

Jacques, F. 1982. *Différence et subjectivité*. Paris: Aubier.

Jenkins, J. 1996. 'The Impress of Extremity: Women's Experience of Trauma and Political Violence', in Carol Sargent and C. Brettell (eds), *Gender and Health: An International Perspective*. New Jersey: Prentice-Hall.

Kakar, S. 1997. *The Inner World: A Psychoanalytic Study of Childhood and Society in India*. Oxford: Oxford University Press.

Karlström, M. 2004. 'Modernity and Its Aspirants: Moral Community and Developmental Eutiopianism in Buganda', *Current Anthropology* 45(5): 595–618.

Lacan, J. 1992. *The Seminar of Jacques Lacan*, Book VII, J.A. Miller (ed.). New York: Morton.

Lambek, M. (ed.). 2010. *Ordinary Ethics: Anthropology, Language, and Action*. New York: Fordham University Press.

Levinas, E. 2003 [1972]. *Humanism of the Other*. Illinois: University of Illinois Press.

Lutz, C. 1988. *Unnatural Emotions: Everyday Sentiments on a Micronesian Atoll and their Challenge to Western Theory*. Chicago: University of Chicago Press.

Malkki, L. 1995. *Purity and Exile: Violence, Memory and National Cosmology among Hutu Refugees in Tanzania*. Chicago: The University of Chicago Press.

Marriott, McKim and R. B. Inden. 1977 'Toward and Ethnosociology of South Asian Caste Systems', in David, Kenneth (ed). *The New Wind: Changing Identities in South Asia*. Hague and Paris: Mouton Publishers.

Merleau-Ponty, M. 1962 [1945]. *Phenomenology of Perception*. London: Routledge and Kegan Paul.

———. 1964. *The Primacy of Perception*, J. Edie (ed.). Evanstone, IL: Northwestern University Press.

Migliorino, N. 2008. *(Re)constructing Armenia in Lebanon and Syria: Ethnocultural Diversity and the State in the Aftermath of a Refugee Crisis*. New York and Oxford: Berghahn Books.

Moore, H.L. 2011. *Still Life. Hopes, Desires and Satisfactions*. Cambridge: Polity Press.

Nussbaum, M. 1986. *The Fragility of Goodness: Luck and Ethics in Greek Tragedy and Philosophy*. London: Cambridge University Press.

Rouse, R. 1991. 'Mexican Migration and the Social Space of Postmodernism', *Diaspora* 1(1): 83–99.

Safran, W. 1991. 'Diasporas in Modern Societies: Myths of Homeland and Return', *Diaspora* 1(1): 83–99.

Schiller, N.G., L. Basch, and C. Blanc-Szanton (eds). 1992. *Towards a Transnational Perspective on Migration*. The New York Academy of Sciences. 645. New York: The New York Academy of Sciences.

Sideris, T. 2003. 'War, Gender and Culture: Mozambican Women Refugees', *Social Science & Medicine* 56(4): 713–24.

Simmel, G. 1950. *The Sociology of George Simmel*. New York: Free Press.

Wadley, S. 1977. 'Power in Hindu Ideology and Practice', in K. Davis (ed.), *The New Wind: Changing Identities in South Asia*. Hague and Paris: Mouton Publishers.

Zmegac, J.C. 2007. *Strangers Either Way: The Lives of Croatian Refugees in Their New Home*. New York and Oxford: Berghahn Books.

Chapter 2

THE DANGER OF KNOWLEDGE

EXERCISING SAMENESS, BOUND
TO DIFFERENTIATION

Giovanna Bacchiddu

This chapter explores the relationship between knowledge and danger, focusing on the implications of knowledge perceived as threatening in social interactions in two different research contexts. The first setting, the small island of Apiao in southern Chile, demonstrates that knowledge is part of everyday life and an indispensable tool, yet it can be fraught with danger. In a community where people strive to ensure lack of differentiation, knowledge is dangerous because it promotes differences between people, entailing different access to sources of power, and to witchcraft. The same issues of dangerous knowledge, and the presence or lack of differentiation, are further explored in the second research context, one that concerns children adopted in Chile and taken to Sardinia. The concept of dangerous knowledge informs and affects everyday life and relationality, both for the adoptees and their adoptive parents. Ways of overcoming the painfully experienced asymmetries include strategic manipulation of differentiation and sameness, according to contingent needs. In both research settings the ethnographer's presence and enquiry gave rise to perceptions of representing a dangerous threat, and at the same time was invested with knowledge expectations, raising yet again issues of sameness versus differentiation on the part of informants and ethnographer alike.

The knowledge discussed in this chapter is not moral-oriented knowledge: it is rather knowledge intended as possession of information about the world and about the other. While certainly agreeing with Michael Lambek (2010) in his consideration that the ethical pervades social life in all its direct and indirect manifestations, the knowledge I refer to deals specifically with the subtle implications of the pairing up of knowledge and perceived (social) danger, and the way this specific dyad gets entangled with differentiation and its contrary, sameness; and its consequences for the social dynamics in the settings under study.

The various ways and modes in which and through which people create and share knowledge via relations and commitments are the object of philosophers' enquiries about common features of humanity; anthropology is increasingly engaging in a dialogue with such philosophical debates (again, see Lambek 2010), articulating connections that enrich and substantiate its ethnographical roots in the effort to describe and interpret social mechanics.

Anthropologists have always been interested in discerning and conveying the sophisticated ways in which people in society organize their thinking, with the task of rendering other people's world views intelligible. A recent shift in the discipline has called for a focus on the relational over the systemic as a locus of knowledge creation; in the words of Henrietta Moore (1996: 9) 'We are now no longer looking for ontological categories, but for interwoven patterns; what was once systemic is now mobile'. This chapter captures the subject matter of this volume with a reflection on relational knowledge through a few themes that have recurred throughout my research in two different settings, southern Chile and Sardinia.

Knowledge and the process of its creation, accumulation and exchange are firmly entwined in the unfolding of all social relations. I take knowledge to be a form of social capital, as drafted by Bourdieu, who described it as 'the aggregate of the actual or potential resources which are linked to possession of a durable network of more or less institutionalized relationships of mutual acquaintance and recognition – or in other words, to membership in a group' (1986: 51). Knowledge, strongly relational, is developed through connections; it allows people to be socially active, hence socially meaningful. It becomes a profitable tool in dealing with everyday life in its social aspects: through its application people earn social esteem and build alliances. Bourdieu observes that making and maintaining connections is a process requiring continuous effort, but this effort is necessary because through such ties the group is reproduced. As Bourdieu notes (1986: 56), however, efforts to obtain profitable outcomes do not guarantee equal results to all actors involved. Different individuals may obtain unequal profits from equivalent capital: hence the possibility of differentiation, and the consequent danger.

Children learn early in life basic information about themselves, the place they inhabit and the people that surround them; they learn what is expected of them, and the rules that inform social life. Adults refine that knowledge, slowly accumulated in years of experience, adding further acquisitions to their exploration map. Knowledge is formed, exchanged and passed over in each social interaction. In perpetual development, knowledge grows and is constantly updated, enriched and adapted to yet another social situation, adaptation that entails continuous efforts. Knowledge of oneself, of others and of the world is what sociality is made of. Its benefits, however, are accompanied by some liabilities: it may promote difference between individuals and inequality. In the contexts under discussion, knowledge appears intimately connected to notions and expressions of sameness and difference. Sameness, a value that encompasses inclusion, belonging to a group, 'shared localness' (Cohen 1987: 48) is to be achieved and maintained, whereas difference epitomizes exclusion, is the negation of belonging and simultaneously an inescapable feature of social individuals. Sameness and difference, I argue, are articulated around the notion of knowledge, a social tool that may guarantee substantial gains, but also cause considerable losses. My reflections will revolve around these double aspects of knowledge, highlighting the correlation between knowledge and danger, illustrating how knowledge can be experienced as empowering but also produce constraints and social conflicts, to be warded off by careful and strategic negotiation.

Sameness and difference are concepts lying at the heart of the project of anthropology as an academic discipline and a scientific endeavour. While anthropology's interest has shifted from a study of exotic difference (such as the 'sensational, wild and unaccountable world of "savages"', Malinowski 1922: 10) to an 'understanding of the interconnected and changing worlds of experience' (Ortner 2002: 8), anthropologists are always interested in local categories, formulated by their hosts, as crucial loci of significance. In the research contexts discussed in this chapter, some of the categories that regularly emerged were expressions of sameness and difference, as vehicles of inclusion/exclusion, categories whose existence and articulation presupposes a relational context. The categorization of sameness and difference contains the intrinsic danger of transforming alterity into what Moore calls 'processes of radical othering' (1996: 6): in the dialectic of oppositions, the other's difference is charged with negativity and used as grounds for exclusion or discrimination.

This chapter explores issues of communication and knowledge in two different communities, focusing on contrasting aspects of sameness and difference, visibility and invisibility, gain and loss. The first context is a small Amerindian community, characterized by insularity and prone to thinking of itself through articulations of sameness and difference, viewed as extremes along which social life dialectically unfolds. The second part considers issues of sameness and difference in a group of Chilean-born adoptees and their Sardinian parents. Both settings experience a pairing of knowledge and danger; these instances, illustrated and analysed through ethnographic data, offer an opportunity to reflect on the anthropologist's involvement – and entanglement – with these same facets of relationality.[1]

I. Apiao, Chiloé, Chile

Apiao is a small island in the Chiloé archipelago, in southern Chile. Completely rural, the island lies three hours away by boat from a town on a bigger island, with electricity and facilities such as a bank, post office and local government office. Apiao's 700 inhabitants live in households scattered across the territory, subsisting on agriculture, small animal farming, fishing and shell collecting. Strongly egalitarian, the islanders are related to the Mapuche – the main southern Chilean indigenous group – although, unlike them, they quickly converted to Catholicism in the seventeenth century. They lost their language, but retain their indigenous heritage in their surnames and place names.

Apiao people define themselves as 'island people'. Their insularity shapes and informs their lifestyle, their world view and the way they communicate and share knowledge with one another and with strangers. Apiao people consider themselves to be alike. They often state: 'Here we are all equal, all the same'. This statement expresses their perception of themselves as a compact group, comprising those born and living on the island and excluding whoever does not belong there. They share a common origin, engage in the same activities, share interests and concerns; they have the same duties and everyday tasks to accomplish. It is extremely difficult for Apiao people to choose a person to represent them, because this implies declaring someone different from the others. And they are 'all the same'.

Apiao stated sameness is the pre-requisite for meaningful social relations, which always entail reciprocal exchange between people who consider themselves as equals. Both Cohen (1987) and Byron (1986) report the exact same assertion by Scottish islanders of Whalsay and Burra, showing how insularity and marginality favour what Cohen defines as normative egalitarianism (1987: 60) in small-scale communities.

Knowledge: An Indispensable Tool

All children follow the same routine to acquire the knowledge necessary to become autonomous individuals, which is the definition of adulthood in Apiao. They learn from an early age how to do things in and around the house, the basic knowledge needed in everyday life. They learn through careful observation, rarely asking questions or seeking explanations; they especially do not ask how to do things, nor do their parents tell them; they constantly observe the adults, following them and imitating them in their playtime. Children reach full adult status only when able to perform certain tasks responsibly and independently. Social knowledge, or the proper way to engage in social relations, is never taught either: children observe it and learn it from an early age, being immersed in a social group that adheres to an unwritten code of decorum (see Bacchiddu 2010). The application of knowledge that regulates social commitments revolves around the principle of reciprocity. This corpus of information includes the social duties involved in annual events connected with the agricultural cycle, religious rituals and the perpetuation of alliances with fellow islanders. This knowledge is essential and defines individuals as active members of the community.[2]

Social knowledge aside, having knowledge of any kind, such as that acquired travelling or working elsewhere, is a desirable condition, always empowering. Conversely, just knowing one's surroundings denotes lack of experience of the world, an undesirable state that causes complaints and discomfort vis-à-vis outsiders and strangers.

The Danger of the Others

Communication with fellow islanders – the volume of one's social capital per Bourdieu – requires skills that children learn through observation and continuously practise and refine. These skills are relatively predictable because shared by all islanders. Dealing with islanders entails negotiation and effort; interacting with outsiders requires skills of a different order. I will consider various degrees of otherness and difference as experienced by Apiao people, starting with outsiders such as occasional visitors, continuing with non-local residents, and finally I will look at nuances of sameness and difference amongst Apiao islanders themselves.

There are different degrees of alterity that Apiao people confront. Outsiders, townspeople and strangers are always dangerous (on outsiders' radical diversity, see also Rapport 1997). Coming from a different social world, they have different orders of knowledge. This implies that they know more than the average Apiao person and might not understand or appreciate the way things are done there. This becomes manifest in the reactions to the hospitality ritual, which involves offers of food and drink. While fellow islanders, familiar with the hospitality imperative, always accept whatever is offered eagerly, strangers are well known for their erratic behaviour when offered food and drink in Apiao households. They might be suspicious, judge the food as below their standards, or even refuse the offers. This is considered a serious insult and a grave offence. The ignorance of the hospitality rule (the obligation of the host to offer food and drink, and the obligation of the guest to receive it) reveals the difficulty of engaging with otherness, and the danger implicit in difference. Discourses of marginality and backwardness, inherited from discourses of government officials or town dwellers, interested in forcing people into categories and identities, are internalized and emerge when the islanders feel their vulnerability is exposed. This happens when they are confronted with outsiders and strangers, encounters that, they believe, highlight their lack of knowledge. Insularity and being a peripheral, peasant community, in a country where indigeneity has strong political implications and carries a stigma, further contributes to the Apiao experience of marginality.

Potentially dangerous individuals are the occasional visitors that travel to the island yearly: priests and missionaries, government officials and guests of the non-locals (see Bacchiddu 2012). The visitors' unpredictability, their lack of familiarity with the local ways and the fear of being judged is what makes Apiao people sensitive to strangers, perceived as threatening.

Apiao schoolteachers, health service staff and technicians of the salmon farms implanted on the island's waters are resident outsiders. Fairly dangerous at first, they slowly familiarize themselves with the Apiao social world and their danger diminishes with time. The professionals are compared and contrasted by the locals in terms of 'difference' rather than in terms of positive/negative value. This ontology discourse is the Apiao version of the 'us/them' distinction. Teachers (for decades the main category of difference in Apiao), for example, are reputedly profoundly different from the locals due to their education-acquired knowledge. They are considered high status because of their position and income – enormous by Apiao standards. Marrying a teacher is considered highly profitable and male teachers are always the object of female attention; having a child with a teacher, even as a single mother, is a desirable choice. At the same time, although this would never be stated explicitly, their work is not considered proper work. In commenting on a lazy woman, who does nothing, people would say 'Look at her, as if she were a teacher!' *('Parece profesora!').* Teachers can boast of education, but they lack knowledge acquired with experience (see Edwards 1999: 310) and do not know 'real' work (i.e., agricultural work) and how to do it properly.[3] Their high status and money endow them with knowledge of a different order from the one that makes up life in Apiao. Despite long-term residency, active participation in the community's life and familiarity with locals, teachers are perceived as outsiders, different and dangerous. They are, however, taken in high consideration and often sought to be part of alliances. Apiao people use relational knowledge fruitfully, by deploying communicational strategies profitable to their end. The benefit consists in a richer network of connections with which to entertain gift exchange, work party exchange, etc. However, Apiao people are conscious of the levels of sameness and difference that are part of their social world and they choose whom to include and whom to exclude from their attempt at networking. Apiao sociality reveals the danger of social interaction (= knowledge of the other), and the necessity of it.

The Risk of Exclusion

If outsiders are perceived as different, and as such threatening, the flip side of this is the safeness enjoyed amongst people that are 'all the same'. Not only do Apiao people perceive themselves as equal, they also entertain balanced reciprocity in all of their social exchanges, and include supernatural beings in their social world (see Bacchiddu 2011). The world is conceived of and experienced as a network of exchanges that are always reciprocal. The rules that govern interaction are clear, and shared by all parties involved in the exchange. Interaction and exchange, requiring 'unceasing effort' (Bourdieu 1986: 52), is necessary 'in order to produce and reproduce lasting, useful relationships that can secure material or symbolic profits' (ibid.). If the starting point is an often-mentioned equality, in the words of Apiao people sameness acquires a strong levelling value and becomes a crucial aspect to be preserved in order to maintain social equilibrium on the island. Indeed, sameness is not only an obvious characteristic of Apiao inhabitants; it becomes a near-moral value to achieve, maintain, defend and exhibit.

Whenever someone acquires something out of the ordinary, earns unusual sums of money, secures alliances with powerful strangers or radically changes lifestyle, they are somehow leaving sameness behind and joining differentiation; in other words they are becoming more like outsiders and strangers and less like Apiao people. Their perceived difference is dangerous; it questions values and characteristics that up to then had been shared: identity, network alliances, complicity and knowledge. If sameness protects, difference leaves one's vulnerability exposed, and this can happen not only with outsiders, but with fellow islanders too. By acting differently, some Apiao individuals jeopardize their position, running the risk of being excluded. There is danger on both sides: if individuals act differently they are dangerous to the others, who find them threatening; at the same time their behaviour is dangerous to themselves, as it puts them at risk of social exclusion (which is what happened to the evangelical converts described in Bacchiddu 2009). Such individuals lose the 'backing of the collectivity', the 'credentials' in Bourdieu's words.

Practising Sameness: Antagonism Reversed

When Apiao people mention their sameness, it is because, as we have seen, it protects them from outsiders perceived as threatening, and it allows constant reproduction of the group through reciprocal exchange, which is vital. Declarations of sameness are accompanied by its practice, a continuous rehearsal of it. This way of being could be described as antagonism reversed: a constant tension towards ensuring that one's behaviour, possessions and choices are always predictable, and indirectly accepted and ratified by the community. This is done to avoid standing out, becoming noticeable, which would give rise to gossip, judgemental remarks and, ultimately, conflict.

How can sameness be practised? Much of everyday life in Apiao, with its expressions and uses of knowledge, is enmeshed in issues of visibility and invisibility. People strive to make everything that they experience as invisible as possible. This is because showing equates to showing off, a strong statement in a community of people who are alike. My friend Luz expressed generous and sincere affection whenever I visited her in her household, but kept a discreet distance in public. She explained that she preferred to refrain from being demonstrative in public, to avoid becoming the target of judgemental remarks because of our friendship. She could have been judged as wanting to rise socially, wanting to appear different by displaying a relationship. In Apiao, people strive to ensure lack of differentiation.

One form of knowledge regularly practised, and an integral part of everyday social life, is the intimate knowledge of one's fellow islanders. People appear interested in whatever their neighbours are doing, and spend a considerable amount of their time observing them and their activities, and speculating about them. This attitude is generally divested of malevolence: it is simply part of the everyday lived experience, of the social world as it is. Knowing the other helps shape the way to relate to everyone, to each one in a specific way. Being part of a small-scale group, it is imperative for people to avoid conflict, and at the same time keep boundaries in order to protect themselves. People tend to be reserved, and track the knowledge that others have of themselves. They are aware of the danger of disclosing too much information, and shield their private life as much as possible. Hence people are trying on the one hand to acquire knowledge about others, and on the other to prevent others from acquiring knowledge about them. Access to information about others is definitely empowering; allowing others to access information about oneself denotes loss of power. This knowledge differs from gossip; there is no interest in circulating precious information about other individuals or in discussing it within a circle of friends. It is rather the contrary: accessing information about others allows a certain control over them in interpersonal interaction, in specific circumstances such as trying to obtain favours; in Bourdieu's terms, it increases one's capital. Control over others is not to be shared amongst many. This is why people are tendentially extremely reserved; sharing information is not in their best interests.

Apiao specific topography, with households scattered on both sides of the main path and surrounded by wide fields, allows people both to see and be seen from a distance. The path is monitored by households on its margins, affording a good view of passers-by. Householders gaze out of their windows and wonder aloud about the traveller's journey. Households that sit above the coast have a wider control of information on any occasional or regular traveller, boat owner or activity taking place at the beach. Those enjoying a particularly good view of their neighbours openly comment on whatever they see beyond the fence. This is a favourite pastime, usually not implying any malice; visitors would join in and participate in observing the scene: 'Look at Francisco! What's he doing?' 'He must be getting organized to work on his orchard!' 'What's he cultivating?' 'Cabbage, it must be!' 'Look, he's walking down, what's he carrying in that sack?' 'Potatoes, it must be!' 'And where's his wife? Why is she not helping him?' 'Doing the washing, she must be!' 'She spent a whole week at her mother's; I doubt she'd have done any washing there!' 'That must be it, then!' And so on. When those observed are engaging in a lucrative project, such as gathering and processing seaweed for sale – an activity practised by most – quick calculations are made in order to guess the amount of cash that will be earned by zealous workers.

Being 'all the same', people know the implications of being constantly monitored, and make great efforts to prevent possible judgements or accusations from others. After I spent a day with the neighbours observing their pig slaughtering, they insisted I take home a gift of sausages, so that my host could see that I had been treated with generosity. It was not convenient for me – I had other commitments before returning home – yet my neighbours insisted I carry the meat gift home, to prevent an accusation of greed from those who enjoyed a full view of their everyday activities. A woman visiting a distant neighbourhood scolded her grandson for playing with a piglet found on the path. 'Stop doing that or people will say you sent their pig away from the household!' Aware of being under people's gaze, and particularly so since she was not in her own area, the woman knew the implications of what seemed an innocent game: accusations, consequent social disruption, conflicts to avoid at all costs.

'One look is enough' to detect some news, a friend told me. 'We all know each other, there are no secrets here; eventually everything emerges', she said, telling me that she had seen her neighbour with a man other than her husband, and that just by looking at her, she knew. Individuals are well aware of the constant gaze of others, and perfect the art of dissimulation, developing a strategy to prevent conflict.

Dissimulation: An Exercise in Negotiation

If 'everyone being the same' translates into everyone knowing everything about each other, individuals employ colourful negotiation techniques in their dialectical engagement with the others. Negotiation allows for flexibility and fluidity of boundaries; through clever negotiation people avoid hostility and friction and restore balance. People perfect the art of negotiating, employing various strategies to influence, convince and attract the other into small and contingent alliances, to be renewed each time there is an encounter.

Resourceful Don Bastian sometimes managed to obtain financial help from the local government by adhering to rural unions. His success caused envy in his extended family, whose members were not as quick-witted, but they appreciated the benefits from any funding he secured. Sara, passing by the man's house, noticed some fledgling chickens that she quite liked. Once home, and after commenting on the man's luck in obtaining the domestic animals, she quickly developed a strategy and decided to return to see the man and ask him to sell her at least one: *'me vende?'* 'Would you sell me (one of your chicks)?' The expression 'me vende?' in some circumstances acquires a specific meaning that differs from its original one. As such, the verb 'to sell' is not appropriate, yet it is the one used in such instances. Angela was regularly asked for milk by her mother-in-law, who always assumed she had some to spare. She invariably introduced her request by asking, 'me vende?' Angela told me that she would not accept money from her mother-in-law, and that it was easier to give her the milk for free whenever she asked for it.

When uttering the expression 'me vende?' neither woman actually meant to offer money in exchange for something. As it was inappropriate to ask for something directly, they communicated their desire to acquire the item by the verbal expedient of mentioning an economic transaction. They wanted the item to be given for free, but offering money for it shielded them from being in the awkward position of asking for a gift – gifts are given, not requested. Those who were asked found themselves obliged to gift the items, since asking for money for such small items would have been inappropriate. All actors were familiar with the nature of the game; while those who were asked might have considered the technique questionable, the aim being to hand over something that belonged to them, those doing the asking proved the virtues of negotiation, and reciprocity.

Another episode shows the disguise of some aspects of reality for personal benefit. Fernanda visited a relative and gave her some fish her son had caught the previous night, saying that he had caught 'very little, not much at all' and that the sea bass were 'very small'. She offered the fish as payment for a debt she owed her relative. Hours later, a visiting neighbour commented on the 'miraculous fishing' of the previous night, with fifty kilos of fish caught between the two fishermen. The same event is alternately portrayed as 'not much at all', and 'miraculous' by two different people; they had a reason, however, to see the same event in a different perspective. Or more correctly: to appear to be seeing it differently. Fernanda's interests were better protected by downplaying the success of her son's fishing expedition. No one could fish for months on the island, and the two men's accomplishment was remarkable. Fernanda's son decided to sell all his catch, while his companion chose to smoke and keep his share. Fernanda's son's choice could cause envy, and speculation on his earnings and his reasons for wanting cash. Fernanda was right: people did speculate about all this, despite her verbal strategy of communication. To protect her family from spitefulness, she added some extra fish to the amount owed, as a gift.

These examples portray an exercise in 'sameness'. Whenever people acquire something that might make them appear different from the rest, they become the target of theorizing, conjectures and discussion. Negotiation becomes crucial whenever individuals, through a stroke of luck or a successful initiative, become somehow publicly different from others. Visibility is critical here: the news had become available, both fledgling and fish were seen by the neighbours. Differentiation is not problematic as such, it only becomes dangerous when noticeable: the knowledge that others have about someone can cause friction and dangerous conflicts.

A Different Kind of Knowledge: Witchcraft

While negotiation is a relational tool allowing people to reverse unfavourable situations and avoid potential conflicts, in some contexts negotiation is ineffective. Witchcraft is considered the most dangerous non-negotiable situation, one that denies and contradicts the imperative of equality, cross-cutting any category of sameness or difference. It is believed that organized witchcraft, historically associated with Chiloé for centuries, is still strong in the area (Rojas Flores 2002). In Apiao some individuals are considered extremely dangerous for possessing a kind of knowledge that is shared only by a few and is so powerful and otherworldly that it cannot be named. The witches, fittingly described euphemistically as 'those who know', are islanders who somehow acquired special powers through connections with evil. Some are rumoured to be witches, but rumours cannot be proven and people avoid the topic, adopting a taboo-like silence. The only sensible attitude is to avoid conflict, maintaining relations of respectful acquaintance.

Witches appear outwardly like everyone else, but have the knowledge to transform into animals, to turn into the spirits and bodies of dead people and to hunt the living. Witches can destroy lives and possessions; they hurt and kill people. They know how to fly – the hallmark of their difference – and most islanders have witnessed some witchcraft-related event at some point in their lives. Witches are greatly feared, because their special knowledge makes them extremely powerful and impossible to counteract. Witchcraft powerfully influences relationality, altering social rules. People avoid going out after sunset, and do not greet people at night – even if they look like family or friends. The imperative is to mistrust familiarity: in some contexts sameness may be the most dangerous otherness in disguise.

In Apiao relational knowledge is the social capital lying at the base of the existence of the group (Bourdieu 1986: 53). Knowledge of the others (relational knowledge, acquired through effort via negotiation, exchange, etc.) is necessary to produce and maintain group dynamics. This is especially crucial in a small-scale society whose experience of marginality is intrinsic to their perception and definition of themselves – geographically, socially and culturally – as it emerges in encounters with otherness.

II. Sardinia, Italy

The second part of this chapter is devoted to a different research setting: that of internationally adopted children in Sardinia, Italy. Another island, another context of geographical marginality within a country, Sardinia experiences the contrast between its role as a luxury holiday destination and its long-term receding economy. The island is part of the economically disadvantaged Mezzogiorno, an area of southern Italy where lack of economic progress is combined with an extremely rich cultural heritage and complex social realities. Sardinia, with approximately 1.5 million inhabitants, is a region with a special political and juridical status within Italy, home to a cultural and linguistic minority.

From the end of the 1970s into the 1980s, a considerable number of Sardinian couples adopted Chilean-born children. While available statistics are unofficial, it is generally believed that a few hundred children travelled from Chile to become Sardinian, their ages ranging between less than one year and eighteen. The data discussed in this chapter refer to lengthy meetings and in-depth conversations with approximately fifty adoptees and twenty-five adoptive parents.

The theme of dangerous knowledge has been a recurring one throughout my encounters with the adoptees and their adoptive parents. Marilyn Strathern quotes incisively that 'the perception of knowledge as gain must inevitably proceed hand in hand with the perception of knowledge as loss' (1995: 10). This exemplifies a common predicament in the life of individuals who have gone through the experience of adoption. Behind each child adopted by willing parents, there is a mother who for whatever reason relinquished that child.

The Revelation of Adoption: Same or Different?

The perception of knowledge as gain, coupled with the perception of knowledge as loss, is the essence of the predicament faced by adoptive parents dealing with the disclosure of information of their child's past. The acquisition of this information changes forever the life of adoptees, who must now deal with this knowledge throughout their lives.[4] While current policies instruct adoptive parents to reveal their origin gently to their children from as early an age as possible, in the past there was hardly any such encouragement and several Sardinian adoptive couples were left to ponder on the lesser of two evils. This often meant that children learned their story traumatically, sometimes from third parties. Once individuals acquire the knowledge of their adoption, contrasting sentiments of gain and loss alternate. If they lost their biological parents and were removed from their country, they gained a new set of motivated parents and a new, relatively comfortable life. Reasons for feeling connected to their adoptive parents are sometimes coupled with motivations to feel disconnected from them, and the dilemma of an imagined life somewhere else haunts adopted children throughout their lives, as does the dramatic awareness of having been unwanted and abandoned. These truths emerge regularly, arising unexpectedly even in innocent social happenings, producing or replicating extremely painful and unsettling experiences of exclusion and loss (see Bacchiddu 2013).

In her work on assisted conception, Bonaccorso interviewed Italian couples that ruled out adoption because it would have exposed the lack of genetic ties between parents and child, highlighting the 'family difference' (2005: 42ff.). Recurrent references to 'normality' by Bonaccorso's informants reveal the need to achieve conformity, to mingle with the mass of couples that they defined 'normal'. Discourses of 'normality' – feeling 'like all the others', 'appearing like all the others' are frequent among my Sardinian informants (adoptees, adoptive parents), similar to Bonaccorso's informants. Most adoptees I met spend considerable time and energy building strategies for dealing with issues of sameness and difference in a Sardinian context where they are often singled out as 'different'. These issues spring out of the knowledge of their history and the knowledge they inhabit and share with society.

Adoptees' knowledge of their difference becomes for them an intrinsic way of being in the world. This is often manifested in the strong sense of responsibility towards their parents. 'You grow up knowing that you are perceived as privileged, and you have the responsibility to demonstrate that you didn't waste the opportunity you were given. That's the bad thing about adoption. The more adopted children receive, the bigger their responsibility', one informant told me. The knowledge of being adopted shifts into a heavy sense of responsibility: the privilege becomes a debt, to be repaid by leading a meaningful life. Adoptees say that while natural children might not feel this pressure, they sometimes feel they have to spend their life being grateful or demonstrating that adopting them was worth it. This knowledge will always mark and differentiate them from non-adopted children. The theme of privilege is frequently mentioned in the adoption literature, where adoptees reportedly feel haunted by a pressing sense of duty and the ensuing guilt of not achieving what they feel is expected of them (for a vivid account of this, see Monestier 2005).

Some Sardinian adoptees wish to feel an integral part of the group, while people around them constantly point out their difference. Society's attitudes and discourse reveal strong awareness of difference, experienced as faulty, as lacking something crucial. The perception of adopted children's difference is indirectly conveyed by the often-heard comment that the child is a fortunate one. Indeed, this might be the most frequently heard phrase by adoptees. It is used as an apparently innocuous comment, but also as an admonishment whenever children or adolescents express their pain with rage. 'How can you behave like this? You are so fortunate!' This comment is so recurrent that some internalize it, and refer to themselves as 'lucky'. Nevertheless, not everyone appreciates these imposed definitions. Anna (adoptive mother) recalled her irritation on hearing that comment while on a walk with her young child, finding it a prejudiced statement. Just like, 'He really looks like he's your child!' to which she emphatically replied 'He *is* my child!' Someone told another mother, 'You chose really well!' commenting on her foreign daughter's beauty, perhaps against all expectations. According to Anna, Sardinians are unprepared to welcome foreign children, the idea being that the latter should best remain in their 'own' country. Later on she had to answer her child's worried question about whether or not she was 'real'. 'Some classmates' parents must have told their child that I was not "his real mother", hence the question about "realness"', she recalled. In another case, people's curiosity towards the relationship established between a foreign child and a Sardinian mother was often expressed even when the adoption process had long been forgotten and the child, who arrived as a toddler, had become an adolescent. 'Does he call you mother?' enquired an acquaintance upon meeting mother and child on the street. The knowledge of his otherness, expressed by a stranger, impinged on the boy's perception of himself as a 'different' child, as an external appendix to a local couple.

The expression 'imitation of biology' (Bartholet 1993: 48) comes to mind. Bartholet argues that the 'as if' model of adoption implies that 'adoption is an inferior and not quite as real form of family which can at best aspire to look like the real thing' (ibid.). Adoptees internalize this concept: 'I love my mother – even if she's not the one who gave birth to me', an adoptee told me. Another adoptee said she was grateful for an adoptive family that never made her feel 'different', despite the fact that she has Chilean blood. The 'real' kinship ties discourse is recurrent, and it reflects the experienced hierarchy of biogenetic ties versus social ties. Bowie (2004), amongst others, comments on how the primacy of biological ties over social or spiritual ties is reflected in Western academic models but does not necessarily represent indigenous categories. The obsession with 'real' categories of kinship according to Howell (2006: 228) is a Western one, and in a similar vein Overing (1985: 5) comments on the elusiveness of the notion of truth.

Whether conveyed by positive comments or negative remarks, the biased perception of adopted children as different, and of their relation to their adoptive parents as unusual and somehow difficult to grasp, is prevalent in the narratives of both adoptees and adoptive parents, who experience subtle and not so subtle discrimination. The knowledge of adoption cannot be undone and it consciously or unconsciously influences the groups' view of individuals and kinship relations.

Resemblances: Looking for Sameness

Sameness (between parents and children and within the rest of the group) then becomes a value to achieve for adoptive families. Achieving sameness gives the impression of erasing differentiation and its negative implications, which international adoption inevitably carries. Adoptive families often experience their effort to achieve sameness endorsed by resemblance, both in character and physical appearance. The resemblance discourse appears repeatedly in the narratives of adoptees, who enjoy tracing and finding lines of connection with their adoptive parents; an emotional expedient, supported by happenstance, to feel safely grounded, part of a concrete, stable unit. Resemblance is also sought and found by other family members, friends or casual acquaintances, who also need to ground the relationship in physical connections (See Howell and Marre 2006: 306ff.).

The concept of resemblance is so powerful that it becomes a vehicle that sustains imagined relations that emerge unexpectedly. Clara was adopted at two months into a fairytale-like family. Her happiness was so complete that she declared to have never felt any wish for or curiosity about her natural mother. When a fellow Chilean adoptee told her of his successful trip to find his own natural mother, showing her the woman's pictures, she was impressed by their physical resemblance. 'She's identical to him! She's just like him in feminine form. Now I'm curious; I'd love to know if I look like someone', she said. And referring to her natural mother: 'I'd like to see her, at least once, even from a distance. I'm not really interested in establishing a relationship – that would have to be maintained, and I don't feel I need it'. However, her friend's enthusiastic account of his experience made Clara rethink the value of sameness. Feeling similarity with her natural mother – someone she otherwise did not wish to spend time with – was perhaps a dormant necessity that materialized unpredictably, prompted by her fellow adoptee's experience (see also Howell 2003: 481, where she discusses adoptees' wish to meet biological relatives in order to see who they look like).

Resemblance, or lack thereof, is always used as a signifier. A woman recently found both her Chilean parents via the Internet. While she quickly established a loving connection with her father, she learnt with sadness that her mother had never been interested in her. 'I was sent her picture, and I saw that we don't look alike; I'm grateful for that, as I was annoyed to know that she never loved her children'. She added that upon learning of the existence of four siblings she was in shock at first, but then she was really glad; she particularly enjoyed realizing that they all look alike. Lack of physical resemblance to her natural mother is paralleled by the woman's lack of motherly love; resemblance with her new-found father and siblings resonated in their willingness to strengthen ties with their estranged family member.

Embracing Difference

Sometimes it becomes an empowering practice to embrace one's own contested identity, which is used as a strategy of self-protection. A young adoptee gave her two babies Chilean names. Aware of her physical difference within her community, she told me how she often has to answer enquiries about her nationality, which she finds insensitive and irritating. And yet she chose to epitomize that difference with the names she chose for her children, turning her passively received difference into a voluntarily chosen differentiation. The same strategy was recently deployed at their wedding by a couple who were both adoptees. The *bomboniera* – a box containing the Italian wedding sweets to present to each guest – was a symbolic synthesis of their identity: each sweet sachet, made with a Sardinian fabric and design, had a Chilean ocarina tied to it. Another adopted woman makes a point of regularly celebrating her arrival into her adoptive family by doing something 'Chilean': this year she had her fingernails painted with the Chilean flag.

Embracing their difference is, for adoptees who become parents, a way to explain their origin to their own children. Natalia told me how she always shared her story with her children, who experienced their mother's unusual origin with curiosity and serenity. This enables them to satisfy their classmates' doubts and answer provocative questions. 'But', says Natalia, 'they learned to defend themselves'. Having to explain alternate forms of kinship is experienced as an attack. The children appear proud of their mother's origin and have learnt some Spanish to communicate with their distant cousins, something they do regularly online. Supported by loving adoptive parents, Natalia transmitted to her children the possibility of parental love that comprehends adoption; in turn her children embraced their mother's adoptive origin and managed to turn a threatening knowledge into a distinctively enriching experience.

Forgetting Difference

The effort to achieve sameness entails the risk of succeeding, clearing the path of any perceptions of difference, an extreme that might have dangerous underpinnings. Adopted parents and children alike told me of how often they forget about the adoption and think of themselves as genetically related. They urge each other to do health check-ups if one of them shows particular symptoms; expecting daughters find themselves asking their adoptive mother about their own pregnancy – forgetting that such an event never took place. When this occurs, it provokes laughter and confirms the intimacy that the family have built throughout the years. Perceived sameness, however, may also harm, when it blanks out adopted people's history, assimilating them to the larger group of children naturally born to their parents. This happened to an adoptee while discussing the possibility of adopting a child with her husband. She froze when her husband candidly admitted that he was not inclined towards adoption, being strongly convinced that he would never love an adopted child as much as a natural one. The man had indirectly denied the possibility of love between parents and adoptive children, thereby declaring his wife's history a defective one, and her experience a pale reflection of the way things ought to be.

When Mario was adopted, at eighteen years of age, he had one living family member in Chile, his grandfather. More than twenty years later, having lost touch with the old man, he manifested strong discomfort at the idea of trying to locate him. He would rather not know anything about his grandfather than have to deal with the news of his death. He also expressed resentment towards his adoptive parents for excluding the man from their family project. They wanted to make a Sardinian of their adoptive Chilean son, disregarding the fact that at eighteen he was a young adult, with parental and emotional connections that could not be truncated. As a result, Mario had to manage the dangerous knowledge of a double abandonment: first as a victim, having been let go by his mother, then as a perpetrator, having left his only relative, an elderly man. The awareness of being somehow responsible for his grandfather's abandonment following his adoption is for Mario so crippling that it prevents him from actively seeking reconnection with this Chilean family member.

Managing Dangerous Knowledge

Arriving into her adoptive family at the age of eleven, having experienced repeated abuse, Marina spent the first months in bliss, enjoying a loving family that expected nothing of her but happiness and peace. Eventually one evening she crumbled and her manifest cheerfulness disappeared, giving way to a violent desperation. Through her tears, she confessed to her mother details of her previous life, sharing information that she had never before dared to bring up. Since her arrival she had fostered the belief that her adoptive parents would not understand or accept such a past, and would never forgive her for it. Having found a loving, non-judgemental family, she was terrified of losing it. She feared that knowledge of her experiences might alienate her adoptive parents' love; in order to prevent such a failure she attempted to detach from her previous self, until it forcefully emerged. With the loving help of her Sardinian parents, she learned to accept her past, acknowledging that she was loved irrespective of her history.

One of the most difficult experiences that Chilean-born adoptees have to face upon returning to their country of origin, and succeeding in reconnecting with lost relatives, is the expectations of their Chilean family. These are often economic in character; for many lower-class Chileans, being European automatically signifies a high social and economic status, incomparable to the one experienced in Chile. The label of 'privileged' extends to the Chilean part of the adoptees' world, and they are forced to manage the consequences of other people's imagined knowledge of them.

Adopted at the age of three, Carlo argues that people have always declared him privileged, for having been rescued from extreme poverty and backwardness. Once in his thirties he travelled to Chile, determined to find his natural parents. While there, he discovered the reason for being given up for adoption: his young parents went partying for days, leaving their little children alone in the house. The neighbours called the police after hearing the children crying for hours; the police broke in and the children were declared abandoned. While in Chile, Carlo managed to find his father, and took him along on a trip to meet his mother. The couple had separated two decades before, never to meet again, and they were reunited for the occasion. What surprised Carlo was that the etiquette of privilege, imposed on him since his adoption, was even stronger in Chile. His parents were impressed by his generosity and wealth; he paid for the plane trip to bring his father and himself to meet his mother, he took them out for lunch, spending what they thought was an exorbitant sum; he rented a taxi for a whole day. Soon after they met, both parents asked him for money. Carlo said he was disappointed; this was a confirmation of an opinion he had nursed for a while, that he was part of an economic exchange. He refused to give economic help, explaining that he did not see a reason for it. After all, he had travelled to Chile for himself, not for them. 'My real need was to complete my life's story. They asked me for money, but I did this trip to save my own life, not anyone else's life. I came here to feel better. I came here with my money, my motivations; I did it for myself, not for others'. After years of imagining his parents, and questioning their reasons for abandoning him, once Carlo accessed the knowledge of how the events had truly unfolded, he realized he needed to preserve his individuality. The will to embark on a journey to find completeness gave him the strength to face whatever dangerous knowledge he had to face; the certainty that he was not a passive object anymore, but a decision-making subject, allowed him to embrace his project fully, putting himself at the forefront and everyone else in the background (cf. Carsten 2000: 698). 'It used to be that I was Carlo, son of X and Y. Now things have changed: now it's X and Y that are the parents of Carlo. This is what I earned in life', he told me. Carlo experienced being identified as 'someone's child' – an identification that defined him for decades – as severely limiting, and he thus claimed back his individuality, freeing himself from the constraints of his role of son. The re-appropriation of his individuality included full control of his economic value, a difficult task when one is invested with expectations, and showered with requests from individuals who represent crucial emotional connections, such as one's estranged parents.

The Danger of the Anthropologist's Knowledge

The attitudes I met in my encounters with informants have been mixed. I was welcomed with enthusiasm, shy curiosity, elusiveness, and I also experienced scornful refusals to meet. I was asked questions regarding my knowledge of Chile, of adoption cases, of several adoptees. Parents were curious about the number of adoptees that had married, that had fathered children and that enjoyed a successful professional life. Some were curious about Chile, which they associated with the happiness of becoming parents, and wanted their children to know more about it. Nevertheless, my knowledge and willingness to discuss this topic produced at times strong reactions that the Freudian concept of the uncanny (Freud 1990 [1919]) aptly describes. This concept combines complex feelings of fear produced by something familiar, belonging to one's past, but that has been somehow repressed because it was painful or frightening. These feelings tend to be concealed, and become problematic when they emerge. In most cases my enquiry, or the reflections generated upon the simple announcement of my research topic, caused precisely this sort of feeling, and as such it was experienced as unsettling. While some informants agreed to expose their vulnerability and agreed to share their emotional story, others declined my invitation to meet. Reactions included postponing requests, indirect negations, cancelling after agreeing to meet and irritated remarks on the telephone followed by hanging up. If in some cases my familiarity with Chile facilitated connections, in others it represented a dangerous closeness to a country and to events that were best kept at a distance. Parents who had worked hard at erasing their children's difference saw my proposal to meet and discuss their experience as a retrograde step, as a reminder that those children were not born in Sardinia. 'I don't even want my daughter to know that you are doing this research!' an angry adoptive mother told me, adding that her child was doing fine, was a respectable professional and that no one had any right to enquire about her private life. After spending hours in pleasant conversation with another adoptive parent, she admitted that were I Chilean, she would never have agreed to meet me. Eventually, she made me understand that I had better avoid meeting her son. I was not Chilean, nevertheless my long-term familiarity with Chile made me dangerous enough; the threatening aspects were kept at bay during our meeting, but she could not equally control a conversation between her son and me. And yet, a part of her strongly wanted us to talk: throughout our encounter she had hinted at what her son and I could have discussed.

Sometimes I met parents before being introduced to their children; they openly shared their adoption memories, occasionally requesting to keep details of our conversation *inter nos*. Similarly, I met adoptees that later introduced me to their parents; however, they talked to me privately, to shield their parents from intimate reflections that could have hurt them or made them feel uncomfortable. I became a channel for two lines of information to be unravelled, information that had to travel in parallel lines because it was potentially dangerous. Nevertheless, the opportunity to voice such data gave the informants the feeling of rendering painful memories as somehow controllable.

Conclusion

All are Different, but Some are More Different than Others

Writing on American social class, Ortner (2003) said that success is always comparative. The same can be argued for knowledge: one is more or less knowledgeable compared with other people. This, I believe, is the essence of the question. Defining 'difference' is difficult, because a term of comparison is always needed. To forge a definition of themselves, people need others.

Nigel Rapport (1997) discusses these same themes in his portrait of a small rural community in England, whose members adamantly defend themselves from outsiders interested in their land. Cohen's Whalsay ethnography (1987) deals with issues of identity to be protected, and boundaries. Jeanette Edwards' informants convey issues of inclusion/exclusion (1999). These are just a few studies highlighting questions of sameness or differentiation in small communities. People perceive otherness, and act upon their perception, according to local values, always invested of a specific morality, as Overing (1985: 23) reminds us. Local values are used to categorize others in various degrees of otherness. Paraphrasing Orwell, I suggest that we are all different, but some are more different than others. For Apiao people, the different others range from town dwellers to teachers to next-door neighbours; for the adoptees the range of otherness includes strangers, family acquaintances, adoptive parents and Chilean estranged kin. Difference is experienced simultaneously by all actors involved, in a prism-like situation with everyone's definition and experience of it affecting their individual perceptions. Stating difference is a way to raise boundaries between themselves and others – a way to handle alterity. Returning to Bourdieu, engaging meaningfully with alterity is necessary and profitable, but it requires effort. Success/profit is not guaranteed: it depends on many variables. The way people use their knowledge to engage with others is shaped by values informed by concerns with protecting one's physical and emotional space. When this is threatened, the boundary of difference is set off, like a defence mechanism. This was manifest in Apiao locals and their visitors; in the adoptees and their parents, vis-à-vis society and the enquiring anthropologist.

Caught in Dangerous Knowledge?

In both research settings my role was mostly that of a silent listener. In Apiao I soon learnt to ask only superficial questions; the rest I observed and practised as part of everyday life, just as local children do. While the circumstances in Sardinia were different because I had solicited the meetings, during the research into adoption I was, again, silently listening. My decision to ask few or no questions, encouraging the informants' free stream of consciousness, allowed them to evoke memories according to their lived experience and personal wishes.

In both contexts, however, people invested me with knowledge expectations, imposing an identity foreign to me. Apiao people initially treated me with hostility, due to prejudices accompanying my difference. My access to the community was determined by my willingness to downplay my difference, and my success in articulating my eagerness to be 'almost like them'. My ignorance of the local ways balanced my perceived superior status that accompanied my foreignness: I was like a youngster that needed to be socialized. A peculiar individual, partly adult and partly child, I possessed some knowledge, but lacked some other knowledge: [5] my ambiguity was feared as threatening for a good portion of my first long-term stay on the island.

An issue at stake, in both settings, is the anthropologist's knowledge of private and intimate details of other people's lives. Is it possible, or desirable, not to be affected by such acquired knowledge? In Apiao, while visiting friends in different households, I had access to opinions voiced on neighbours, relatives and professionals living on the island. These people were part of my world, too, and were included in my routine visits. I had to negotiate my own knowledge of people about other people, and practise detachment. Managing my own preferences and opinions, naturally formed after long-term acquaintance, and put to the test with the acquisition of further knowledge about my friends, was often challenging. Is the awareness that everything constitutes data enough to counterbalance a flux of information intermingled with a flux of emotions and personal opinion? I had to face this predicament not only in Apiao, but in Sardinia too, when trying to organize focused meetings with adoptees who happen to be my relatives. Dealing with elusiveness, indirect refusals to collaborate, and the withholding of names of fellow adoptees represented a serious impasse when I was starting the research. Furthermore, such reticence was unexpectedly coming from individuals I was fairly close to. I had to assume the fact that my knowledge, or my attempt at knowledge acquisition, was experienced as threatening to the point that my research was to be brushed off, or even unconsciously boycotted.

It seems to me that the position of anthropologists is similar to the experience of both Apiao people and the Chilean-born adoptees I talk about in this chapter, in their attempts to reach sameness, and their obligatory management of difference. In order to conform or fit into the host community, we engage in operations of assimilation, imitation and adaptation with the objective of being accepted and perceived not as the threatening other but as 'someone almost like us'. We slowly shift into different versions of ourselves to suit the circumstance better, hoping that by downplaying our difference this will be forgotten, and remain confined to the first batch of field notes. Just like Apiao people when confronted by outsiders, and like the adoptees, who must always take into account other people's perception of their difference, we have to face the unpleasant certainty that, when doing research, our difference defines us, and is the engine behind the uncomfortable questions we pose to amenable or unresponsive people. Irrespective of how often and how successfully we exercise sameness, we will always be bound to differentiation.

Giovanna Bacchiddu is a social anthropologist currently working as a Lecturer at the Pontificia Universidad Católica in Santiago de Chile. She is the author of several scholarly articles on sociality, kinship and religion as experienced in Apiao, southern Chile. She recently researched the adoption of Chilean children by Italian families.

Notes

This chapter is based on ethnographic fieldwork conducted in Apiao over fifteen years, and in Sardinia from 2010. Research in Chiloé was financed with grants from the Regione Autonoma della Sardegna, and the Interdisciplinary Centre for Intercultural and Indigenous Research – CIIR. The adoption project was originally sponsored by the RAS within the FSE 2007–2013 and the L7/2007. Many thanks go to all informants; to Craig Lind for 'naming' the lack-of-differentiation issue years ago; to Peter Gow and Sandro Poddesu for insightful conversations on the themes discussed; to the editors, for constructive comments on earlier versions of this chapter; and to Máire Ní Mhórdha.

1. This chapter is by no means an exhaustive Apiao ethnography, or an extensive foray into international adoption studies; its main goal is to explore specific issues through material displaying a recurrence of those same themes.
2. I have elaborated on this topic elsewhere; see Bacchiddu 2009, 2011 and 2012.
3. An Apiao friend would gently tease me for spending hours writing notes, stating that one day he would do the same and leave all other work aside – the irony being in the nonsensical nature of the statement.
4. Cf. Carsten on acquisition of kinship information, and her discussion of Strathern's work (Carsten 2007).
5. Rapport (1997: 92) describes how he was caught in a similar predicament.

References

Bacchiddu, G. 2009. '"Before We Were All Catholics": Changing Religion in Apiao, Southern Chile', in R. Wright and A. Vilaça (eds), *Native Christians: Modes and Effects of Christianity among Indigenous Peoples of the Americas*. Farnham and Burlington, VT: Ashgate, pp. 53–70.

———. 2010. 'Getting Tamed to Silent Rules: Experiencing "the Other" in Apiao, Southern Chile', in A.S. Grønseth and D. Lee Davis (eds), *Mutuality and Empathy: Self and Other in the Ethnographic Encounter*. Herefordshire: Sean Kingston Publishing, pp. 21–34.

———. 2011. 'Holding the Saint in One's Arms: Miracles and Exchange in Apiao, Southern Chile', in A. Fedele and R. Llera Blanes (eds), *Encounters of Body and Soul in Contemporary Religious Practices: Anthropological Reflections*. New York and Oxford: Berghahn, pp. 23–42.

———. 2012. '"Doing Things Properly": Religious Aspects in Everyday Sociality in Apiao, Chiloé', in L. Debevec and S. Schielke (eds), *Ordinary Lives and Grand Schemes: An Anthropology of Everyday Religion*. New York and Oxford: Berghahn, pp. 66–81.

————. 2013. 'Come un Trapianto d'Organo: Questioni di Uguaglianza e Diversità in un Contesto di Adozione Internazionale', in F. Bachis and A.M. Pusceddu (eds), *Storie di Questo Mondo: Percorsi di Etnografia delle Migrazioni*. Roma: CISU, pp. 91–111.

Bartholet, E. 1993. *Adoption and the Politics of Parenting*. Boston: Houghton Mifflin.

Bonaccorso, M. 2005. *Conceiving Kinship: Assisted Conception, Procreation and Family in Southern Europe*. New York and Oxford: Berghahn.

Bourdieu, P. 1986. 'The Forms of Capital', in J.G. Richardson (ed.), *Handbook of Theory of Research for the Sociology of Education*. New York: Greenword Press, pp. 46–58.

Bowie, F. 2004. 'Adoption and the Circulation of Children: A Comparative Perspective', in F. Bowie (ed.), *Cross-Cultural Approaches to Adoption*. Abingdon and New York: Routledge, pp. 3–20.

Byron, R. 1986. *Sea Change: A Shetland Society 1970–79*. St. Johns: Institute of Social and Economic Research, Memorial University of Newfoundland.

Carsten, J. 2000. '"Knowing Where You've Come from": Ruptures and Continuities of Time and Kinship in Narratives of Adoption Reunions', *The Journal of the Royal Anthropological Institute* 6(4): 687–703.

————. 2007. 'Constitutive Knowledge: Tracing Trajectories of Information in New Contexts of Relatedness', *Anthropological Quarterly* 80(2): 403–26.

Cohen, A. 1987. *Whalsay: Symbol, Segment and Boundary in a Shetland Island Community*. Manchester: Manchester University Press.

Edwards, J. 1999. 'Why Dolly Matters: Kinship, Culture and Cloning', *Ethnos* 64: 3–4, 301–24.

Freud, S. 1990 [1919]. 'The Uncanny', in *The Penguin Freud Library, Volume 14: Art and Literature*. London: Penguin.

Howell, S. 2003. 'Kinning: The Creation of Life Trajectories in Transnational Adoptive Families', *The Journal of the Royal Anthropological Institute* 9(3): 465–84.

————. 2006 *Kinning of Foreigners: Transnational Adoption in a Global Perspective*. New York and Oxford: Berghahn Books.

Howell, S. and D. Marre. 2006. 'To Kin a Transnationally Adopted Child in Norway and Spain: The Achievement of Resemblances and Belonging', *Ethnos: Journal of Anthropology* 71: 3, 293–316.

Lambek, M. (ed.). 2010. *Ordinary Ethics: Anthropology, language, and action*. New York: Fordham University Press.

Malinowski, B. 1922. *Argonauts of the Western Pacific: An Account of Native Enterprise and Adventure in the Archipelagoes of Melanesian New Guinea*. London: Routledge.

Monestier, B. 2005. *Dis merci! Tu ne connais pas ta chance d'avoir été adoptée...* Paris: Editions Anne Carrière.

Moore, H. 1996. 'The Changing Nature of Anthropological Knowledge: An Introduction', in H. Moore (ed.), *The Future of Anthropological Knowledge*. London: Routledge, pp. 1–15.

Ortner, S. 2002. 'The Death and Rebirth of Anthropology', *Ethnos* 67: 1, 7–8.
———. 2003. *New Jersey Dreaming: Capital, Culture, and the Class of '58*. Durham, NC and London: Duke University Press.

Overing, J. (ed.) 1985. *Reason and Morality*. London: Tavistock.

Rapport, N. 1997. 'The Morality of Locality: On the Absolutism of Landownership in an English Village', in S. Howell (ed.), *The Ethnography of Moralities*. London and New York: Routledge, pp. 75–98.

Rojas Flores, G. 2002. *Reyes Sobre la Tierra*. Santiago: Editorial Biblioteca Americana.

Strathern, M. (ed.). 1995. *Shifting Contexts: Transformations in Anthropological Knowledge*. London and New York: Routledge.

Chapter 3

ON THE SHIFTING ETHICS AND CONTEXTS OF KNOWLEDGE PRODUCTION

Tamara Kohn

Anthropological fieldwork – as I have known it – is a journey into the unexpected. The journey is ever mediated by the reflexive gaze and writing of the ethnographer, as well as changing historical, social and political contexts. The interest in grasping a 'native point of view' (à la Malinowski) through local expression and action has long been seen as a foundational interest in the discipline, even as this interest has been shaped through time and its practitioners have come to recognize the reflexive creative aspects of the 'knowledge' that is produced from their writings. Native points of view generate a multiplicity of not always overlapping understandings, and our critical tolerance of difference makes us quite sympathetic to these dissonances – we know that in understanding them we come to explore our fields 'thickly' and 'deeply' rather than search for generalized answers to questions. What might be expected at the beginning of the process often has little to do with what is understood by the end, and this includes, of course, questions about methods and ethics. It is, I would like to suggest, the idea of this exploratory ethos, the idea of possibility of experimentation and revelation at any point in the research process, that has not only defined the discipline, but has opened a door to worlds never imagined (even those right in one's own backyard).

It is against this suggestion about the power of the idea of creative process that I wish to think about the development and implementation of ethics review boards and the degree to which institutional regulation (or in some cases its circumvention) impacts upon researchers' creativity from the onset. I am not trying to suggest that institutional review is dispensable nor am I suggesting that it does not serve a very important function in some cases. I am, however, flagging the possibility that its effects extend well beyond the acceptance or not of research ethics applications or the lost time and energy spent on the endless forms. Indeed, it affects the range of the possible and interacts with one's sensitivity to different ways of being ethical, with ways of perceiving one's field from outside and from within and of the research process as a whole. It shapes ways of seeing relationships between method, ethics and anthropological knowledge.

Annually, I lead an intensive honours-level seminar on fieldwork ethics that generally follows one on 'the interview'. Theoretical discussions give way to more practical advice on how students should successfully complete University ethics forms, write 'plain language statements' and concoct possible interview questions. Often students would begin rethinking their planned field projects' aims and objectives or even their whole research topics based on the potentially unmanageable hurdles that their first ideas produced in working through the forms. I feel extremely uneasy about the stifling power of the form, but also need to make the students complete them! Then, one year, I heard about a recent Ph.D. graduate who had been researching in a retirement home and had earlier presented the institution with full ethics approval to conduct interviews with people in the home. Apparently he offered to help with the washing-up in the kitchen one day and an elderly woman in the home took issue with this, suggesting that he was trying to learn about things outside the purview of the interview. This escalated to an investigative tribunal involving the supervisor and senior faculty managers at his university (and this is even before the production of the ethnographic text).[1] In pursuit of 'the ethical', universities have, unknowingly, refigured the very nature of anthropological 'questioning' as well as participation. And yet here I would like to argue that 'the ethical' does not exist outside of the contexts that shape it in each instance. Ethics is relational – institutional interest in the construction of procedural rules for social research must somehow be tempered by an understanding of the degree to which fields, contexts and histories of relations are emergent rather than planned for and are expressed differently and produce different meanings through alternate media and methods. Various critics have distinguished these different points of ethical concern in qualitative research. For example, Guillemin and Gillam (2004) describe the formal application for research permission in terms of 'procedural ethics' as opposed to the problems of actual everyday conduct within the field, or 'ethics in practice' (cited in Chenhall, Senior and Belton 2011: 13). Procedural ethics, according to the authors, have little or no impact on the way researchers reflexively engage with ethical problems that confront them during the process of fieldwork (ibid.).

I agree that these different dimensions coexist, but in this chapter I will argue that the former does impact upon what becomes possible in the second dimension. Indeed, the two dimensions transform one another in profound ways that change how our discipline is imagined and experienced by new generations of practitioners and their subjects. In the following reflexive sections I will demonstrate how different fields at different times produce different questions, different methodological possibilities as well as different fields of knowledge transaction.

Part I: Musing on Knowledge Gleaned from Past Fields

I 'grew up' in a relatively form-free anthropological world during my studies in the 1970s and 1980s, so any limitations on how I variously introduced myself in my 'fields' and how I elicited data were largely self-imposed, based on intuitions and feelings and sensitivities that all of us spend our lifetimes developing in our relations with others. Good and productive fieldworkers are those who are personable, who make friends and communicate well, who are able to put people at ease, who interact with spirit and generosity, and those who are sensitive to people's needs and desires and who attempt to protect their subjects as well as themselves when situations call for this. Reflecting on my various field experiences, I have often found the most interesting ideas expressed at that disjuncture between what is elicited through questions and focused discussion and what is learned from others through observation and in local unhurried interactions – both verbal and embodied. Ethical dilemmas and their solutions often emerge from those moments. Members on ethics boards today peering into my various fields would most likely not have signed any application I might have submitted (based on today's requirements) that attempted to predict the serendipitous procedures I would eventually follow.

Example 1: 'Belonging' on a Small Scottish Island

I conducted my D.Phil. research on a small island in the Inner Hebrides, supervised (until his untimely death) by Edwin Ardener at Oxford. Before Edwin, my mentor at the University of Pennsylvania was Dan Rose, who conducted fieldwork with African Americans in Philadelphia in the late 1960s. Dan was a student of Erving Goffman, who had encouraged him to work covertly – posing as a mechanic and hanging out on street corners with the black community. Political and social constraints of the time meant that covertness was felt to be the only option for that particular work, which took some seventeen years to emerge in text as the narrative monograph *Black American Street Life*. In the book, Dan expressed the ethical anguish that such covert work made him feel – he wrote that unlike Goffman, he 'lacked the desire and ability to play the role of actor' and conceal his identity as anthropologist (Rose 1987: 22). In contrast, Edwin Ardener's fieldwork in the Hebrides was far from covert, as he beautifully cultivated his role there as the aging Oxford scholar, which provided him a particular vantage point from which he could work: observing, talking, learning Gaelic.

I ended up somewhere in the middle on the relative covertness scale in my D.Phil. research – I had lived on the Scottish island for the initial year as an incomer (on an island largely inhabited by other incomers) with my then husband, who had a job there. My 'relationships' with locals were already well formed by the time I went off to Oxford for long periods of library work in advance of my fieldwork proper on the island. My attempts to explain my research and 'researcher' identity on my return from the university fell on deaf ears and were converted in local discussion to a dalliance in local history and 'culture' (past). My primary research question had emerged out of serendipitous circumstance in the site itself. I learned early on that local farmers, who were descended from incomers in the nineteenth century, were considered in every respect the 'real islanders' of the community. I also learned that asking 'local' people about identity status (e.g., islander/local 'belonging' categories) largely elicited answers following spoken and written (e.g., parroting popular history) expectations about deep genealogy, blood connections, clans and land. My question was to explore how those descendants of incomers moved into their islander status despite a popularized discourse that would exclude the possibility. So back in the mid 1980s my question required a study not of what island residents thought I would want to hear in that particular place and time, but of what people did in their daily activities and interactions, which would demonstrate how some incomers, through embodied action, gossip, raising children, etc. could move rather rapidly along the incomer/islander continuum in the community.

I interacted much the same way as I did quite naturally as a pre-research 'incomer' trying to belong. I visited friends, joined the knitting bee, the keep-fit group for women, the Church of Scotland Women's Guild; I helped farmers with their sheep, I baked cakes and grew rhubarb for the island 'show'. I conducted only a handful of purposeful 'conversations' (with overtly taken notes) that might have resembled 'interviews' over the three years I lived on the island, because I had come to feel that I could not get to where I wanted to go that way. I took scratch notes on scraps of toilet paper in the hotel bar toilet, or jotted in the margins of my knitting patterns. I felt ethical anguish when I was invited to speak at the high school on the mainland in Oban about my research and later when I had to decide how to write the thesis and publish its findings (particularly about material that dealt with 'sensitive' information that I was privy to through my research access at the Scottish Records office, where I did have to sign confidentiality papers). My first publication was an outlet for this anxiety (Kohn 1987). I arranged for an embargo on my D.Phil. to give me a few years' distance from the material before it became accessible to the public. Publications used pseudonyms and scrambled various characters into new ones, even though I knew that anyone on the island could reassemble themselves through the contexts and events described (see Kohn 2002). If I could take a time machine back to the mid 1980s on that island, but with the institutional 'ethics review' constraints of today, I wonder what I would do and what I would (or would not) find?

Example 2: Risky Choices in East Nepal

Just two weeks after my D.Phil. 'viva', the oral defence of my thesis that was based on my work in Scotland, I embarked on postdoctoral research in East Nepal. There was no ethical review required for my unfunded research, and Andrew (my then husband, who was beginning his ESRC[2] funded D.Phil. research) and I lived for nearly two years in a 'remote' village with the Yakha, a Tibeto-Burman community in the middle hills of Sankhuwasabha district in the foothills of Mount Everest. Westerners had not lived in that village before we arrived there. There was no possibility of not explaining our reasons for being there. We had to explain our presence almost daily to any new person that we met. We opted initially for a rather mundane and general answer – for instance, that we were learning the language 'and the way you live here'. This refined as time passed because our interests evolved into something that had local relevance and also resonated with our own research interests and personalities.

I learned by asking and observing. Unlike Scotland where most interaction was in English so notes seemed somehow more comprehensive in their possibility, in Nepal I constantly struggled to understand the meaning and nuance in people's speech in Nepali and certainly felt lost when people interacted with each other at speed or in the Yakha language. I found myself making more from less (learning everything you can in any way possible), finding a connection and homing in on it. Interethnic marriage became a topic that drew me in and coalesced with my previous empirical and theoretical interest in incomers, mobility and change. Ethnographic gems and meaningful questions to pursue emerged unexpectedly out of serendipitous social interactions and my daily observations and reflections in the field. Such interactions I could never have planned for and could never have encountered without first fostering trusting relationships with the people involved. In a contribution to Hastrup and Hervik's edited volume, *Social Experience and Anthropological Knowledge* (Kohn 1994), I described one particularly revealing story about a set of interactions with an untouchable family in the village. I described how the Yakha family I lived with reacted negatively to my visiting and sharing food and drink with these people, because they said I would carry the pollution of untouchability back into their home. I was initially shocked by their direct instructions, limiting my social interaction with my Kami (blacksmith/untouchable) friends, as I thought that my foreignness would exempt me from caste pollution (ibid.). So it was against this backdrop that I took a great risk and secretly continued to visit the family. In a sense I was acting true to my own liberal cultural ethic of egalitarian action while I was at the same time acting against a promise made to abide by an 'other's' local ethical stance. But in doing this I discovered that I was not the only one to take such a risk. Out of my own experience in a place I stealthily inhabited, I was able to witness local high caste visitors, who also came to visit the family, consume food and drink and cross the polluting threshold of the house, blatantly and silently enacting a challenge to caste rules during a politically charged moment in Nepalese history. The knowledge I gleaned about how local people broke rules and acted out their political and social beliefs long before they spoke of them was significant in my work. I took a risk in not heeding my family's request, in breaking a promise made, but it allowed me a vantage point from which I could witness how I was not alone – how some local people would take risks with their bodies to demonstrate to each other their changing and challenging ideas that in turn interacted with caste rules.

If I had put together a research project proposal to study challenges to caste in a time of political change, where would the very subtly approved transgression of certain caste rules fit in my ethical planning and in the reception of a gatekeeping ethics committee with no understanding of the nuances of Nepalese social interactions around caste? Where is the place for serendipitous knowledge production in the process of fieldwork? Furthermore, what are the consequences of prescriptive planning for ethics approval in terms of one's ability to respond freely to events and opportunities that arise out of the research process? Later in this chapter I will test some of these questions that arise out of my own reflections on my field experience against empirical examples of how such questions are confronted by others in current institutionally audited fieldwork practice. The following example, however, arises out of a very different field context to illustrate how power relations in the field may affect the content and shape of enquiry even before the additional powerful gaze of ethical review is applied to it.

Example 3: Understanding Leisure, Respecting Authority

I have been involved in studying a transnational community of martial artists I have come to know since the early 1990s, and in my research and writing on this 'field' I have focused on embodied knowledge as it is expressed through shared practice and how this interacts with what practitioners tell you about such knowledge (eg. Kohn 2007, 2011). I conducted detailed taped interviews over several years with my aikido master and his senior students. As in the above examples from Scotland and Nepal, the questions I wanted to answer (regardless of method) had emerged from the experience of being there and listening and watching and interacting with others in situ and would not have occurred to me before that.

The master teacher always requested that I show him the questions I wished to ask of him, well in advance of our meetings. Initially I thought this was because of his limited English fluency, so that he would be sure to understand, but over time I realized that there were quite different issues at the heart of his request. As a revered elder in this community he was often interviewed for publication in martial arts magazines that would then be read by his own students as well as others and thus needed to be 'right' – to be educative and wise, not just informative. By requiring the questions in advance and then indeed transforming them to meet his needs as well as mine, he was able to craft a message to his followers and a larger public (both through what I would publish as a result of the interview as well as through works he would subsequently author for magazines or orally represent for training seminars with his students). He was simultaneously attending to my interests (sanctioned and given authority through my overt positioning as an outside academic researcher) while maintaining a position of control over me as a student and conduit of his larger message. This authority as master teacher was enacted daily in training on the mat with his students as well as off the mat, and I was one of his students.

The questions prepared in advance for a long interview in 1999 were generated out of several weeks of full-time training in Chiba Sensei's dojo in San Diego, made relevant and productive out of my notes from discussions, observations and experiences. They ranged from queries about teaching/mastery, aikido and change, the 'aikido body' and Sensei's life story. The pleasantries and tea preparation over, Sensei began to work his way through several of my questions, and he chose what to discuss and when to move on. I asked him to share some of his hopes, worries and dreams for the future of aikido in the United States and Europe after the ageing Japanese Shihan (senior teachers) retire, which was avoided entirely. Such concerns were very much part of his consciousness, however, as the organizational structures for the art in the United States, Europe and Japan were being severely challenged, but on that day he was not yet ready to talk about them. Over the next few years, answers related to those issues emerged in various communications to his students and teachers. A question I asked on that occasion in 1999, however, did get a very detailed and evocative response, related to his memories of his childhood in Japan. It was a desperately sad tale of guilt and the loss of his baby sister, who drowned after following him to a stream on a very hot day after school. He attached the story to an earlier part of the interview where we were discussing the place of women in aikido and a perception of his own protective role towards women in his personal and martial life. Years later in a national summer school, with his most dedicated students around him (including me), he told the story of his baby sister's drowning – a different connection entirely was drawn from it, but it was clear that he was in charge – he orchestrated and gave meaning to questions he redesigned and organized. I was ever aware of the complexity of our various power relations as I considered the effect of these on the various ways in which knowledge was proffered.

Planning interview questions in advance requires careful construction with the knowledge that the answers will be far from spontaneous. This does not sit well with the participant observer who thrives on the serendipity of rich and unexpected moments of interaction. However, if interview questions are worked out in the field and have an immediate relevance to ideas and behaviours that are displayed in that field, especially if, as in the case above, they shift to accommodate the needs, relations and statuses of the people who are expected to answer them, then one could say that sensitive interviewing can display a type of spontaneity. This raises a new question, however, that needs addressing in a contemporary ethical review context: is such ability to be spontaneous and work collaboratively in an interview context supported formally in any way by the initial review process or is it potentially hindered by it? To what extent is the idea of the appropriately framed and ethically approved interview necessarily prescriptive, inflexible and authoritative? Subsequent interview flexibility in the field may indeed be understood as an act of subversion rather than a creative practice – by the review committee but also by the researchers and even the subjects. These questions will be explored after the following final reflexive example.

Example 4: Death Row Inmates: Interviews versus Letters and the Production of Posthumous Knowledge

My sister (Jessica) is an attorney in the Office of the State Public Defender in California who represents men on death row at post-conviction stages in their appeal. In the early 1990s she took me with her into the world of San Quentin where I met with her client, Manny Babbitt. In this first of a number of visits to the prison's death row waiting room, I conducted a pre-planned informal 'pilot' interview. I had constructed questions around a wish to begin to understand something about the social world of death row for this man who had lived there since his murder conviction in the 1970s. I wanted to learn of his friendships and conflicts and daily routines and concerns. Manny's answers were fascinating and disturbing: 'You never get too close to nobody – it's like 'Nam – you get moved around and any of us will be dead tomorrow'. Almost every answer about his routines and life made reference to Vietnam – a place where the horrors of war had effectively crippled his life decades earlier with (then undiagnosed) post-traumatic stress disorder (PTSD). Based on this, I began to consider planning a research project to look at the relationship between veteran trauma, victimization and criminality. Veterans of war comprise a large proportion of the population on death row in the United States. Interestingly, despite the call for such research by Jessica and her legal colleagues, they also informed me that most defence attorneys would not permit access to their clients for independent research interviews, as the material may, no matter how innocently and sensitively 'extracted', contravene in the development of the case material. Just as a prisoner's body is controlled, so are his words surveyed and politically charged.

The first interview with Manny had led me straight to a prioritizing of the past in the formation of his identity in the present. After this, Manny and I started to correspond by letter and he 'introduced' me through letters to his friend and fellow inmate Jay. The letters I wrote to these men occasionally asked questions about their lives, but mostly I wrote about what I was doing and seeing – my travels and studies and young motherhood experiences. Their letters to me, perhaps partly due to their reciprocal dialogic nature (responding to my own missives on my own 'productivity' and action), and written in the context of their private cells, allowed me a very interesting window into a very different framing of self-identification. The past haunting the space of those initial interview answers was almost completely replaced by the present, of creative production and looking to the future – the 'selves' produced in the letters flagged the people they had become in prison through the arts, writing and crafts that they had taught themselves to produce (see Kohn 2009 and 2012). It is only now, years after the men were executed, and in the context of considering research ethics and knowledge production, that I can understand the powerful effect of method over the differential elicitation of lived 'truths' as they are filtered through me and the institutions of power that control what I can do and what my 'informants' can do with me.

Where to Now?

There is no singular objective world that any qualitative research method elicits and records. Each way of knowing is productive in its partial way – each door to 'understanding' opened through an interview or observation closes other doors. Even partial truths are only meaningful against our personal understandings of what is interesting, right and important at any time. It is not enough to work towards 'giving voice' to our informants' views; we must also recognize the effect of method on what voice is given with what partial view.

Likewise, there is no set of ethical rules that should be applied to all cases. Ethicality should be located in the effort to achieve it, rather than the successful addressing of rules (Swiffen 2007). The effort to achieve it, when based on experience in situ, may indeed deeply challenge ideas of 'best practice' that are generated from outside in some perceived ethical administrative 'centre'. Also, the responsibility in the end remains with the researcher situating his or her own point(s) of view. Points of view are so often unfurled through interaction (and occasional dilemmas that occur in the research process), so surely the ethics of research are likewise processually revealed. There might be guiding principles that, for example, a professional organization (like the American Anthropological Association) might provide for researchers to consult before they engage in what Fluehr-Lobban calls a process of 'active decision-making involving appropriate ethical conduct in a given set of circumstances' (2009: 8). These decisions revolve around a process of discussion and debate that accompanies the elucidation of knowledge in the field.

The philosopher Hans-Georg Gadamer emphasized the situated and subjective nature of the researcher and the way in which knowledge is produced rather than just elicited through particular methods (1979). Following this lead, Cerwonka and Malkki (2007) have reflected on the improvisational features of fieldwork practice through the dissection of their own year-long email correspondence (between a student in 'the field' in Melbourne and her supervisor in the United States). Their long discussion is tangibly generative and reflections on ethics are arrived at through the research process (as they were for me in the examples sketched above). Knowledge production, therefore, is deeply affected by changes in our understandings of what ethical practice might look like in a particular case and time and how social institutions and personal experiences and histories may shape and enforce particular ways of 'being' with 'the other'.

The examples from my fieldwork above begin to point to the emergent and often unspoken performative elucidation of knowledge in the field, and how this relates to different possibilities and limitations in method. Senses that allow for such processual understanding are never like new; they have been preloaded with information by particular teachers, theoretical engagements, preliminary researches and bodily experiences. They are also laden with an active imaginary of what will happen, what one might find. It is this same imaginary that is activated in the construction of a project or grant proposal and of course for an ethics document.

I will now move on from a reflexive consideration of my field practices and how knowledge generation has always emerged from the particularities of relations and fields to consider the place and 'problem' of formal ethical review. I wish for the reader to read on with an understanding that the most meaningful questions and observations grow from an embedded and dialogic experience in situ. With these possibilities in mind, I begin Part II by tracing a history of the development of ethical review boards and then look at how people on the receiving and delivering end of the review process [3] see the process and recognize (or not) its shortcomings, before thinking about how we can best tend to the future of ethnographic knowledge production.

Part II: A Glimpse into a Present State of Affairs: The Making, Implementing and Challenging of RECs and IRBs

Research Ethics Committees (RECs in the United Kingdom, Australia and New Zealand, also known as Institutional Review Boards (or IRBs in North America)) have been created in the last forty years and are continually developing and proliferating to monitor the planning of all institutionally affiliated research on human subjects in order to prevent potential harmful effects. Chalmers and Pettit have usefully charted three stages of development of the REC/IRB in various disciplines (1998). The first stage relates to the call that we all have to be fair and treat others properly – to a lived 'ethics in practice'. The second stage is when professional research bodies (such as the AAA, ASA and AAS[4] in anthropology) produce discipline-specific guidelines for their members. The third stage is when independent authorities (universities, hospitals, governments) take control of processes of ethical review – when suggestions (or 'guidelines') are often replaced by less nuanced directives (ibid.).

Pettit has documented how terrible tales of dangerous practice result in public scandal that in turn generates more surveillance and regulatory action (1991). Famously outrageous stories stimulate the escalation in regulation: the injection of cancer cells in elderly patients in New York without informed consent; the withholding of treatments that led people to their deaths, as in the famous Tuskegee study of syphilis in Alabama in 1972 when researchers had decided that black subjects were too 'uneducated' to provide consent (ibid.). Interestingly, most of these outrageous cases have involved medical procedures and health threats, and yet the movement from the earlier disciplinary guideline stage to the larger external review stage would come to affect all researchers working with human subjects and would make the same demands upon them. You would guess that research processes that would lead to subjects' deaths would not so easily be compared with the consequences of washing dishes without permission in a home for the elderly, but ironically these scenarios, if put through institutional review, would follow similar procedures and identical forms for approval. They also would result in the same type of outcome – an outcry (from a community and discipline on the one hand to a single elderly voice on the other) that, if loud enough, would contribute to a cumulative escalation of restriction. They would both result in increased power vested in institutional review boards, and such RECs/IRBs would ostensibly offer rigorous protection to the research (and institutional) community and uphold 'professional standards' for the future (ibid.).

There is a plethora of literature for the interested reader that examines the emergence and expansion of audit culture more generally (Shore and Wright 1999, 2017; Strathern 2000) and ethics review processes more specifically in various national and institutional contexts (Caplan 2003; Schrag 2010; Schneider 2015). Zachary Schrag's comprehensive study of IRBs and the social sciences in the United States is entitled 'Ethical Imperialism' and he not only charts the history of the development of the IRBs, but makes a strong case to demonstrate ways in which they limit or even silence benign research (2010).

For my purposes here, I am particularly interested in how such committees operate or 'think' about the proposals put to them, and, on the other side of the coin, how researchers think about the processes of review that they engage with. Inevitably I look at both through the reflexive lens of one who has not had to subject much early research planning to the ethics board gaze but who does understand how field knowledge is generated around questions of ethics and method.

I have had the opportunity to serve for several years on the Humanities and Applied Sciences Human Ethics Sub-Committee (HAPS HESC) for my Australian university. I have also been told many tales of woe about such committees and their verdicts from researchers' (more particularly, ethnographers') points of view. Through my involvement in discussion and interaction around specific proposals, certain patterns emerged that supported general observations that Pettit has made for the operations of these boards in Australia (made up of academics and members of the public). He has suggested that committee members clearly feel that they have to legitimate their presence and the time spent in such meetings, so finding something to correct or object to does, alas, demonstrate their rigorous contribution to the process, or what Lederman has called 'regulatory hypervigilance' (2006b). A useful point Pettit raises is that there is little or no penalty for the false negative (1991: 17). This means that if a panel stops or delays a worthy research project, you only end up with a few sour people and email complaints from supervisors, for example. If, on the other hand, a decision is too 'adventurously liberal' and this ends up leading to problems, then there is the risk of a huge public outcry with serious penalties (ibid.). This implicit line of reasoning inevitably drives ethics committees towards conservative and restrictive decision-making (ibid.).

Experience of dealing with this restriction first-hand or even through stories from others often leads researchers and/or their supervisors to adopt a defensive minimal-information mode in an effort to achieve clearance and save time and effort. At my university, for example, honours students who only have one year to design, execute and write up a field-based research project are urged to avoid certain topics and remove any words in their application that would trigger a 'high risk' categorization (and thus a significant if not disabling delay) from the online system such as 'ethnicity', 'nationalism', 'trauma', 'stress', 'conflict', and of course, for Australia, 'indigenous Australians'. From this we see that the very idea (borne from experience) of an obstructive process leads to a constriction in the pre-field anthropological imagination and consequently in the field experience and anthropological understanding that can be produced through it. Conservative and defensive advising on new projects and on the teaching of methods produces a sad irony that as the anthropological community grows in numbers and the discipline grows in popularity at tertiary level the research gaze shrinks!

To understand how this constriction might happen, one must also look at how it is actively resisted by some, particularly in this interesting betwixt and between era when people like myself hold memories of a less formally monitored age and yet have to deal now with a rigorously upheld system of audit and control around ethics for their own work and for their students. At my university I have been able to learn what some aggrieved ethnographic researchers feel about their interactions with the process. They describe the ethics committee using words such as 'punitive', 'increasingly adversarial', 'self-righteous', 'heavy-handed', 'distrustful' and 'undermining of student confidence'. They feel the committee always begins with 'what can go wrong?' rather than with asking 'is this ethical research?' They describe consent forms as 'unwieldy and intrusive' and the whole judgement as often directed at assessments of project quality and method (but not ethics) and made by committees lacking the relevant disciplinary qualifications. One colleague described a very long saga with ten extensive email exchanges for a Ph.D. student's ethics application that took the best part of a year to receive clearance. The process can be conceived of as a battle. That project was about a community of migrants in Melbourne and their experiences with a particular disease, and comments from an ethics committee that clearly demonstrate a lack of understanding about participant observation and ethnographic field methods include:

> – Can you please confirm that the in-depth interviews will take place before the observational stages of the study?
> – Members still felt that the observational aspects of the study were potentially intrusive for participants, for example, being observed while shopping, eating at functions.

If these show a lack of understanding about exploratory qualitative field research engagement that includes participant observation, the next example from a colleague at another Australian university indicates an extraordinarily high level of very general mistrust and paranoia about field knowledge as potentially (and subconsciously!) misused intellectual property:

> The ethics committee requested that I demonstrate that I will not subconsciously take something I learned as a researcher and use it against informants in my capacity as a citizen.

It is hard to know how one would react to such a request, except to send it out into the larger academic community to fuel even further the negative stereotypes of ethical review process.

Inside the ethics review process, experienced panel members speak about themselves being misunderstood. Ethics, they say, is a public relations disaster – supervisors tell their students not to worry about the process – that it is just bureaucracy. Regarding the frequent complaints that they are policing methodological designs rather than ethics, they tell each other that they have to do this in many cases – that if people are not very clear about their methods through every step of the research process, then it is not clear if consideration of risks and ethical consequences meet the national guidelines or not. On a number of occasions people on the panel I was a part of suggested that the misunderstandings could be resolved by inviting the aggrieved scholar(s) to observe the process in person. There is a curious irony here: fieldworking researchers want committees to come to understand the intersubjective, negotiated and processual nature of ethnographic research that emerges out of face-to-face encounter in the social world, and the research ethics committee members want academics to understand through face-to-face encounter the 'fair and reasonable' discussion amongst good educated folk that produces its directives. The irony is that 'understanding', from the committee's perspective, is serviced by face-to-face encounters when it comes to dealing with researchers who have not agreed with their directives, and yet these directives have been predetermined in an institutional vacuum without any face-to-face contact with people who 'know' the relevant research field sites and disciplines deeply.

The ethical position that emerges from face-to-face human encounter has been explored most famously by Emmanuel Levinas (1961). His humanistic philosophical stance focuses on the mutuality of responsibility that is built up through the encounters we have with others – just being with others creates through the interaction a drive to care and to act responsibly (ibid.). To accept this philosophical position is to shift one's gaze from the deontological rule-based stance of institutional ethical review to a more practice-oriented view. It allows us to consider how we might privilege experience gleaned through encounter over potential risks that are imagined through uninformed eyes.

In addition, risks have often been found to be produced as a result of researchers' attempts to comply with research ethics committee decisions. The rules, when followed (the application passed, the plain language statements and consent forms created and then presented to institutions and individuals), while very helpful in some cases, may, in other cases, generate problems of their own out of the uncertain space that is the future in the field. The story at the beginning of this chapter about the researcher getting in trouble for washing-up dishes in a retirement home is an interesting example of this, where a resident took the limits of research outlined in the forms literally and felt the researcher's casual interaction in his field was necessarily suspect. Another example is when 'plain language statements' and lists of trauma counsellors (all required for ethics clearance) were given to a Ph.D. student's interviewee, an indigenous and highly educated elder, who became angry, throwing the forms back to say that they were not only patronizing but racist. For this to come at the beginning of a project from a key informant is surely casting more than a mere shadow over the work to come.

Those who recognize the negative possibilities that could arise from the proper application of institutionally sanctioned ethical procedures in the field think, quite naturally, about how to subvert them. In some cases this is not even a choice. Institutional ethics review boards may determine rules of interaction and process for a project where compliance becomes impossible due to the unpredictable nature of participant observation (Katz 2006) or indeed of any 'method' applied in the field. In some cases the institutionally agreed rules need to be

broken in order to meet the 'ethical' requirements of the community
in a field context (see Swiffen 2007). For example, an NGO project in
Bangladesh involving children using cameras was embarked on by
following external ethical review procedure to seek informed consent.
Community members all agreed they would not participate unless the
photos the children took were shared publicly (contradicting external
reviewers' determination that they must be kept 'confidentially' so as
to 'protect privacy'). The gathered community insisted: 'That's how
we do it here – there is no private ownership – we do not value confidentiality – and we believe it is unethical to destroy the pictures the
way you suggest – they are precious and must be kept for the future'
(Kate Ramsay, personal communication).

Sometimes it is the call to act morally as a person and react in any
given moment to a sense of a shared humanity – to decide to admin-
ister a life-saving drug without qualifications to do so, to lie and go
undercover to get to the heart of illegal organ trafficking (see Scheper-
Hughes 2009) – that leads to intentional neglect of externally
determined rules for best ethical practice.

Along similar lines, an Australian Ph.D. student working with
victims of rape in Eastern Europe had been advised by the ethics board
to attend various training workshops in advance of her trip so she
could deal with the reportage of traumatic memories of violence. The
people running the workshops insisted in no uncertain terms that
informants who have been raped, anywhere in the world, must not be
physically touched during any interview or during any other social
interaction – that this would consist of another bodily invasion of
space and safety, etc. The researcher left for the field with an armoury
of tactics she had come to believe in, but in her first arranged interview her gentle practised avoidance of physicality almost lost her
the woman's support. To be a human being and talk of such difficult
things in that part of the world requires intimacy. She discovered that
holding back a hug or comforting arm – regardless of one's position of
power or one's relatively new arrival status in the field – closes down,
rather than opens up, channels of communication and trust.

This brings us back to the idea that the core of ethicality in field-
based research is inevitably embedded in the practice itself, in feeling
responsible to do the right thing, in working towards protecting others
from harm, in altering one's expectations about what is needed or
right based on what the field itself teaches us. And yet one cannot
always achieve all of these things. In most human research there is
inevitably at least some small risk involved – some person who might
be hurt or offended, some confidential information that leaks out to

a broader audience. The trick is learning to adjust, to react and to creatively negotiate a way through it.

Many scholars who write about ethnography and institutional ethics review have made suggestions for ways forward. Plattner has suggested that the level of oversight by institutions should be relative to the level of risk (2006). Chalmers and Pettit encourage ethical self-evaluation as best practice and suggest the delegation of some responsibility to professional organizations (1998). They urge institutional ethics review bodies to stop their obstructive posing while also discouraging researchers' defensive posing that puts them into the respective roles of police and offenders (ibid.). Clearly stepping back to look, one can see how destructive such posing can be, not only in the design and approval stages, but also to the research itself. Chenhall, Senior and Belton have recently drawn from case studies to consider how ongoing self-evaluation leads to the idea of an 'ethics of practice' and the important role of reflexivity in its articulation (2011).

Personally I have found it very useful to reflect on a number of my contrasting fields to consider how an ethics of practice is designed and produced not only from a singular reflexive awareness in that field alone, but a relational one that can see how easily everything can serendipitously shift and change in social life. Each change in context and relation evokes different sets of questions, different requirements of method and different fields of knowledge transaction.

Of course we need to have a mechanism in place to monitor ethics in some research scenarios, and, as Lederman reminds us, if institutional review boards were not reviewing ethnographic proposals, other organizations may need to do so to satisfy funding agencies' requirements (for example IRB Advisor, 2006). However, even with monitoring, we can work to change the oppositional framing described above to a flexible and collaborative one. Heidegger has described the act of research as coming to an understanding through 'unveiling' over time (1996). We have seen, from my unveiling of ideas through different fields earlier in this chapter, that the most significant knowledge is not reducible to a series of social facts collected from contemporary anthropological research contexts, but it develops from an intersubjective and processual experience of being there and developing rapport and sensitivity. It emerges out of real relations with persons, not with 'subjects', in a gradual manner through biographical and other shared disclosures that come with responsibilities (Strathern 2006). Not only does good questioning, engaged observation and productive thinking develop out of such research, but so too does 'good ethical practice'. The material that is produced is connected initially to the particularities of encounters, but it then becomes filtered through ideas, policies, memories, formalized practices and finally the authorship of texts. Through other paths, other methods and other possibilities emerge. The clamping down on what is possible in the audit space that precedes entry to the field may be necessary to protect individuals and institutions in some cases, but in the vast majority of cases it is wholly inappropriate and only restricts researchers' imaginations and ability to be flexible and open to the lessons from serendipitous encounters of the field. By whatever means possible we need to foster faith in the good judgements that emerge out of such interactive field experiences. We need to reach out and work together with those scholars in positions of institutional power who have not yet been properly exposed to this way of working, learning and knowing.

Tamara Kohn is Associate Professor of Anthropology at the University of Melbourne, and Chief Investigator on two Australian Research Council grants. Selected publications are 'Crafting the Self on Death Row', in *Emotion, Identity and Death* (2012); and 'Posthumous Personhood and the Affordances of Digital Media', *Mortality* 20(4) (2015).

Notes

I presented earlier versions of this paper for anthropology seminars at Monash University, Macquarie University, and Melbourne University, as well as for the University of Melbourne's HAPS Human Ethics Sub-Committee, and I am grateful for the useful discussions and debates these generated. I have also published two other pieces that were inspired by the initial work done for this chapter (see Kohn 2014 and Kohn and Shore 2017). I especially wish to thank Jacky Angus, Richard Chenhall, Rena Lederman, Martha Macintyre, Sarah Quillinan, Kate Ramsay, Buck Rosenberg, Cris Shore, and Lisa Wynn for their invaluable input and advice, as well as the editors of this volume.

1. The ethics review board did conclude in this case that the elderly informant was vexatious and so there were no repercussions for the student, at least at the university end, but the important point here is that interactive possibilities can be detrimentally shaped by the limits the form requires – for both the researcher as well as for the participants in the study.

2. Economic and Social Research Council.

3. Note that most of the examples that follow in this chapter were drawn from research projects at Australian universities. The editors of this volume have helpfully asked me whether institutional ethics review boards are indeed more restrictive in this part of the world than in the United Kingdom or United States. While I am, alas, not sure of the answer to this, I would emphasize instead that the patterns are recognizable and that the basic principles iterated here are generalizable, even if the examples are amongst the more extreme.
4. These stand for the American Anthropological Association, the Association of Social Anthropologists, and the Australian Anthropological Society.

References

Caplan, P. (ed.). 2003. *The Ethics of Anthropology: Debates and Dilemmas*. London: Routledge.

Cerwonka, A. and L.H. Malkki. 2007. *Improvising Theory: Process and Temporality in Ethnographic Fieldwork*. Chicago: University of Chicago Press.

Chalmers, D. and P. Pettit 1998. 'Towards a Consensual Culture in the Ethical Review of Research', *The Medical Journal of Australia*. Retrieved 31 October 2016 from https://www.mja.com.au/journal/1998/169/2/ethics

Chenhall, R., K. Senior and S. Belton. 2011. 'Negotiating Human Research Ethics: Case Notes from Anthropologists in the Field', *Anthropology Today* 27(5): 13–17.

Fassin, D. 2006. 'The End of Ethnography as Collateral Damage of Ethical Regulation?', *American Ethnologist* 33(4): 522–24.

Fluehr-Lobban, C. 2009. 'Guiding Principles over Enforceable Standards', *Anthropology News* 50(6): 8–9.

Gadamer, H-G. 1979. *Truth and Method*. London: Sheed and Ward.

Guillemin, M. and L. Gillam. 2004. 'Ethics, Reflexivity and "Ethically Important Moments" in Research', *Qualitative Inquiry* 10(2): 261–80.

Heidegger, M. 1996. *Being and Time: A Translation of Sein und Zeit*, trans. J. Stambaugh. New York: State University of New York Press.

IRB Advisor. September 2006. 'Ethnography Proposals Pose Problems for IRBs'. Retrieved 31 October 2016 from https://www.princeton.edu/anthropology/faculty/rena_lederman/pdfs/Lederman-2006-IRB-Advisor-articles-09-06.pdf

Katz, J. 2006. 'Ethical Escape Routes for Underground Ethnographers', *American Ethnologist* 33(4): 499–506.

Kohn, T. 1987. 'Field Residence and Textual Responsibility: A Scottish Case Study', *Proceedings of the Association of Scottish Ethnography* II: 50–54.

————. 1994. 'Incomers and Fieldworkers: A Comparative Study of Social Experience', in K. Hastrup and P. Hervik (eds), *Social Experience and Anthropological Knowledge*. London: Routledge.

————. 2007. 'Bowing onto the Mat: Discourses of Change through Martial Arts Practice', in S. Coleman and T. Kohn (eds), *The Discipline of Leisure: Embodying Cultures of 'Recreation'*, New York and Oxford: Berghahn Books.

————. 2002. 'Becoming an Islander through Action in the Scottish Hebrides', *Journal of Royal Anthropological Institute (JRAI)* 8(1): 143–58.

————. 2009. 'Waiting on Death Row', in G. Hage (ed.), *Waiting*. Melbourne: University of Melbourne Press.

————. 2011. 'Appropriating an Authentic Bodily Practice from Japan: On 'Being There', 'Having Been There' and 'Virtually Being There', in V. Strang and M. Busse (eds), *Ownership and Appropriation*, Oxford and New York: Berg Publishers.

————. 2012. 'Crafting Selves on Death Row', in D. Davies and C. Park (eds), *Emotion, Identity and Death: Mortality Across Disciplines*. London: Ashgate, pp. 71–83.

————. 2014. 'Ethics Review and the Limited Gaze: a plea for an intervention', *The Australian Journal of Anthropology* 25(3): 379–81.

Kohn, T. and C. Shore. 2017. 'The Ethics of University Ethics Committees: Risk Management and the Research Imagination', in S. Wright and C. Shore (eds), *The Death of the Public University*, New York and Oxford: Berghahn Books.

Lederman, R. 2006a. 'Anxious Borders between Work and Life in a Time of Bureaucratic Ethics Regulation', *American Ethnologist* 33(4): 477–81.

Lederman, R. 2006b. 'The Perils of Working at Home: IRB "Mission Creep" as Context or Content for an Ethnography of Disciplinary Knowledges', *American Ethnologist* 33(4): 482–91.

Levinas, E. 1961. *Totality and Infinity*. Leiden: Martinus Nijhoff.

Macdonald, S. 2010. 'Making Ethics', in Melhuus, M., J.P. Mitchell, H. Wulff (eds), *Ethnographic Practice in the Present*. New York and Oxford: Berghahn Books.

Mitchell, R.G., Jr. 1993. *Secrecy and Fieldwork* (Qualitative Research Methods Series 29). London: Sage Publications.

Pettit, P. 1991. 'Instituting a Research Ethic: Chilling and Cautionary Tales', *Academy of the Social Sciences in Australia 1991 Annual Lecture*.

Plattner, D. 2006. 'Comment on IRB Regulation of Ethnographic Research', *American Ethnologist* 33(4): 525–28.

Rose, D. 1987. *Black American Street Life*. University of Pennsylvania Press.

Scheper-Hughes, N. 2009. 'The Ethics of Engaged Ethnography: Applying a Militant Anthropology in Organs-Trafficking Research', *Anthropology News* 13–14.

Schneider, C.E. 2015. *The Censor's Hand: The Misregulation of Human-Subject Research*. MIT Press.

Schrag, Z.M. 2010. *Ethical Imperialism: Institutional Review Boards and the Social Sciences, 1965-2009*. Baltimore: Johns Hopkins University Press.

Shore, C. and S. Wright. 1999. 'Audit Culture and Anthropology: Neo-Liberalism in British Higher Education', *Journal of the Royal Anthropological Society* 5(4): 557–75.

Strathern, M. 2000. *Audit Cultures: Anthropological Studies in Accountability, Ethics and the Academy*. London: Routledge.

———. 2006. 'Don't Eat Unwashed Lettuce', *American Ethnologist* 33(4): 532–34.

Swiffen, A. 2007. 'Research and Moral Law: Ethics and the Social Science Research Relation', *Political and Legal Anthropology Review* 30(2): 210–28.

Wright, S. and C. Shore (eds). 2017. *The Death of the Public University*, New York and Oxford: Berghahn Books.

PART II

The Ethics of Indirect Mediated Ethnography

The chapters in this section (by Laura Huttunen and Tamsin Bradley) are built on two forms of ethnographic indirectness. The second concerns ethnography at a distance in a literal sense, when fieldwork is delegated to local persons, who have their own social positions to maintain. Not only is the research filtered through them, but their findings are grounded in their own local relations rather than in any relations the ethnographer might have established. The first form of indirectness is conceptual, in that the ethnography is carried out in the context of an entirely different concern. In neither case is the fieldwork determined by the ethnographer in one to one relationships, or in relationships that place her or him in a direct position of control. In one case, the anthropologist is a mouthpiece for a doubly alienated man: first as a refugee and second as a patient undergoing psychotherapy. The ethnography thus passes through several filters, drawing analogies between the work of the therapist and that of the anthropologist, but ultimately turning to the patient's strategies for understanding the intentionality behind the mise en scène. In neither case is it a question of a one-to-one relationship with an informant, and both cases raise the question of ethical responsibility.

Chapter 4

TROUBLED CONJUNCTURES

ETHNOGRAPHY, PSYCHOTHERAPY AND TRANSNATIONAL SOCIAL FIELDS

Laura Huttunen

Introduction

This chapter is an exploration of knowledge practices in therapy with people with a refugee background. In many Western countries there are established institutions offering psychological counselling and therapy to those categorized as 'refugees'. Thus migrant people from various social and cultural backgrounds are often drawn into the sphere of therapeutic practices in their new countries of settlement. I am interested in the therapeutic relationship as a space for knowledge production, as well as in the ways in which ethical questions resonate with such encounters.

In this chapter I will look at the broader questions of (ethics of) knowledge production through a case study of a Bosnian man with a refugee background attending psychotherapy in Finland. The man invited me, an anthropologist, to attend his therapy sessions. I will disentangle the complex intentionalities that met in this encounter. Moreover, I will address the ways in which these intentionalities relate to aspirations of being ethical. The modes of knowledge transacted and negotiated in this encounter, and the ethical questions connected with them, have implications beyond the therapeutic space, concerning issues of refugee settlement and transnational social relations, as well as ethics of social scientific enquiry.

On the one hand, my focus on the therapeutic encounter calls for an understanding of the ways in which ethics is an aspect of all social life (Lambek 2010). Both the therapist and the patient bring their own ethical aspirations into the encounter, as well as their own ethical dilemmas. On the other hand, my engagement with the case as an anthropologist calls for a consideration of research ethics. The minimal requirement of standard research ethics is, of course, that the researcher does not harm those researched in any way. Already this requirement posed some serious questions for me as an ethnographer. Moreover, there is a rather strong current in anthropological thought suggesting that ethical research should benefit those who are the subjects of research in one way or another, or benefit society more generally, at least through offering a critical or analytic voice in public discussion. As Wiktor Stoczkowski (2008) puts it, the ultimate aim ('the fourth aim') of anthropological enquiry is often nowadays considered to be that of transforming the social reality we are studying. The other aims of anthropological research, those of 'describing-understanding-explaining' are often considered primarily as tools to attain the fourth one. Sometimes, however, the ethical imperative for 'truth' may collide with the other ethical imperative, sustained by some, for political commitments. To avoid such a collision Stoczkowski suggests that the ethics (or morality) of the observer/ the anthropologist should be analysed alongside those of the people observed (ibid.: 351–52). I will come back to these points in the concluding discussion.

Stephen Collier and Aihwa Ong introduce the idea 'global forms' as social forms capable of travelling across national, social and cultural boundaries, thus having potential for universality and arranging social relations across the globe (Collier and Ong 2005). Psychotherapy as a practice has pretensions of being such a global form. Even if psychoanalysis as an intellectual tradition and institutional practice is firmly embedded in Western modes of thought, it is often presented as a universal theory addressing human nature beyond cultural difference. Within anthropology, the subfields of psychological and psychiatric anthropology have addressed these issues for a long time, questioning the universality of psychological and psychoanalytic concepts and theories (see e.g., Kleinman 1987; Briggs 1998; Weiner 1999). My aim here is not to take part in these controversies, nor do I address psychoanalytic theory. Rather, my aim is to look at psychotherapy as a practice of knowledge production and a particular 'global conjuncture', where people from various social backgrounds are drawn into specific relations prescribed by therapeutic practices. I will briefly compare it with another global form, that of truth commissions.

In the vocabulary of Collier and Ong (2005), 'global assemblages' are conjunctures where global forms are articulated in specific contexts. I will look at my particular ethnographic case as such an 'assemblage'. I will ask: how is knowledge produced in psychotherapeutic encounters? How are different forms of knowledge used in these encounters? How is ethics as an aspect of social life in general, and as an aspect of therapeutic practices, played out in these encounters? And further: how should anthropologists relate to such a form of knowledge production? Or to put it differently: how could anthropologists ethically address psychotherapy with refugees as a form of knowledge production? In the next section I will frame these questions in debates over the nature of the predicament of refugees – that is, should we understand 'refugeeness' first and foremost in psychological or in political terms?

Framing the Case:
Debates over 'Psychologizing' Refugeeness

As noted above, in many Western countries there are established practices of offering psychological help to refugees. The modes of such psychological interventions vary, from state-sponsored systems to centres run by NGOs; from long-term psychotherapy to various forms of group sessions, solution-focused therapies and art therapies. There is a strong ethical commitment among the therapy professionals to help traumatized people with such practices. The focus of such an ethical commitment is on the individual, supposedly in need of a therapeutic intervention.

Many anthropologists, however, with their focus on the social and the political, have criticized the tendencies to 'psychologize' the situation of refugees; according to this critique, questions that are ultimately political are turned into individual and psychological problems (see e.g., Eastmond 2005; Grønseth 2010; Kleinman and Kleinman 1997; Malkki 1995b, 1996). These critics have emphasized (both the ethical and analytical) importance of understanding refugees, or people categorized as such, as deeply embedded in social and historical contexts, in complex societal relationships that are not reducible to individual trauma. Some writers foreground the situations in refugees' countries of origin and the complex historical processes that in each case force people to leave their original homes (e.g., Daniel 1996; Malkki 1995a, 1995b, 1996), while others focus on life in countries of asylum or new countries of settlement, where people need to negotiate again complex social relationships that are often hierarchically ordered and politically tense (Eastmond 2005; Grønseth 2010; Hautaniemi 2010; Juntunen 2009; Prato 2009). Such critique resonates with claims that victims of political violence need arenas for giving public witness accounts of experiences of injustice; various forms of truth commissions are needed, instead of individual therapy. According to such claims, having a public voice would have a healing effect.[1]

I agree with much of this critique. I argue, however, that we should not jump to conclusions too quickly; we should not dismiss all therapeutic practices as mystifying the 'proper' questions, or as simply useless. Rather, I will place the connection between the individual trauma and the larger political context into the focus of enquiry, and ask how practices of knowledge production in each sphere relate to each other. In other words, I wish to look at the connection between the therapeutic, the political and the ethical more closely. As I argue elsewhere (Huttunen 2014), the act of claiming an audience beyond the therapeutic relationship may be simultaneously a political and a therapeutic act for the patient. Negotiating the relations of knowledge production is a key element in building this connection between the therapeutic, the political and the ethical.

Framing the Case 2: Transnational Social Fields

The case that I discuss in this article is embedded in my long-term ethnographic research among Bosnians in diaspora.[2] I have conducted fieldwork among Bosnians in Finland since 2001, focusing on their transnational and diasporic relations. Most of the Bosnians in Finland are of Bosnian Muslim or Bosniak origin, or from ethnically mixed families, and practically all of them came to Finland as refugees during the war in Bosnia-Herzegovina (1992–1995) or soon thereafter through various modes of family unification. I have looked at modes of relating to their country of origin through travel and family relations, as well as through rebuilding activities in Bosnia. My actual field sites included both Finland and Bosnia-Herzegovina (hereafter 'Bosnia'; see Huttunen 2005, 2007, 2009a, 2009b, 2010). The fact that my informants, including the one discussed in this chapter, engage in transnational social networks means that their meaningful social relations span social fields that cross borders of nation states. This fact has implications for the modes of knowledge production in this case, as well as for the contestations over ethics. I will return to these implications below.

Conducting research in such a transnational setting had two implications for my actual research process. First, I did multisited ethnography (Hannerz 2003; Marcus 1995) with fieldwork both in Bosnia and in Finland. My strategy of building a multisited research setting involved applying Marcus' formulation 'follow the people'; accordingly, I have chosen field sites that were relevant for my informants' lives. For them, these various sites in Finland and Bosnia were naturally connected to each other through their social relations, and practices of communication and visiting. Secondly, when interpreting knowledge produced in each setting, such as interview material or episodes observed, I attempted to situate them analytically within the transnational field. In other words, when interpreting my informants' actions and words, I kept in mind that their active social fields included several geographic locations.

When there are several field sites, there are also more audiences that will potentially use our research findings for their own purposes. This is a relevant point also in the case discussed in this chapter. As I will suggest below, my interlocutor had several audiences in mind when telling his story to the therapist, and to the anthropologist. Contested interpretations of Bosnian history have different implications in Finland and in Bosnia. While in Finland stories of violence in Bosnia are most often read within the framework of refugee settlement, as warrants for refugee status, in Bosnia they are enmeshed in an ongoing bitter struggle over the 'truth' of the wars in the Balkans in the 1990s. In this struggle not only the past is at issue, but also the legitimacy of the present political structure, and beyond that, possibilities of imagining an alternative future for Bosnia. Even if my focus in this chapter is on face-to-face negotiations of knowledge production, I am acutely aware of this larger embeddedness of my ethnographic case study. I will argue that the larger frame was present in the face-to-face encounters in various ways.

The Case Study

In 2005 I was actively engaged in fieldwork among Bosnians in Finland. In the spring of that year I visited various social gatherings and meetings arranged by Bosnian associations. I spoke about my research project, and took the opportunity to invite people to come and talk to me about their lives. I told them that I was interested in their experiences both in Bosnia and in Finland, and especially in their experiences of living between these two places. At that time I meant 'living between places' in a concrete sense – that is, the practices of visiting Bosnia or sharing their time between Finland and Bosnia, of keeping relationships alive across borders via material and symbolic exchange. But 'living in-between' could also be interpreted more psychologically and symbolically, as referring to lacking a sense of being at home, or a troubled emplacement both in the new country of settlement and the radically changed social and political landscape of Bosnia (cf. Jansen 2008; see also Gronseth and Davis 2010; Jackson 2002). I conducted several formal interviews and countless informal ones in pursuit of this research.[3] Most Bosnians had a permanent residence permit in Finland; some had even acquired formal citizenship. Their situation in Finland is framed by welfare state practices with a pronounced agenda of integration (alongside other immigrant groups) into Finnish society. The other end of the diasporic social space, Bosnia, was still characterized by political and economic instability (see e.g., Jansen 2007; Stefansson 2004).

To my surprise, I was contacted by a psychiatrist working with people with a refugee background in one of the urban centres in southern Finland. He told me that he had a patient: a man in his late fifties who had come to Finland as a refugee from Bosnia during the Bosnian war. The man, whom I will call Mustafa Hadzić, had asked his therapist to invite me to attend their sessions. He had heard me talk about my research when I attended a social club meeting organized for elderly Bosnian refugees in a suburban centre some six months earlier. I gladly accepted the invitation, even though it made me uneasy. I was not sure about my role in the sessions, neither was I clear about the patient's expectations. Starting with the very basic questions of research ethics I wondered if I would disturb something with my presence in the therapy sessions. Could I harm Mustafa Hadzić or his therapeutic process? Or the other way round, could I be useful in any way? Here my thoughts were fuelled by debates on research ethics in anthropology, described by Stoczkowski (2008). Despite my doubts I decided to accept the invitation.

I attended two therapy sessions. I learned that Mustafa Hadzić came from a rural area in eastern Bosnia. He had little formal education, and had earned his living as a farmer and a manual worker in Yugoslavia. He came from a Bosnian Muslim or Bosniak family. My role in those sessions was rather a passive one: after the initial introduction, I sat in a chair in the corner of the therapist's office and listened to the discussion that was taking place between Mustafa and the therapist. The sessions were conducted through an interpreter. Mustafa talked in Bosnian and the therapist talked in Finnish, and a translator

mediated between them after each utterance. This is a common practice with patients with a migrant background in this institution. Both
sessions began with a brief discussion of Mustafa's medication, and
the therapist would ask about his general moods. Mustafa would talk
about being tired, but also about having a feeling that the medication
helped him. During both sessions that I attended Mustafa would then
move away from his current condition to talk about events during
the Bosnian war. He would talk about some recurring memories of
atrocities that he had witnessed during his imprisonment in a prison
camp during the war. Then he would bemoan the fact that the rest of
the world had allowed the atrocities to go on for such a long time. He
had visions of using technology, such as filming from aeroplanes and
helicopters, to document the atrocities that took place in Bosnia. His
speech conveyed a strong conviction that the outside world did not
know what 'really' happened in Bosnia.

Due to the special nature of this ethnographic encounter, I did not
record anything that took place during these sessions; I have only
my own field notes, jotted down after each session and based on an
exchange that took place via the interpreter. As a consequence I
cannot quote Mustafa directly here. There were, however, some recurring themes in his speech that are significant in this context. He would
repeatedly talk about his bodily feelings of tiredness and anxiety, and
consider, in dialogue with the therapist, whether medication helped
these feelings. Another recurring theme was certain incidents of
violence that he had witnessed during the war, especially violence
committed against children. He would himself explain his anxiety by
these memories. Furthermore, he would repeatedly imagine helicopters, equipped with film cameras, documenting the atrocities that took
place in Bosnia, and disseminating them 'to the world'. While in the
first theme sensations and feelings located in his body anchored him
to his current life in Finland, the two latter themes referred to social
spaces beyond Finland. Events that took place in Bosnia, and politically loaded questions of accountability in post-war Bosnia, occupied
his narrative. 'The transnational', referring to social spaces or fields
created through social relations and practices, was thus present in
the therapy sessions. Simultaneously, the 'in-betweenness' in a more
symbolic sense was formed in these acts of narrativization, as efforts
to come to terms with his current life repeatedly turned his mind back
to Bosnia.

To my surprise, at the end of the first session he handed me a
folded piece of paper. As I opened it I realized that it contained a long
handwritten text in Bosnian. He told me that there, in the paper,

he described events during the 'previous war' – that turned out to mean the Second World War – that were told in his family and that he thought the world should know about. He assured me that everything in the paper was true, and that I could do whatever I wanted with the story. Then he asked if I wanted him to write something about the 'last war', meaning the war in Bosnia in the 1990s. I said that I would appreciate that. Thus, after the second session he handed me another paper, again handwritten in Bosnian.

Both accounts were written as a chronicle, listing concrete events with exact dates and names of villages and houses; also listed were the full names of actual persons who had been the victims of horrendous violence. The first story covered events in Yugoslavia during the Second World War, while the second one covered the Bosnian war between 1992 and 1995. The first story had the heading: 'Crimes committed during the Second World War', and before going into details he placed himself as the interlocutor within the landscape of the historical changes that were taking place:

> Written by Hadzić, Mujos's son, Mustafa, born on the 3rd of May, 1953, in the village of Borovac,[4] in the municipality of Srebrenica, in Bosnia-Herzegovina ...
>
> Before the Second World War the Serbs demanded all the inhabitants in the area to hand over all the fire arms. Those municipalities that were demanded to do that mostly agreed. The arms were taken away and given to Serbs, as those making demands were mostly Serbs. Later, a Serbian rule was established.

Then he chronicles the story, relying on exact details:

> I will give this witness account from the region where I was born and grew up. There were five villages, which were: Borovac, Kupuvice, Vrtaze, Ljubomislja and Grno Gore.
>
> In these villages, 230 inhabitants were killed or disappeared in various ways. In these five villages it means 50% of the total population.
>
> I will give here some examples, those that I find most horrifying:
>
> One evening they burnt three houses, with 114 women and children inside:
>
> In the village if Kupovice, the house of Haris Filipović:[5] 72 people
>
> In the village of Ljubomislja the house of Mehmet Fazlić: 35 people
>
> In the village of Grno Gore, the house of Meho Agić: 7 people
>
> In the village of Borovac there were even more people, but some of them survived. There they locked in over 40 women and children in a house, and they set the house on fire, and after that they even threw some bombs into the house. They left the house and took some wounded persons with them. Among those was Sabiha Batinić, who is still alive.

He closes the story with a moral assessment of the consequences of this violence, as well as of the forced silence regarding these events:

> And we were not allowed to speak about such things. As if nothing ever happened. If the perpetrators would have been made responsible for their deeds then, there would certainly have been fewer crimes during this last war.

He opens the second story by again locating the story in a historical framework, this time the events in the former Yugoslavia in the 1990s, moving from more remote locations towards his home region:

> I want to tell briefly about some events during the hellish war in Bosnia.
> The war in former Yugoslavia broke out first in Slovenia, then in Croatia, and after that in Bosnia-Herzegovina. In Bosnia it started in 1992. ... In April 1992 they closed all the main roads, and we could not move along them anymore. This happened also in Žepa, in Rogatica ...

Again, he chronicles the horrendous details:

> During the siege in March 1992 there were hundreds of bodies floating in the Drina from Višegrad. The bodies came along the waterfall. Our people lifted up a big amount of bodies from the river and buried them on the river bank. Those people who lifted and buried the bodies told us, that these bodies were mutilated, and some even nailed to wooden boards.
> On the 5th of May, 1992, the Serbs set a birch plain on fire. I saw with my own eyes Mehmet Hasanović and his wife and children, as well as Esad Zejkić and his wife and two children among those bodies. Marko Kordić's throat was slit, as well as Leijla Begović's who was approximately 80 years old. The grandmother of my wife, Fatima Ajanović, was burned alive, and she was almost 100 years old. I saw with my own eyes how they burned a stable, and the cows and goats were burned there too. They killed the cows, the goats, the dogs, the cats, the old people, the young ones, everything that happened to be in their way.

He ends the text by situating the places within the political geography of post-war, post-Dayton Bosnia-Herzegovina, with the division of the country into the Serb Republic and the (Muslim-Croat) Federation:

> 2000 houses were burned in the Žepa area, a lot of people were killed and their belongings were destroyed. In the area round the River Drina, along the Serbian border, there were many towns that were Muslim towns before the war. Like Foča, Goražde, Rogatica, Bratunac and Zvornik. Now these towns belong to the Serb Republic, except Goražde, which remained in the Federation.

The written accounts expanded the themes discussed during the therapy sessions. Both the oral and the written accounts are emplaced in the Bosnian landscape, but the written accounts expanded the time frame backwards from the 1990s to the Secord World War. Moreover, in the written form, Mustafa's personal feelings and sensations were subdued; instead he was present in the text as the narrator of others' experiences and witness accounts, as well as of his own witness accounts.

Mustafa was born after the Second World War. Thus, in the first story he talks about events that he has only heard about, while in the second one he talks about events that he has lived through himself. The style of writing and modes of producing truth are, however, surprisingly similar: exact names, dates and places, counting victims and recognizing dead bodies with full names. Moreover, there are some striking visual images, such as bodies drifting in the Drina River as well bodies nailed to wooden boards. In the written form, the Second World War and the warfare of the 1990s merge into a continuous narrative of violence committed against civilian populations. The enforced silence over the earlier events provides explanations for the repeated violence in the 1990s.

In the context of violence committed by German troops in Tuscany, Italy, during the Second World War, Francesca Cappelletto (2003) analyses the formation of group memory as a process of intersubjective storytelling after 'extreme events'. She claims that a mnemonic community is formed through a process of repetitive, interactive storytelling in narrative sessions. During such a process individual and group memories get intertwined, or in other words autobiographical memory and historical memory are merged, so that detailed events witnessed and then told by individuals become a shared memory. According to her, visualized images serve a special function in the formation of such a shared historical memory: images are 'emotions in visual form' (Cappelletto 2003: 251), and as such they function as bridges between the individual experience and the historical representation (Cappelletto 2003).

Cappelletto analyses the social formation of memory in a context where people who had lived through extreme events were able to meet face-to-face, and produced their shared historical narrative in actual social interaction. In the Bosnian case, while the memories of the Second World War were circulated within the local community that stayed in the area, the events of the 1990s created a worldwide diaspora separated by long geographical distances. In such a transnational setting, written accounts gain new importance, as they are able to travel and communicate across distances. In his writing, Mustafa employs surprisingly similar tools to build a narrative as Cappelletto's informants: he intertwines his own first-hand experiences with

witness accounts by others; he localizes accounts to a carefully constructed local landscape that is familiar and recognizable to those
involved; and he presents strong visual images loaded with emotional
content to convey the ultimate meaning of the stories. Mustafa's
written accounts may be read as utterances in a narrative process of a
mnemonic community in the making. This time, however, in a transnational setting, the process of forming a historical narrative is done,
at least partly, via written mediation.

Elsewhere (Huttunen 2014) I have analyzed the written accounts
in more detail, paying special attention to the ways in which the
interlocutor tapped into various modes of understanding ethnicity
and history, or giving a shape to history, circulating in the post-war
Balkans. In this chapter my aim is different: I will look at the tension
between the personal/therapeutic and the larger political aspirations that emerges from this case, and how the tension resonates
with various aspects of ethics. I will analyse the case in relation to
the transnational setting, as well as to the idea of psychotherapy as a
'global form'. Below I consider the therapeutic encounter as a space
for knowledge production in more detail. My key aim is to understand
how various ends and intentions of knowledge production meet each
other in this case, and how these various intentionalities with their
ethical commitments are negotiated in the process.

'Will to Knowledge', Ethics and the Psychotherapeutic Conjuncture

As a 'global form', psychotherapy brings (usually two) people together
who cooperate to produce an understanding of the patient's condition.[6] This usually happens through verbalizing experiences that are
problematic or painful for the patient. The core idea of most forms of
psychotherapy relies on the interaction, the mutuality of the relationship – even if the relationship is asymmetric or unequal by default.
Usually the co-production of narratives, or knowledge, takes place
between the patient and the therapist.[7] In this case, the anthropologist was also involved in the relations of knowledge production,
complicating the picture. I will first outline psychotherapy as a mode
of interaction in abstract terms; after that I will relate to the actual
ethnographic case.

If we think of psychotherapy as an abstract model, then we can see
that the creation and transaction of knowledge has specific purposes
and uses in the therapeutic process – or we could say, specific ethics.

The patient ideally 'gets better', recovers or recuperates through the transactions, while the therapist uses her own expert knowledge to diagnose, to prescribe medication and, ultimately and ideally, to heal the presumed trauma[8] or at least to facilitate ways to live with it. The ethical imperative of the therapist is to elicit knowledge in the form of the patient's narrative, and to use her expert knowledge in ways that help the patient to heal. For the patient, verbalizing the most hurtful memories often activates the deepest moral and ethical questions of being a human in the world. The anthropologist, invited to attend the sessions, has her own expert knowledge, geared towards 'understanding' and theoretical considerations; anthropologists tend to look at the social, cultural and political context of each event. The anthropologist also brings her own professional ethics as well as general research ethics into the encounter. In other words, each participant has her own 'will to knowledge' and own ethical aspirations.

There is a widely shared belief in the Western countries that narrativizing one's experiences – that is, putting them into verbal form – is therapeutic in itself (see e.g., McLeod 1997). Thus, the patient is encouraged to 'tell her story' – that is, to 'give' knowledge to the therapist. Another widely shared understanding within Western psychology is that traumatized people have 'suppressed' memories: experiences that are not verbalized, not given a discursive or narrative shape (e.g., Kirmayer 1996). Memories that are not verbalized are thought to be the most agonizing for patients – or, to look at it the other way round, the patient is not able to face and to narrativize the most painful memories. Thus the patient's knowledge is not just 'there', to be given; rather, it is something that needs to be produced, woven into verbal forms, given narrative shape.[9] In this process, the therapist is supposedly of help, giving tools and support in this often painful project of knowledge creation. The patient's knowledge, or the form of the knowledge, is cooperatively produced in a mutual, dialogic relationship (if the therapeutic relationship is functioning properly).

Correspondingly, the therapist's expert knowledge is useless without a functioning relationship with the patient. The therapist uses her expert knowledge to monitor the trajectory of interventions needed. But if the patient does not cooperate, the therapist cannot do her work properly: the healing qualities of the relationship cannot develop without mutual engagement. Ultimately, the therapeutic relationship cannot function without mutual cooperation.

This outline of relations in psychotherapy helps me to open up the ethnographic case at hand in more detail. In this case, various kinds of knowledge were transacted in the therapy sessions, and various ethical aspirations became entangled. The patient's emotions and sensations, both bodily and mental, were discussed as significant pieces of knowledge. Moreover, his memories from Bosnia were discussed; the therapist's questions, and gestures, opened the space for Mustafa's narrativizing activity around these memories.[10] I could observe the dialogic co-production of knowledge, a process where the therapist's questions (such as 'How have you felt lately?' or 'What has been on your mind lately?') invited Mustafa to reflect on his thoughts and feelings and to formulate them in verbal form.

Interestingly, Mustafa also brought in topics that were beyond his personal experiences. It was obvious that memories from the Bosnian war were a 'legitimate' topic, and the subject opened up a whole social world that is transnational in character – that is, spanning Finland and Bosnia. On the one hand he referred to politically and ethically charged events during the Bosnian war; on the other hand he commented strongly on the role of the 'international community' in the Bosnian war, and on atrocities in the former Yugoslavia in the 1990s in general. As mentioned, he even envisioned technically elaborated efforts to document and produce evidence of the violence 'for the world', such as filming Bosnia from helicopters. Deeply ethical issues of being human in this world were at issue here: how to encounter extreme forms of violence? Who bears the responsibility in such cases?

Such an evocation of the 'global audience' or 'global opinion' made me speculate if I was sitting there as a surrogate for that opinion – or as somebody seen as having the means to reach this larger audience and to address this 'global opinion'. The relations of knowledge production were transformed by my presence.

Mustafa's written testimonies affirmed this interpretation. There are several aspects worth noting in this act: first, he gave those written accounts to me, not to his therapist; [11] secondly, writing, as a technology, fixes things and enables the dissemination of knowledge, in some cases more effectively than oral communication (see e.g., Goody 2000); and thirdly, he had written them carefully in a form that sought to produce a certain truth value with exact dates, names of locations as well as real names of real people. The written testimonies brought in complex local histories from his country of origin, making the transnational frame explicit. Simultaneously, the written testimonies complicated the relations of knowledge production: they enlarged the presumed audience from the therapist to me, and to all putative readers of the texts.

The fact that he gave those accounts to me actively engaged me in the relations of knowledge production in the therapeutic process.

Even if I mainly sat and listened during the therapy sessions, I argue that my presence changed the configuration of the relations, at least momentarily. My role or my place in that process was different from the therapist's. The relationship between Mustafa and the therapist was a space for reflection, and for verbalizing difficult experiences, for seeking verbal form for that which is difficult to talk about. The therapeutic space is confined by confidentiality, and as such it enables the painful work of verbalization. The therapist used the cooperatively created knowledge to monitor Mustafa's well-being. The ethical imperative of therapeutic intervention is to help the individual in need. I was there to open up the therapeutic space to the 'outside world' when some of the knowledge had found its verbal form.

What was Mustafa's 'will to knowledge' when inviting me as a surrogate for larger audiences to his therapy sessions? What did he want to do with his stories in the world beyond the therapy room?[12] I can think of at least three different uses to which his stories may be put: I presume that first and foremost he wanted to talk to the Finnish audiences, the people with whom he shared his everyday life in his new country of settlement. The stories presented a strong warrant for his and his fellow Bosnians' situation as refugees in that country. However, the stories build simultaneously a history for his predicament, and they situate his personal condition within a field of social and political relations in Bosnia. By this narrative move he presents himself and his fellow Bosnians as people with histories, not just prototypical 'refugees' (cf. Malkki 1995b and 1996). I do not know much about Mustafa's personal relationships with Finns, as these were not discussed during the sessions that I attended or in the written accounts. However, my fieldwork among Bosnians had given me some insights concerning the relationships between them and Finns. The Bosnians in Finland were in general rather frustrated over the Finns' understanding of the events in the Balkans in the 1990s. Furthermore, the Bosnians often felt that on many occasions they were treated as 'refugees' rather that equal citizens.

Thirdly, the accounts have implications for audiences beyond Finland as well. We may read them as claims in the ongoing battles over the 'truth' of the recent history in the Balkans. In this sense, Mustafa participates in the contested process of writing history (e.g., Andrews 2007). Beyond that, Mustafa's style in the accounts, with exact dates, locations and names of the victims, is reminiscent of witnessing in court rooms, including, significantly, the Hague tribunal for war crimes (International Criminal Tribunal for the Former Yugoslavia, ICTY). As many Bosnians follow keenly events taking place in the Hague, they know that such a witnessing mode is a consequential mode of remembering, a way of translating private memories or private knowledge into the public and political sphere.

The ICTY is one version of a truth commission. Molly Andrews, writing on the Truth and Reconciliation Commission of South Africa, argues that one of the most important functions of such truth commissions is to transform knowledge into acknowledgement (Andrews 2007: 161). In other words, silenced experiences are brought into the public sphere and incorporated into public narratives as truth, or as a part of the truth. Mustafa's accounts could be read as reaching for recognition both in the Finnish public sphere, and in the Bosnian public sphere. I suggest that Mustafa is actually making a strong ethical claim that engages all these various publics. He insists that shared humanity makes us all responsible to intervene at the face of such atrocities. The actual perpetrators should be made responsible, but beyond that, as fellow human beings, we have an ethical responsibility to face the truth and help those in need of protection.

I filter the accounts through my expert knowledge as an anthropologist. My way of looking at things foregrounds the social and the political situation around Mustafa's personal story. I see him, inevitably, as embedded in the complex history of the Balkans, in relationships renegotiated after horrendous violence, in a field of contested memory and forgetfulness, as well as in a recent history of migration and exile. It is perhaps easier for me as a social anthropologist to understand the functioning of truth commissions than the confined logics of individual psychotherapy. However, this case made me rethink the dimensions of psychotherapy. In order to understand better both psychotherapy and truth commissions as ethical practices, I will try to disentangle the questions of voice and audience in the two instances, as well as the charged relationship to 'silence' in both.

Psychotherapy and Truth Commissions: Interlocutors, Audiences and Silence

In his written account, Mustafa points to the forced silence concerning partisan violence during the Second World War as a root cause for the eruption of violence in the 1990s. He sees silence as carrying enormous power to shape history. As the flip side of silence, 'voice' must similarly have the power to change the course of history. But how are silences broken, and voices formed?

The way in which Mustafa addressed the global audience, or 'the West', and their responsibility for allowing the bloodletting in Bosnia in the 1990s to continue, resonates well with my field data. Most Bosnians I met during my fieldwork seemed to be perplexed, angry and frustrated over the events and of the role of the Western powers (Huttunen 2009a). Moreover, such formulations are not unique to the Bosnians. Liisa Malkki, for instance, reports that the Burundian refugees in Tanzania in the 1980s were particularly active in their efforts to reach the 'international opinion' (see Malkki 1994). In both cases, there is a sense that the voice of the locals is in not heard in larger arenas.

Such a call for larger audiences seems to suggest that truth commissions or war crime tribunals would be the proper way to deal with traumas caused by genocidal projects or totalitarian governments terrorizing their own citizens. Empirical research, however, shows that such a public witnessing is not necessarily a healing experience for the individual. Quite the contrary, it could even traumatize the victim further, at least in the short run (see e.g., Andrews 2007: 167–69). The relations of knowledge production in such public hearings are very different from the confidentiality and mutuality of long-term therapy relationships; strict formulas for acceptable knowledge, such as printed forms with ready-made questions and limited space for answering, are typical, as well as preconceived procedures for accounting. The relationship to the audience is characterized by one-way communication and strict time limits. Moreover, audiences are typically large, and they do not engage in such a dialogic relationship with the witness as therapists usually do. The well-being of the witnessing individual is not the ultimate focus of such commissions but rather a 'public' or collective recovery; the individual is giving her knowledge for collective ends. However, as noted above, such commissions are able to transform knowledge into public acknowledgement. In other words, they provide a forum for a shared process of making history. Within such forums, individual knowledge may be included in the process of making new history after major ruptures, even if it is multivocal and contested history.

To sum up, the presumed audience in psychotherapy is the therapist, while in truth commissions the audience is 'the world', or at least the different parties of political processes in question. In psychotherapy, the narrative is produced in the idiom of individual experiences, while in truth commissions the language is of social groupings and power relations. In therapy, the ethics is geared towards the individual, while the ethics of such commissions is geared towards the collective. In both cases the interlocutor may refer to exactly the same events, but the language of knowledge production is different in each case. However, individuals engaged in processes of narrativizing their experiences in either one of these institutions probably do not think in such bipolar terms; rather, they look for hinges that would connect the individual and collective dimensions. Mustafa's act of inviting me to his therapy sessions, and the written accounts that he gave me to be disseminated further, worked to produce such a hinge between the personal and the political.

The different ways to understand 'silence' and recognition in psychotherapy on the one hand, and in truth commissions on the other, help us to see the transformations of knowledge that take place in this case. In psychotherapy, 'harmful' silence is understood to be caused by psychological trauma, whereas in truth commissions silence is understood to be caused by oppressive power relations. In psychotherapy the harmful silence is healed by verbalization of traumatic experiences within the therapy process, and the patient's emerging voice is heard and recognized by the therapist. The ethical commitment of psychotherapeutic practice is to help the patient to create a voice. In truth commissions, on the other hand, a remedy for forced silence is sought through gaining public recognition of one's experiences. The ethical commitment in such institutional practices is to ensure an audience for one's voice. However, whereas psychotherapy recognizes the difficulty and painfulness of the process of verbalization, truth commissions expect the stories to be there, ready to be told and asserted to the public.

The premise of strict confidentially between the therapist and the patient in psychotherapy, however, builds another kind of silence around the therapeutic relationship. The voice gained in the therapy room does not necessarily reach the world outside, and the therapist remains the only audience, the only one to acknowledge the accounts of the patient, often framed in the language of individual trauma. Psychotherapy as a global form creates social relations that enable the narrativization of certain silenced experiences, while it simultaneously threatens to silence their larger political implications through the practices of confidentiality and individualization. This is exactly the core of anthropological critique of psychotherapy.

Anthropological Contributions: Ethnographic Contextualization

The core of anthropological expertise is perhaps in the deep contextualization of ethnographic data. Here my question is: how to use ethically the knowledge that Mustafa was offering me? I am not a historian and my project is not one of producing the historical truth of what 'really' happened in Bosnia in the 1990s[13] (or during the Second World War). In this chapter, my project has been to contextualize the therapeutic in two senses: first, I have contextualized the case within the transnational field of social relations between Finland and Bosnia. Secondly, I have explored the 'global form' of psychotherapy in relation to truth commissions as public forums of making political claims, another institutional form having pretensions to be a 'global form'.

I suggest that psychotherapy and truth commission-like institutions have complementary ethical claims: the first aims at supporting the individual in a struggle to create a voice, while the latter works towards creating a consequential audience for such a voice. Sometimes the confidentiality of the therapeutic relationship is the space that enables the verbalization of knowledge that may then be disseminated further. The nature of the knowledge is transformed in this move, from personal/therapeutic into socially sharable/politically significant. Both forms of knowledge have their ethical importance.

The anthropological project of contextualizing the case carries two interlocking ethical implications. First, instead of understanding the interlocutor as a generalized victim of trauma, the anthropological project seeks to contextualize him in time and place, and consequently to take his public voice, and public agency, seriously (cf. Malkki 1996). The case discussed in this chapter evokes a deeply historical context for specific ethics cum politics in Bosnia and in the former Yugoslavian territories. Second, conceptualizing both therapy practices and truth commissions as 'global forms' opens them up to be analysed as spaces for knowledge creation and as spaces of ethical endeavours.

Moreover, I suggest that addressing extreme experiences in both kinds of institutions – therapeutic and public commissions – evokes ethics as a pervasive aspect of human life. In today's world, many people live through what we might call 'extreme events' (Cappelletto 1993) that leave deep imprints in individuals' minds and bodies (often literally), and at the same time dramatically reorganize social relations, and conditions for living. In Katherine Verdery's words, such events often entail 'a loss of one's moral world' (Verdery 1999). Such a loss is thoroughly social, and the painful process of rebuilding moral worlds is likewise necessarily social. Mustafa's call for larger audiences suggests that we share a responsibility as human beings at the face of such extreme atrocities.

In my initial framing of Mustafa's case I asked whether we should understand 'refugeeness' primarily in psychological or in political terms. I conclude by claiming that such a dichotomy is not the most fruitful way to approach the question. Various 'global forms', such as psychotherapy and truth commissions, as well as competing forms of narrating and writing collective histories, all seek for a proper language to talk about 'the unspeakable'. Each of them entails their own formation of social relations of knowledge production, as well as their own sore points of ethical dilemmas.

Laura Huttunen is Professor of Social Anthropology at the University of Tampere, Finland. Her recent publications include the chapter 'Remembering, Witnessing, Bringing Closure: Srebrenica Burial Ceremonies on YouTube' (in Hajek et al. (eds) 2016); 'Protective Barriers and Entrapping Walls' (*Journal of Borderland Studies* 2016); and 'Liminality and Contested Communitas: The Missing Persons in Bosnia-Herzegovina' (*Conflict and Society* 2016).

Notes

1. For a discussion of the topic, see Hayner 2001, also Andrews 2007, 148–76; Borneman 1997.
2. I understand transnational social fields as comprising of multiple interlocking social relationships that cut across national borders, and through which ideas and resources are exchanged, and transformed (see e.g., Faist 2000; Vertovec 2009).
3. During the research period I conducted twenty-two taped interviews. In addition there are various discussions, sometimes turned into short interviews, recorded in my research diary.
4. I have changed all the names of the villages as well as persons. I was hesitant to do this: Mustafa Hadzić's hope was that I would tell his story as a true one. But I am not a historian and I cannot check the verity of various factual claims; rather, I wish to discuss other implications provoked by his stories.
5. All the names have been changed.
6. 'Will to knowledge' as a formulation refers, of course, to Michel Foucault's work (1981 [1976]). I use it here as a heuristic tool to think about the relationship between agency, knowledge and discursive practices.
7. There are, of course, competing views on the therapeutic relationship among psychotherapists. My description here is not necessarily how psychotherapists would describe their practice, or how some of the theoretical literature in the field defines the relationship. This description of the relationship relies on my own experience as a patient in therapy, and in my informal discussions with some psychotherapists. As I emphasize in

the introduction, my aim in this chapter is not to discuss the validity of psychological or psychoanalytic theorization as such, but rather to tease out some aspects of therapeutic practices with refugees (for textbook definitions, see e.g., Lazarus and Zur 2002).

8. More precisely, it is usually not the therapist who is thought to 'heal' the patient, but rather the relationship between the patient and the therapist, and the mutually produced therapeutic process is understood as 'healing'. But the therapist uses her knowledge in order to facilitate such a healing process.

9. For discussions over the production of the self in narrative, see Josephides 2008, also Jackson 2002.

10. For a situation in which the listener's verbal response and body language did not allow the interlocutor to freely seek for narrative form, and to bring in topics, see an account of a case in the South African Truth and Reconciliation Commission , in Andrews 2007, 167-168.

11. As I mention above, Mustafa gave the written accounts personally to me. Afterwards I talked with the therapist, who confirmed that he had not received the stories. With Mustafa's permission I gave a copy of the stories also to the therapist.

12. Molly Andrews, writing about narrative testimonies given for the South African Truth and Reconciliation Committee, reminds us that those who participated in the process of the commission had various, sometimes even contradictory motivations for their participation (Andrews 2007, 161–76; see also Hayner 2001; Wilson 2000).

13. Of course, as an anthropologist I can also present the cumulative evidence of my interlocutors' experiences, as I have done elsewhere (see e.g., Huttunen 2009a and 2009b).

References

Andrews, M. 2007. *Shaping History: Narratives of Political Change*. Cambridge: Cambridge University Press.

Borneman, J. 1997. *Settling Accounts: Violence, Justice, and Accountability in Postsocialist Europe*. Princeton: Princeton University Press.

Briggs, J. 1998. *Inuit Morality Play: The Emotional Education of a Three-Year-Old*. Yale University Press.

Cappelletto, F. 2003. 'Long-term Memory of Extreme Events: From Autobiography to History', *The Journal of the Royal Anthropological Institute* 9(2): 241–60.

Collier, S.J and A. Ong. 2005. 'Global Assemblages, Anthropological Problems', in A. Ong and S.J. Collier (eds), *Global Assemblages: Technology, Politics and Ethics as Anthropological Problems*. Oxford: Blackwell, pp. 3–21.

Daniel, E.V. 1996. *Charred Lullabies: Chapters in and Anthropolography of Violence*. Princeton: Princeton University Press.

Drakulic, S. 2004. *They Would Never Hurt a Fly: War Criminals on Trial in the Hague.* London: Abacus.

Eastmond, M. 2005. 'The Disorders of Displacement: Bosnian Refugees and the Reconstruction of Normality', in R. Jenkins, V. Steffen and H. Hessen (eds), *Managing Uncertainty: Ethnographic Studies of Illness, Risk and the Struggle for Control.* Copenhagen: Museum of Tusculanum Press, pp. 149–71.

Faist, T. 2000. *The Volume and Dynamics of International Migration and Transnational Social Spaces.* Oxford: Oxford University Press.

Foucault, M. 1981 [1976]. *The History of Sexuality, vol. 1: The Will to Knowledge.* Harmondsworth: Penguin.

Goody, J. 2000. *The Power of the Written Tradition.* Washington: Smithsonian Institution Press.

Grønseth, A.S. 2010. *Lost Selves and Lonely Persons: Experiences of Illness and Well-being among Tamil Refugees in Norway.* Carolina: Carolina Academic Press.

Grønseth, A.S. and D.L. Davis (eds). 2010. *Mutuality and Empathy: Self and Other in the Ethnographic Encounter.* Herefordshire: Sean Kingston Publishing.

Gutman, R. 1993. *A Witness to Genocide.* London: Macmillan.

Hannerz, U. 2003. 'Being There...And There...and There! Reflections on Multi-Site Ethnography', *Ethnography* 4(2): 201–16.

Hautaniemi, P. 2010. 'Transnational Family Ties and the Resistance of a Welfare State', *The Journal of the Finnish Anthropological Society* 35(4): 42–45.

Hayner, P. 2001. *Unspeakable Truths: Confronting State Terror and Atrocity.* London: Routledge.

Huttunen, L. 2005. '"Home" and Ethnicity in the Context of War: Hesitant Diasporas of Bosnian Refugees. *European Journal of Cultural Studies* 8(2), 177–195.

Huttunen, L. 2007. 'Between 'the World' and a Pear Tree: Memory and Belonging in Bosnian Diaspora'. In *On Foreign Ground: Moving between Countries and Categories.* M-L.Karttunen and M. Ruckenstein (eds), Helsinki: Suomalaisen Kirjallisuuden Seura, pp. 174–87.

———. 2009a. 'Historical Legacies and Neo-colonial Forms of Power?: A Postcolonial Reading of the Bosnian Diaspora', in S. Irni, S. Keskinen, D. Mulinari and S. Tuori (eds), *Complying with Colonialism: Gender, 'Race' and Ethnicity in the Nordic Region.* Aldershot: Ashgate.

———. 2009b. 'Undoing and Redoing Homes: The Bosnian War and Diasporic Home-making', in K. Saarikangas and H. Johansson (eds), *Home at Work: Dwelling, Moving, Belonging.* Helsinki: Suomalaisen Kirjallisuuden Seura.

———. 2010. 'Sedentary Policies and Transnational Relations: A "Non-sustainable" Case of Return to Bosnia', *Journal of Refugee Studies* 23(1): 41–61.

————. 2014. 'From Individual Grief to a Shared History of the Bosnian War: Voice, Audience and the Political in Psychotherapeutic Practices with Refugees', *Focaal* 68: 91–104.

Jackson, M. 2002. *The Politics of Storytelling: Violence, Transgression and Intersubjectivity.* Copenhagen: Museum Tusculanum Press.

Jansen, S. 2007. 'The Privatisation of Home and Hope: Return, Reforms and the Foreign Intervention in Bosnia-Herzegovina', *Dialectical Anthropology* 30.

————. 2008. 'Misplaced Masculinities: Status Loss and the Location of Gendered Subjectivities among "Non-transnational" Bosnian Refugees', *Anthropological Theory* 8(2): 181–200.

Josephides, L. 2008. *Melanesian Odysseys: Negotiating the Self, Narrative and Modernity.* New York and Oxford: Berghahn.

Juntunen, M. 2009. 'Diasporic Silences and Multicultural Encounters', *Finnish Journal of Ethnicity and Migration* 4(1).

Kapteijns, L. and A. Richters (eds). 2010. *Mediations of Violence in Africa: Fashioning new Futures from Contested Pasts.* Africa-Europe Group for Interdisciplinary Studies 5: Wits University Press.

Kirmayer, L. 1996. 'Landscapes of Memory: Trauma, Narrative and Dissociation', in P. Antze and M. Lambek (eds), *Tense Past: Cultural Essays in Trauma and Memory.* New York: Routledge.

Kleinman, A. 1987. 'Anthropology and Psychiatry: The Role of Culture in Cross-cultural Research on Illness', *The British Journal of Psychiatry* 151: 447–54.

Kleinman A. and J. Kleinman. 1997. 'The Appeal of Experience, the Dismay of Images: Cultural Appropriations of Suffering in Our Times', in A. Kleinman, V. Das and M. Locke (eds), *Social Suffering.* Berkeley: University of California Press, pp. 1–23.

Lambek, M. 2010. 'Introduction', in M. Lambek (ed.) Ordinary Ethics: Anthropology, Language and Action. Bronx, NY: Fordham University Press.

Lazarus A. and O. Zur. 2002. *Dual Relationships and Psychotherapy.* New York: Springer.

Maass, P. 1996. *Love Thy neighbour: A Story of War.* London: Macmillan.

Malkki, L. 1994. 'Citizens of Humanity: Internationalism and the Imagined Community of Nations', *Diaspora: A Journal of Transnational Studies* 3(1): 41–68.

————. 1995a. *Purity and Exile: Violence, Memory and National Cosmology among Hutu Refugees in Tanzania.* Chicago: The University of Chicago Press.

————. 1995b. 'Refugees and Exile: From "Refugee Studies" to the National Order of Things', *Annual Review of Anthropology* 24(1): 495–523.

————. 1996. 'Speechless Emissaries: Refugees, Humanitarianism, and Dehistoricization', *Cultural Anthropology* 11(3): 377–404.

George E. M. 1995. 'Ethnography in/of the World System: The Emergence of Multi-Sited Ethnography'. *Annual Review of Anthropology,* 24: 95-117.

McLeod, J. 1997. *Narrative and Psychotherapy*. London: Sage.

Prato, G.B. 2009. 'Minorities in Italy: The Cases of Arberesh and Albanian Migrations', in G.B. Prato (ed.), *Beyond Multiculturalism: Views from Anthropology*. Farnham: Ashgate.

Schäuble, M. 2011. 'How History Takes Place: Geographical and Sacralised Landscapes in the Croatian-Bosnian Border Region', *History and Memory* 22(2): 23–61.

Stefansson, A.H. 2004. 'Refugee Returns to Sarajevo and their Challenge to Contemporary Narratives of Mobility', in L.D. Long and E. Oxfeld (eds), *Coming Home? Refugees, Migrants and Those Who Stayed Behind*. Philadelphia: University of Pennsylvania Press.

Stoczkowski, W. 2003. 'The 'Fourth Aim' of Anthropology: Between Knowledge and Ethics.' *Anthropological Theory* 8(4): 345–56.

Verdery, K. 1999. *The Political Lives of Dead Bodies: Reburial and Postsocialist Change*. New York: Columbia University Press.

Vertovec, S. 2009. *Transnationalism*. London: Routledge.

Weiner, J. 1999. 'Psychoanalysis and Anthropology: On the Temporality of Analysis', in H.L. Moore (ed.), *Anthropological Theory Today*. Cambridge: Polity Press, pp. 234–61.

Wilson, R.A. 2000. 'Reconciliation and Revenge in Post-apartheid South Africa: Rethinking Legal Pluralism and Human Rights', *Current Anthropology* 41(1): 75–98.

Chapter 5

THE PROBLEMS WITH GOSSIP

REFLECTIONS ON THE ETHICS OF CONDUCTING MULTISITED ETHNOGRAPHIC RESEARCH

Tamsin Bradley

Introduction

This chapter presents reflections on the ethnographic methodology and ethics of a multisited project designed to explore the relationships between religious teachings, values, beliefs and concepts of development. The research aimed to assess the extent to which religious teachings inform the values and beliefs by which local people live, and how these religious values and beliefs do or do not shape their ideas about development. In essence the research sought to record local knowledge about the world and explored how this knowledge was used by people as they strove to lead, what they felt to be, a good existence.

The research was carried out in Pakistan, India, Nigeria and Tanzania as part of a larger programme. The research team agreed on a shared methodological approach. As an anthropologist and the component coordinator I felt that an ethnographic approach was the only way insights would be gleaned into how local people do or do not translate religious beliefs into visions of development. Along with the rest of the research team, I felt that the microfocus of ethnographic research would help illuminate not only how religious values and beliefs may influence concepts relevant to development, but also give a sense of the heterogeneity of the social, cultural and religious environments in which development takes place.

The central aim of this research was not to produce a grand theory on how religion and development may or may not intersect. Instead, we wanted to recognize, document and explain commonalities and variations in how local people expressed and experienced the intersections between their religious lives and daily concerns, and visions for the future (Pottier, Bicker and Sillitoe 2003). This objective is similar to that of much anthropological research where the ethnographer seeks to understand and draw out the complexities of a particular situation and often uses her or his research to challenge attempts at producing oversimplified development theories (for example Crewe and Harrison 1998; Mosse 2005; Olivier de Sardan 2005; Peet 2007). The research techniques and approach we adopted needed to support us in this venture of highlighting the nuances in the relationship between religion and development. As a team we felt that an ethnographic approach would allow us to observe diversity in terms of how religion, practices and development are conceptualized at the local level, and how these intersect and reinforce each other.

Despite our determination to use ethnography to seek answers to these questions, we knew from the outset that our chosen approach presented problems. Firstly, most of the fieldworkers were not trained anthropologists and had never before used ethnographic research techniques. Secondly, in order to counter the time constraints placed on this work by the wider programme, our team was entirely made up of local researchers, who would conduct the fieldwork within their own communities. Ethical issues emerged as our local researchers hesitated over recording informal encounters with people in their own communities and found it hard to see how chance conversations and even gossip could represent 'data'. Whilst anthropologists increasingly are choosing to study their own social and cultural environments, our researchers were not trained in reflexive ethnographic practices and found it hard to position themselves as insiders/outsiders within their own field (Lambek 2010; Rabinow 2011; Stoczkowski 2008).

This chapter documents the unfolding story of this research, exploring the problems researchers encountered both practically, in trying to use a methodology that was new to them, and ethically, because they were asked to record informal conversations with people from their community, many of whom they knew personally. At the heart of the practical and ethical problems is knowledge, specifically how to gather different forms and then accurately represent them. The teams were mindful and concerned about being part of a large programme designed to explore the relevance of Western knowledge on development. Western discourses around development centre on neo-liberal economics, which emphasize the importance of free trade and globalized markets as mechanisms for wealth generation (Mosse

2005; Olivier de Sardan 2005; Peet 2007). The research team shared concerns over what might happen if we exposed very different concepts of development that conflicted with this Western model. How might local people be viewed by the project's funder? The researchers were concerned to ensure that local people's knowledge and insights into development were valued equally alongside the prevailing discourse. Ensuring that this happened was an ethical concern, which, as a team, we spent much time debating.

This chapter does two things. First, it presents a narrative detailing how the research team was introduced to ethnography and the various techniques I developed in order to help them in this learning process. One of these techniques was a grid approach to data collection designed to heighten the researchers' awareness of the different spaces in which data could and should be legitimately collected. A second technique involved the use of prompt questions part way through the process, intended to push the researchers to think more critically about the kinds of knowledge their data revealed and help them go back into the field with greater focus.

Secondly, the chapter offers my critical reflections on why the researchers found it so challenging to employ ethnographic techniques. It documents how confused and uncomfortable many of the team were with the ethics of the research. Although the team was involved in the overall design of the project, when the reality of fieldwork emerged members voiced concerns. Some of the researchers were vocal in stating that they felt they were being asked to record gossip or informal conversations often told to them in confidence. Concerns were voiced about how this very personal information would be represented and what kind of outsider views it might shape of local people. As part of this critical reflection I present the narrative of one of the researchers, who simultaneously found the process of conducting fieldwork challenging and personally insightful. This researcher felt that she grew enormously in her own self-awareness of the knowledge she drew on in her daily life and in the way in which this knowledge formed the lens through which she viewed the world. This personal and positive narrative presents a contrast to the ethically problematic aspects of this research.

The chapter is divided into three sections, beginning with background and organizational information detailing how this component fits into the overall structure of the wider research programme of which it was part. The first section also gives details into the aims and objectives of the component. It presents the approach to data collection designed to support first-time ethnographers to unpack what constitutes qualitative data. The second section reflects on how the methodology worked in practice; how the researchers experienced the process of conducting ethnographic research for the first time. This section contains a personal account from one of the researchers, who found that ethnographic fieldwork encouraged her to think about her religious and cultural heritage and the impact it had in shaping how she saw and related to the world. The third section focuses on the ethical challenges individual researchers faced. The section recounts these challenges and considers the impact they may have had on the research process as a whole. The conclusion reflects on what, despite the ethical pitfalls, can be gained from the inclusion of ethnography in multisited and interdisciplinary research.

Background and Organizational Information

This project was one of fourteen projects spread across four themes that comprised the research programme. The overall programme had a director and deputy director, four country coordinators and many component coordinators, all of whom represented the overall management committee. As stated in the introduction, this component covered four countries, India, Pakistan, Nigeria and Tanzania. Each country team was led by a local senior researcher, who selected up to four junior researchers. In each country two field sites were selected. The sites were chosen to complement each other and offer some idea of the diversity surrounding the impact of religion and the differing ideas about development held by groups, organizations and individuals across the country. However, despite our intention to record a diversity of views and influences, we also hoped that the field sites would enable some useful overarching comparative analysis that could be used to argue that religion and development were (or were not) intrinsically linked in the lives of many people.

In each country the senior researcher endeavoured to recruit junior researchers who were proficient in the local language and/or dialects and already embedded into the community. The central role of the junior researcher was to collect the field data, to be analysed by the whole country team led by the senior researcher. The success of this component rested upon the recruitment of junior researchers who could move easily around and observe closely everyday life in the field sites. The approach we took resembles aspects of 'peer ethnography', which selects fieldworkers directly from the context to be studied. In peer ethnography the fieldworkers already work and live alongside those they will gather data from. The peer field-workers are given research training to support their data collection. The knowledge and relationships that the peer researchers have to potential informants means they can gather useful data much more quickly than an anthropologist, who would begin the research as an outsider. Peer ethnography has been primarily used to gather data on sensitive and personal topics such as sexual health or sexuality, which are difficult to approach without a close relationship between researcher and research participant (see Collumbien et al. 2009; Price and Hawkins 2002). Our fieldworkers did not share the same peer relationship with the majority of their participants in that they did not work with their informants or have close friend-ships/family connections to them. However, the researchers were part of the wider community in which all their participants lived and assumed a role within it mostly as university lecturers or devel-opment practitioners. This prior knowledge enabled us to sidestep the lengthy induction period many anthropologists have to go through in order to become assimilated into their 'field site' (Geertz 1973a, 1973b, 1975; Marcus 1998; Nash 2002; O'Reilly 2005; Watson 1999). Each country team was supported by a U.K. coordinator; I was primarily responsible for facilitating the logistics of the fieldwork and maintaining an overarching and uniform frame for the research across all four countries. The following paragraphs give brief details on each of the sites chosen for fieldwork.

In Tanzania, Meru and Tanga were selected. Meru, in northern Tanzania, is a predominantly Christian area, and Tanga or Tanga city, as it has been known since 2006, is located 360 km north-east of Dar es Salaam and has a large Muslim population. In Nigeria the two sites selected were Jos and Ibadan. Jos is in the northern part of the country in Plateau State and has a Christian majority and a Muslim minority. Ibadan is in the south-western part of the country in Oyo State rep-resenting an almost equal population of Christians and Muslims. In Pakistan, Peshawar and Lahore were selected. Lahore is located in Central Punjab and is generally considered a less conservative area than Peshawar, which is located in Khyber Pakhtunkhwa (formally North-West Frontier Province) close to Afghanistan, where there has been a Taliban resurgence in recent years. In India the field sites were Dharamsala and Pune. The largest Tibetan Buddhist community in India is based in Dharamsala, north India, and it is the home of the Dalai Lama. Pune, in Maharashtra, central India, is a city of approx-imately five million people. Its population is religiously mixed with a Hindu majority.

Aims, Objectives and Approach to Data Gathering

Aims

The first aim of this component was to understand in what ways religious teachings are disseminated and interpreted in local contexts in relation to development issues. The issues most focused on were education, gender relations, access to credit and poverty.

Second, the component aimed to understand development concerns from a local perspective, and compare these concerns with those of the Western development discourse. As stated in the introduction, Western development concerns are influenced by neo-liberalism, which advocates economic growth through trade liberalization in order to increase national wealth. This national wealth can then be used to reduce poverty in several ways: by developing employment opportunities, increasing wages, supporting and nurturing small enterprises, and improving education and health services. We were keen to see gender incorporated in all aspects of the work and not merely added on to the research report in a separate 'gender section'. We hoped that a gendered analysis would enable considerations of how power relations play out between different groups. A gendered approach would also encourage critical consideration of whether the prominence of male religious leadership has any significance for the way values and beliefs are interpreted, communicated, and impact on people's lives.

Objectives

The first objective was to identify dominant religious teachings and understand how they are first interpreted by religious teachers and then received and translated into actions by their audiences. The second objective was to investigate how the emerging interpretations inform responses and views on development issues in the communities under study.

Teaching Non-anthropologists How to 'do' Ethnography

The Data Grid

Since the fieldworkers were unfamiliar with ethnographic fieldwork, the senior researchers and I developed a grid to help unpack the different kinds of interviews and conversations we hoped they would have with local people. The grid represents a tool for the purpose of collecting and sorting data and was not necessarily meant to be used rigidly. The grids were designed to help keep the conceptual basis of the methodology firmly in each researcher's/fieldworker's mind. It was designed to enforce the importance of exploring our research questions in a number of different settings, spaces and with a variety of groups. It acted as a prompt that the research should be carried out in two phases; the first, to survey dominant views expressed in public religious and secular spaces. The second grid asked researchers to dig deeper into how local people regard these public views; what really shapes how they see the world and their concepts of development. The grid is in two sections. The first section focuses on material and views that are publicly accessible, including any literature produced by religious and secular organizations on development issues and recordings of the views of key religious and community leaders. In this part of the grid some of the fieldworkers recorded sermons and lectures, or reviewed pamphlets distributed to local people.

The second part of the grid aimed to understand more closely what local people think about the views being expressed by their local religious and community leaders. Are local people aware of the messages being disseminated by them? Who do they listen to and why? Do they share the development goals set out by key local organizations or do they have a different perspective on religion and development? This information should have been gained through direct conversation with local people. This meant that locations needed to be identified where people congregated informally. Fieldworkers had to position themselves at these locations and for a period of time attempt to integrate into the daily pattern of life. They were asked to engage informally in gossip and chats about how people see the world, pulling out concerns that preoccupy discussions. The documentation of informal conversations was vitally important to this component, because it would be possible to gauge the extent to which religion influenced how people reflected on their lives.

The researchers were asked to pay particular attention to how data flowed between these two spheres. In other words, did public-level religious or secular teachings translate into the views and opinions expressed by local people in more informal and private spaces? Were any development concepts (e.g., poverty, debt/credit, women's education, and gender) discussed in either sphere or were other visions of development expressed?

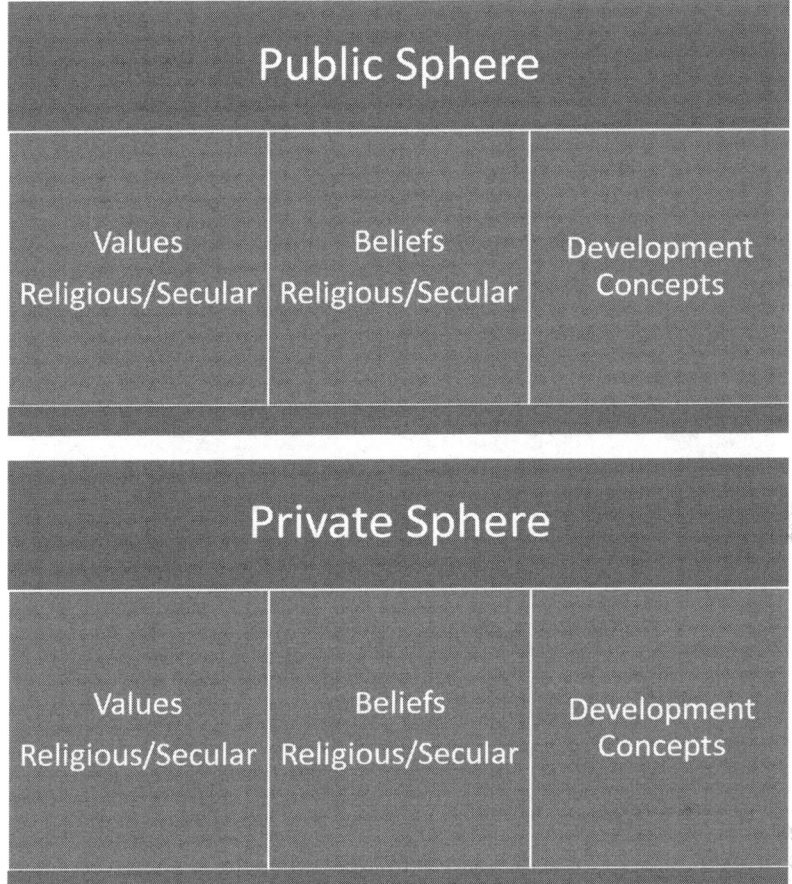

Figures 5.1 and 5.2 At a glance: the grid approach to data collection

Reflections on the Research Process

The Problems with Seeing the 'Informal' as Data

Senior members of the component team met in Bagamoyo, Tanzania, on 17–19 September 2008. Bringing all the researchers together meant that we were able to reflect as a whole on how our methodology had worked in practice, and at this meeting teams honestly recounted the challenges they faced. Our discussions revealed two kinds of difficulty. First, that team members at all levels struggled to conduct ethnographic interviews and frequently fell back on their comfort zones of structured interviews. The interviews involved direct and pre-planned questions that failed to reveal anything about how influential religious leaders are in shaping how people see the world. Furthermore, the questions assumed the informants shared the interviewer's Western knowledge on development. The questions focused on asking local people if they had any problems accessing development (e.g., healthcare and education) and what their views were in relation to debt/credit and gender equality. This very structured approach failed to draw out different types of local knowledge in regard to visions of the future and ideas of social and material transformation. Second, our team discussions revealed ethical concerns some researchers had at being asked to collect the informal views of people alongside whom they lived. This chapter will deal with each difficulty in turn, beginning with the practical challenges of the research.

The grid approach outlined in the previous section was the main data collection tool our teams used. As already stated, the purpose of the grids was to remind our fieldworkers that data collection should occur in two phases: first, the collection of publicly visible data; for example, grey literature from organizations and religious leaders. The second level of data I asked researchers to capture were the views and perceptions of different local people. I asked the researchers to talk with people in relaxed settings in the hope that participants would give more honest answers. Overall I wanted to compare the different visions/world views emerging from each of these levels and explore the extent to which they differed or overlapped. The teams agreed that the grids gave their fieldwork focus, which made it easier for them to plan their daily activities/tasks. In particular, gaps in research data were made visible by the grids, revealing areas where more data were needed. What became clear was that the groups found it much easier to fill out the public level grids than those aimed at recording more intimate and personal views.

The country teams spent time during our component workshop reflecting on data they had collected that could be used to fill out the private sphere grids. What came to light as I facilitated this exercise was a misunderstanding as to what constitutes ethnographic data. Researchers felt uneasy including information gained through very informal encounters and chats, and felt wary about listing observations they had gained through spending time in spaces such as markets, tea shops and places of worship. Gradually the teams teased out encounters and exchanges they had with local people and thought about what they had seen in the social environment that made up their 'field'. In order to help teams reflect back on informal conversations that could reveal opinions relevant to our research I used critical questions. During this process of teasing out more informally

gathered data I stepped into the role of interviewer, pushing researchers to revisit in their heads their fieldwork encounters. I asked questions such as: why do you think informants responded as they did?
The grids enabled the researchers to identify gaps in the data, including the absence of certain groups of informants, and also helped to
identify when researchers did not go far enough with their questions.
In order to help guide the last stages of the fieldwork I went through
each grid and inserted questions, and highlighted where more data
was needed. For example, in one section of the Tanzanian grids given
below, the team documented informal responses on the issues of debt
and women's dress. The team's data is introduced by 'data in grid'
(Dig), my questions then follow.

Data in grid (Dig):   You should not get into debt as it is considered to
be Haraam. However, as indicated above, debt via a secular
lender is considered more acceptable.
Question: Why is this??? Does this mean that most religious people
acquire credit through secular lenders?
Dig: Hijab is only worn in Meru in the coastal areas because
women are working closely with others.
Dig: Outside of these areas in Meru hijab is only worn on Friday.
Question: Can you gather some reflections from men and women on
the importance of hijab for women? Does hijab inhibit or
promote women's increasingly important economic role?

My insertions were intended to be a combination of critical questions
asking teams to get beyond stating a fact but attempting to include
meaning or rather explanations as to why people responded as they
did and force questions over how views are formed. A second type of
probe simply drew attention to places where more data were needed.
Another example is given below where the Nigerian team had documented one man's views on what he valued the most in life.

Dig: People claimed they wanted good things, house, clothing
etc. When asked about material development this is what
they said they wanted.
Question: Does this not contradict the non-material message of
Islam, in other words this seems to be suggesting that
development should be the pursuit of more than just basic
needs but about enjoying consumerism. I am surprised
that charity and helping others does not feature strongly
in his response. PLEASE FOLLOW UP this could be really
interesting. It might suggest that development is a very
separate pursuit from religion in the minds of your informants. They seem to be separating religious knowledge
from knowledge that might enable them to become richer.
Perhaps religion is seen as a vehicle for achieving social
equality but not economic??

The focus of my interviewing and use of critical probes was to force researchers to think beyond presenting descriptions of the dominant views expressed publicly into a more nuanced understanding of how prevailing views may or may not be articulated in people's private lives, and, furthermore, to distinguish between different types of knowledge that people may draw on in various contexts. For example, as my last question indicated, it seemed from the Nigerian data that people clearly differentiated between religious knowledge and the knowledge and skills they felt they needed to become rich. When interviewers asked about development goals people replied by saying they wanted more money so they could buy more things. The data suggested that religion shaped social values, in particular that of equality. These social values were separated from people's personal goals and the visions they held for their futures, which were mostly based on materialism. Those Christian leaders interviewed indicated that they had tapped into the material desires of their congregations by linking religious values to concepts of prosperity. In doing so a new knowledge base has emerged coined 'the prosperity gospel', which essentially argues that if you are faithful to God you will be materially rewarded. One way to display faith is to translate social values into practice and take part in welfare activities. I wanted the researchers to explore the extent to which this bringing together of social and material visions through prosperity has shaped the lens through which Christians, across denominations, see the world, their place in it and development more widely.

In general my questions sought to encourage more reflection on how views are formed. Are religion and religious teachings really very influential in shaping how people see and behave in the world? Perhaps more secular influences have greater impact in determining people's desires, the Nigerian data suggested. Despite my attempts to move the interviewing into the more privates spaces where informal and perhaps more honest opinions are expressed, researchers remained reluctant to extend their gaze this far. The questions I posed to the researchers were made at a midpoint in the fieldwork, giving each team time to go back into the field and collect more focused data. None of the teams did so and no new data emerged. This reluctance to do more fieldwork forced me to reflect on why this might be. As explored in more detail in the previous section of this chapter, researchers expressed concern over how their role as fieldworkers might have compromised their community standing. Some researchers were worried that the data might be used to produce a distorting picture of their community and held back from collecting too much depth and detail. I think the researchers, although they understood why I asked the questions I did, were worried about how the process of collecting this data would impact on them personally. Part of this reluctance was a concern that local people would regard their research with suspicion. This reluctance could also have been because the process of going much deeper into ethnography often involves the fieldworker directing research questions on themselves. This self-reflexive process can be uncomfortable and confusing. When one of the junior researchers did turn the questions on herself, the process of working through them produced unexpected and positive results.

Opportunity for Self-Reflection

In her personal narrative on the research she admitted that the processes of conducting interviews in her country of origin helped her to unpack and reflect on issues of her identity. She realized whilst setting out to fill in the grids that, as with her informants, she too was an amalgam of subject positions and identities. During the process of doing the research she unravelled many layers that shaped her identity: secular, religious, Western and non-Western. Furthermore, she reflected on how her life experiences shaped her assumptions about the views and attitudes she thought she would find in the research. This in turn led to her honest and open acknowledgement when these assumptions were challenged by her informants.

> Working in a predominantly Muslim area as a fieldworker brought back my childhood memories of learning to recite the Koran. I had my early Koran lessons not in the conventional madrassa setting like most Tanzanian Muslim children, whereby children sit on the floor and are whipped upon making a mistake. I was fortunate enough to be taught by my grandmother sitting on a small stool next to her prayer chair. My grandmother had joint problems and I have always seen her praying while seated. It is her who taught me to read and memorize strange Arabic scripts that made no sense to me except that I was told they are sacred. My grandmother would seek pride in telling whoever visited her that her granddaughter could recite such and such verses by heart. And occasionally I was made to display my cramming abilities, which I did with great pleasure. It is during these learning sessions, grandma would tell me how our family migrated from Yemen to Indian then to Zanzibar and then to Dar es Salaam.
>
> Despite our Arab ancestry, my family is affiliated with Kokani Community[1] in Tanzania which used to run religious classes in the afternoons. From the ages of 6 to 12 I attended the classes where all students sat on chairs and used tables to write on. We were taught to

read and write Urdu language, profile and teachings of the prophet Muhammed and some religious "dos" and "don'ts". There was also a period for Koran recitation. Every end of the year we were being examined and graded for every subject. My overall grades were above average but my understanding of Islam would not answer the many questions I had about life and the hereafter. But as a Muslim, I was told I am not supposed to doubt the Holy Book. Just Believe. At some point in life I joined a church group and began to attend bible studies. But then, like the converted Jews, I too felt detached from my roots, from the traditions of my family, from my childhood memories. It was no longer a matter of spiritual search but of identity.

Today, I recite praises to Muhammad in Maulids yet I am as comfortable Chanting Krishna mantra as I am singing "Amazing Grace". What does that make me? A Hindu, a Muslim, a Christian? An Arab by descent, a Kokani by social affiliation, Tanzanian citizen, Urban Swahili Dar es Salaamite or simply a human being and an academic by choice?

When I went to Tanga, I was sure I am going there as an independent researcher, but what were the main assumptions under which this independent researcher operated? There is only one answer to this: I am a puzzle, with all pieces put together, in the right place, all at once.

I visited Women's Islamic College where all the ladies wore black hoods called "jalabibi" covering their heads and the torso. They also covered their faces with black Naqaab and some even wore black hand gloves. The first time I visited them I said to myself "run for your life". I was frightened by tens of people emerging from the corridor all dressed in black, their faces and bodies all covered in black, all I could see was their glaring eyes staring at me until I initiated the greeting with salaam alleykum. They walked past me without saying anything and eventually someone came to escort me to the Dean's office. I was amazed at how people talked to each other without seeing each other's faces.

Dressed in what I would call normal maulidi attire – a skirt, a top, head covering and a wrap, I was obviously not "decently dressed" for most of those ladies. As I waited for the Dean of the college to begin the interview I asked her secretary as to how do people know who they are talking to and she quickly said "unazoea" – you get used to it.

During the interview I asked the dean about Hijab and Naqaab, seeking to understand whether women in Tanga wear Hijab out of conviction as Muslims or as a result of cultural evolution due to the Arab social history in Tanga. The Dean's response was: "You are an Arab, how come you don't wear Hijab?" I could not help but laugh and redirect the focus back to women in Tanga. However her response gave me two shocks: firstly in Dar es Salaam my Arab identity rarely emerges above my South Asian looks – I guess it takes one to know one, and second "I thought the sheikh said I was well covered!"

In another incident I was asked to give a proof of being a Muslim by reciting verses of the Koran to the grandson of a respondent, who later told me he was a Madrassa teacher. My respondent was an elderly woman whom I visited for three nights and helped her sell "mikate" (Coconut bread, a Swahili delicacy) outside her house as we talk. One day her grandson comes questioning me as to why I was asking so many questions to his grandmother, I explained the research I was involved in and he asked me if I was also a Muslim. I said yes, and then he asked me to prove it by reading from the Koran. He first asked me if I was in "Wudhu" (a state of ritual cleanliness). I told him yes, then he asked Koran to be brought and listened to me as I read a couple of verses in Arabic. While I was still reading from a passage he picked, he passed a comment "You are not very fluent, but it is OK". "kazi njema" (all the best in your work) and went away. In his views, it is not good enough to call myself a Muslim; I ought to know how to read the Koran – properly! This was another cultural shock to me, because no one in Dar would ask anyone to prove his/her religious belief.

My most memorable experience was with three Sambaa girls I spoke to as I went to interview their father – Babu Yusufu, an elderly man in his fifties. He has a small workshop where he makes cups and pans out of used iron sheets and tins. Babu Yusufu earns about 5000 Tanzanian shillings (two pounds sterling) a day when the sale is good and is one of the few people who took loan from the credit society on interest. "I know it is haram but do I have an option?" he said. His daughters were a complete contrast to this soft spoken man. They are in the age of 23 to 32, the oldest was married for a year and the day I visited their house they were preparing to take one of their neighbours to a "somo" for a 10 day in-house training on how to be a good wife and care for the husband. The process is called "Kufundwa". One of the girls works as a house girl in Tanga in an Arab household and she spoke with pride that "I earn my own living, so what if it is from scrubbing floors, at least I am independent".

They shared with me a space where religion and traditions converge and diverge for people in Tanga. They shared with me the concept of "Ruhani" and "Ngoma za Mashetani". Whereby, women who possess some spirits call upon the spirit in a communal gathering while others dance around her. Once the woman is in full spirit people who are gathered ask for solutions to their problems and the woman acts as a medium between the people and the spirit. Most of these women are Muslims, who even recite verses from the Koran to call upon the spirit. It is a blend of Islamic mysticism and African Traditional ritual.

To me these women represented originality of thoughts coming from real life experiences free from any form of fundamentalism, pretence or obligation. In some ways I could relate to them better. Was it because there was no age gap between us and we could talk freely or the fact that apart from racial, educational and cultural differences, we share an element of religious and traditional syncretism that shapes and define our identities.

I had many conversations with this researcher about her experiences of conducting fieldwork. She was a postgraduate in social science and therefore understood the importance of trying to develop awareness, as a researcher, of any bias that may skew representations and inter-pretations of other people's lives. However, as she herself stated, the way in which the fieldwork drew her into a reflexive journey took her by surprise. Once she realized that each interview was forcing her to think about her identity and perspective she began to make notes of her reactions. She pooled her notes and produced the narrative above. It is possible that other researchers also went on something of a reflexive journey as a result of the fieldwork but were less willing to acknowledge it or allow their encounters with others to penetrate so deeply. It is also possible that other researchers did allow what they heard and saw to provoke personal and reflexive questioning but found this process too uncomfortable and so buried it.

The passages above weave the researcher's often conditioned responses at what she hears and sees, in particular in relation to female modesty, together with the dialogues she had during her field-work. Her honesty reveals the difficulty that she and perhaps other members of the team experienced at being asked to delve into the religious and cultural values that form aspects of their world view. As Davies (1999) notes, self-reflexivity is an uncomfortable but natural part of the research process. The passages bring out the complexity in how individuals form and express values and beliefs. Upbringing and education are fundamental, but so too are the encounters and interactions individuals have on a daily basis within their community. The impact of many of these interactions will go unnoticed by individ-uals, affecting them subconsciously. Unpacking the process through which opinions and views are formed is highly complex and perhaps impossible to research as an outsider looking in.

Ethical Challenges

In trying to understand more deeply the anxieties of the researchers, I reflected on the possible ethical (conscious or unconscious) tensions they may have faced. In unravelling (from a distance) their experi-ences from many conversations with different team members, I have been helped by the work of Stoczkowski (2008). Stoczkowski draws on his fieldwork experiences working in his home country, where he was positioned as an activist and opponent of the government. At the same time he conducted anthropological research that sought to understand the complexities (or multiple truths) behind the country's authoritarian regime. He identified a contradiction in these positions, which he described in ethical terms as a clash between a moral desire to bring about change motivated by his activism and the quest to understand epistemological knowledge. This knowledge shapes social and cultural phenomena and ultimately the values held by different groups and is the core focus of anthropological research. As he described it, 'the heuristic values of ethnography entered into conflict with the basic values of the background to which I belonged as a political activist' (2008: 112). Anthropological enquiry sought him to expose the truth about his informants (the authoritarian government officials). He was also driven by a sense of moral good as defined by his activism and community membership as part of the opposition. His anthropological enquiry was received harshly by his fellow activists, who felt his attempt to understand the viewpoint of the government undermined their quest for moral political transformation.

In his work Stoczkowski (2008) draws out a conflation in common anthropological enquiry between the seeking of knowledge present in people's actions and reality (as they see it) and the pursuit of moral values. In other words, he uses anthropological insights to transform a society for the moral good of those within it. He argues that the discipline needs to recognize this conflation and separate the two pursuits, not least because anthropological knowledge can come into conflict with political commitment and values. This I believe is what many of the researchers in my team experienced. I am not sure any of us really understand, or recognised at the time, but the personal reflections of one of the researchers certainly implies a series of challenging experiences resulting from the fieldwork. The researchers were all senior, holding community positions. They also held strong political and religious stances that they sought to see through in the daily life of their community, this would have caused the kind of clash outlined so eloquently by Stoczkowski.

As the personal testimony of one of the researchers given in the previous section reveals, researchers were asked to enter into conversations that could force reflection on personal religious and cultural values and lead to a confrontation with aspects of society that contradicted their moral outlook. My conversations with the researcher above certainly suggested this; she admitted that she had always struggled with the way in which women were treated and marginalized. She struggled to remain committed to her religion when she could see the way in which it reinforced gender inequality. She was also concerned not to paint an overly bleak picture of women's agency and held the belief that change would be brought about by women themselves. Focusing on how women are oppressed may, in her view, deter women from exercising that agency. In conversations with the Nigerian researchers, I could sense their discomfort in acknowledging the extent to which members of their community desired material-ism, in many cases above charitable giving. The views collected on debt and poverty fed into the prosperity teachings, which state that a person's financial position was the responsibility of the individual. More devotion to God would bring a turn in fortunes for the poor. The team were concerned that these views revealed harshness in attitude and did not want to create a picture of their communities as uncaring. This view could also have extended to concerns that to reveal such evidence might run counter to their hopes of creating a more equal society.

As the fieldwork unfolded it became apparent that our research-ers themselves had knowledge that was of interest to the compo-nent. Many of them, both men and women, held positions of respect within the communities they were being asked to study. For example, most were university lecturers and some also assumed a religious leadership role offering guidance to local people. Asking them also to report what people shared with them about their lives compromised the trust people placed in them. One researcher raised his concern and although the informants themselves did not raise any objec-tions he was conscious of his position. This researcher was widely acknowledged as an Islamic community leader and people came to his house on a daily basis to receive guidance. He was motivated, so he told me, by a strong desire to counter radical Islamic teaching that he feared was increasing in influence. He used his position as a senior member of the university academic staff to try and prevent extremist ideas filtering into the thinking and actions of the Islamic student organization. Given his community standing, experience, and trusted position, he said he could not record the views of those that came to him for support. When people shared their views with him it was because they trusted him and wanted his opinion as a leader rather than as a researcher. He therefore had to demarcate clearly the time he spent as a researcher for this component from his role as a teacher and leader.

A second researcher, a devout Muslim who held a lectureship in Islamic studies at the local university, struggled with some of the assertions he felt lay behind the development concepts we were exploring. For example, he felt that the focus on gender was designed to assess the extent to which local people believed in equality between men and women. He argued that Islam upholds equality through emphasis on the fair, respectful treatment of men and women but prescribes different gender roles in order to maintain the stability of society through family life. He also believed that Islam endorsed the role of men as household heads and decision-makers. He felt uncomfortable that the data he would collect from those around him would be used to try and expose or highlight his community as one that treated women unfairly. His views also reveal how easy it is for misunderstanding to seep into a multisited research project. Given that the programme was funded by the U.K. government, it was perhaps only natural that researchers outside of the United Kingdom would critically question the motives of the project. In this case the researcher worried that his data would be used as evidence justifying a particular diagnosis over what constitutes the development problems in his country. It was hard to counter this mistrust, which did not seem to exist within the wider research team but was directed towards the donor. The teams remained suspicious of how the data would be used; they were aware that even if they presented a specific interpretation of the data, the donor (DFID) could manipulate it and use it to justify their development interventions.

Conclusion

As with all research, lessons should be drawn from these views and responses, especially given the increase in demand for anthropologists to make up part of research and consultancy teams for international development donors and agencies. Now this research is at an end the ethnographic perspective remains important as a way of getting closer to understanding different forms of knowledge. Additionally, ethnography at its heart draws out the complexities and contradictions that exist in any context or issue under study. However, I feel that more disciplinary debate is needed on the ethical pitfalls and compromises that anthropologists may face in such large scale policy-driven research. Research programmes that engage applied anthropologists such as this one are often policy- or impact-driven in terms of feeding into the creation of practical measures or innovations. This type of research is often, as in this case, tightly managed and monitored by the funder, who has invested in this process and needs to see results. Ethnography should be used not only to gather data but also to ensure that the views of all concerned are heard. Although my retrospective revisiting of this research experience is a little belated, it has made it possible for me to realize how complex the process is of teaching others ethnography.

This chapter has combined analysis into how large multisited ethnographic research can be practically managed, with insights into the experiences of those involved. The grid approach developed by the research team has value as a tool to help those unfamiliar with ethnographic fieldwork gain at least some sense of what it is about. The reflections offered by members of the team give insight into the personal journeys fieldworkers continue to go on regardless of how close or distant they may be to their research participants. Finally, the ethical minefields opened up by involvement in such a large programme have been explored. Each of the three areas, practical, reflexive and ethical represent key dimensions to any research and need continuous debate.

Tamsin Bradley is Reader in International Development Studies at the University of Portsmouth. She is a social anthropologist who works on violence against women and girls, gender inclusion and the intersections of religion and development. Her latest monograph *Women and Violence in India: Gender, Oppression and the Politics of Neoliberalism* is published by IB Tauris.

Note

1. A faith-based organization of Muslims hailing from Kokan in India.

References

Abu-Lughod, L. 1988. *Veiled Sentiments: Honor and Poetry in Bedouin Society.* Los Angeles: University of California Press.

———. 1993. *Writing Women's Worlds.* Los Angeles: University of California Press.

Ahmed, A. 1983. *Religion and Politics in Muslim Society: Order and Conflict in Pakistan.* New York: Cambridge University Press.

Aigbe, S. 1993. *Theory of Social Involvement: A Case Study in the Anthropology of Religion, State and Society.* Lanham: University of America Press.

Alexandra, B. 1997. 'Ritual and Current Studies of Ritual Overview', in S. Glaizer (ed.), *Anthropology of Religion: A Handbook.* Westport, CT: Greenwood Press.

Amit, V. (ed.). 2000. *Constructing the Field: Ethnographic Field Work in the Contemporary World.* London: Routledge.

Angro, M. 2004. *The Culture of the Sacred: Exploring the Anthropology of Religion.* Prospect Heights: Waveland Press.

Atkinson, P. 1990. *The Ethnographic Imagination: Textual Constructions of Reality.* London: Routledge.

Bowie, F. 2000. *The Anthropology of Religion: An Introduction.* Oxford: Blackwell.

Bradley, T. 2006. *Challenging the NGOs: Women, Religion and Western Discourses in India.* London and New York: IB Tauris.

Caplan, P. 1988. 'Engendering Knowledge: The Politics of Ethnography Part 1', *Anthropology Today* 4(5).

Clifford, J. 1988. *The Predicament of Culture: Twentieth Century Ethnography, Literature and Art.* Cambridge: Harvard University Press.

Clifford, J. and G. Marcus (eds). 1986. *Writing Culture: The Poetics and Politics of Ethnography.* Berkeley: University of California Press.

Collumbien, M. et al. 2009. 'Understanding the Context of Male and Transgender Sex Work Using Peer Ethnography', *Sexually Transmitted Infections* 85: 113–17.

Cornish, A. 1987. 'Participant Observation . . . On a Motorcycle', *Anthropology Today* 3(6).

Crang, M. 1992. 'Academic Rules! Studying Sideways, Studying Under', *Praxis* 25: 20–23.

Crang, M. and I. Cook. 2007. *Doing Ethnographies.* London and Chicago: University of Chicago Press.

Crapo, R. 2003. *Anthropology of Religion: The Unity and Diversity of Religions.* Boston, London: McGraw Hill.

Crewe, E. and E. Harrison. 1998. *Whose Development?: An Ethnography of Aid.* London: Zed Books.

Davies, C.A. 1999. *Reflexive Ethnography: A Guide to Researching Selves and Others.* London and New York: Routledge.

Edelman, M. and A. Haugerud. 2005. *The Anthropology of Development and Globalization: From Classical Political Economy to Contemporary Neoliberalism.* Oxford, Malden, MA: Blackwell.

Emoff, R. and D. Henderson. (eds). 2002. *Mementos, Artefacts and Hallucinations from the Ethnographer's Tent.* New York: Routledge.

Esteva, G. and M.S. Prakash. 1998. *Grassroots Post Modernism: Remaking the Soil of Cultures.* New York, London: Zed Press.

Gardner, K. and D. Lewis. 1996. *Anthropology, Development and the Postmodern Challenge.* London: Pluto Press.

Geertz, C. 1973a. 'Deep Play: Notes on the Balinese Cockfight', in C. Geertz, *The Interpretation of Cultures.* New York: Basic Books.

———. 1973b. 'Thick Description: Towards an Interpretive Theory of Culture', in C. Geertz, *The Interpretation of Cultures.* New York: Basic Books.

————. 1975. *The Interpretation of Cultures: Selected Essays by Clifford Geertz.* London: Lawrence and Wishart.

Grills, S. (ed.). 1998. *Doing Ethnographic Research: Fieldwork Settings.* California: Sage.

Hastrup, K. and P. Hervik. (eds). 1994. *Social Experience and Anthropological Knowledge.* London: Routledge.

Hobbs, D. and T. May. (eds). 1993. *Interpreting the Field: Account of Ethnography.* Oxford University Press.

Hume, L. and J. Mulcock. 2004. *Anthropologists in the Field: Cases in Participant Observations.* New York: Columbia University Press.

Jackson, M. (ed.). 1996. *Things as they Are: New Directions in Phenomenological Anthropology.* Bloomington: Indiana University Press.

Kirsch, S. 2002. 'Anthropology and Advocacy: A Case Against the Campaign of the OK Tedi Mine', *Critique of Anthropology 2.*

Lambek, M. 2010. *Ordinary Ethics: Anthropology, Language, and Action.* New York: Fordham University Press.

Lambek, M. (ed.). 2002. *A Reader in the Anthropology of Religion.* Oxford: Blackwell.

Lareau, A. and J. Schultz. (eds). 1996. *Journeys through Ethnography: Realistic Accounts of the Field.* Colorado: Westview Press.

Lassiter, L.E. 2005. *The Chicago Guide to Collaborative Ethnography.* London and Chicago: University of Chicago Press.

Marcus, G. 1998. *Ethnography through Thick and Thin.* Princeton: University of Princeton Press.

Mosse, D. 2005. *Cultivating Development: An Ethnography of Aid Policy and Practice.* London: Pluto Press.

Nash, J.C. 2007. *Practicing Ethnography in a Globalising World: An Anthropological Odyssey.* New York: Altamira Press.

O'Kely, J. 1984. 'Fieldwork in the Home Countries', *Anthropology Today* 61.

Olivier de Sardan, J-P. 2005. *Anthropology and Development: Understanding Contemporary Social Change.* London: Zed Books.

O'Reilly, K. 2005. *Ethnographic Methods.* London and New York: Routledge.

Peet, R. 2007. *Geography of Power: The Making of Global Economic Policy.* London: Zed Books.

Pottier, J. (ed.). 1993. *Practising Development: Social Science Perspectives.* London: Routledge.

Pottier, J., A. Bicker and P. Sillitoe. (eds). 2003. *Negotiating Local Knowledge: Power and Identity in Development.* London: Pluto Press.

Price, N. and K. Hawkins. 2002. 'Researching Sexual and Reproductive Behaviour: A Peer Ethnographic Approach', *Social Science and Medicine* 55(98): 1325–36.

Rabinow, P. 2011. *The Accompaniment: Assembling the Contemporary.* Chicago: Chicago University Press.

Silverman, D. 2001. *Interpreting Qualitative Data. Methods for Analysing Talk, Text and Interaction.* London: Sage Publications.

Smith, A., A. Stenning and K. Willis. (eds). 2008. *Social Justice and Neoliberalism.* London: Zed Books.

Stoczkowski, W. 2008. 'The "Fourth Aim" of Anthropology between Knowledge and Ethics', *Anthropological Theory* 8(4): 345–56.

Watson, C. (ed.). 1999. *Being There: Fieldwork in Anthropology.* London: Pluto Press.

Yedes, J., R. Clamins and A. Osman. 2004. 'Buna, Oromo Women Gathering Coffee', *Journal of Contemporary Ethnography* 33(4): 113–25.

PART III

Bioethics, Bio-politics and Humanity beyond the Local

The chapters in this section (by Kaja Finkler, Marit Melhuus and Lisette Josephides) broaden the question beyond the ethics of the relations of knowledge creation in particular encounters (whether one-to-one, mediated or manipulated) to a consideration of the ethics of knowledge itself. New genetic technologies create new ethical dilemmas, setting biopolitics against bioethics. While the identity of sperm donors must be disclosed because biological origin is constitutive of 'good' kinship identity, foetus defects remain undisclosed during the period when elective abortion is still a legal option, as terminations for 'immoral' reasons threaten the order of society. The use of commercialized and personalized genetic information technologies has further implications for notions of personhood, kinship and society, and for the future of humanity itself. In a world where genetic knowledge is a constituent part of identity and identity is a human right, is knowledge about human life as derived from our genetic make-up less 'local' than cultural knowledge? Finally, a theoretical chapter is offered as a contribution to the enquiry about the cultivation of the kind of selves required for knowledge. It takes up the substantive themes of knowledge, the creation of the knower, and ethics as a linking relationship, in a historical, philosophical and anthropological enquiry. The relationship between ethics and knowledge creation is revisited from these perspectives.

Chapter 6

A MEDITATION ON KNOWLEDGE PRODUCTION BY PERSONALIZED GENETIC TESTING

Kaja Finkler

Introduction

Since the mid-twentieth century there has been an explosion of research in genomics, its role in disease aetiology and its impact on human personality (Pinker 2009). Knowledge produced by the new genetics, including personalized genetics, tends to redefine not only aetiological understanding of health and illness, medical treatment and the doctor-patient relationship, but also bears on multiple levels of contemporary life beyond biomedical concerns, including: definitions of personhood, concepts of ownership, the meaning of intellectual and material property, ethnicity, race, philosophical and religious questions of predestination and free will, and ethics, especially concerning privacy, confidentiality, informed consent, and, in the United States, matters of employment and insurance. Family and kin relationships also may require rethinking and restructuring. At its most fundamental level it is held that the sequencing of our DNA reveals who we are in totality, and the new genetics attempts to address basic questions about the meaning of being human (Fox Keller 1986, 1994: 89; Kay 2000). The one-time head of the Human Genome Project (HGP) in the United States, Francis Collins, invoking a religious dimension, called the findings of the HGP 'the Book of Life' (Collins 1999a, 1999b; Nash 1994).

According to the website of the National Human Genome Research Institute (NHGRI), 'our genes orchestrate the development of a single-celled egg into a fully formed adult. Genes influence not only what we look like but also what diseases we may eventually get. It also promises to usher in an era of molecular medicine, with precise new approaches to the diagnosis, treatment and prevention of disease'.[1] On the current NHGRI website one can read the following: 'Clinical opportunities for gene-based pre-symptomatic prediction of illness and adverse drug response are emerging at a rapid pace, and the therapeutic promise of genomics has ushered in an exciting phase of expansion and exploration in the commercial sector' (National Human Genome Research Institute 2011). The premise of the NHGRI is that the entire genome map will allow for the eventual discovery of cures for all diseases and will profoundly influence biomedicine by moving it from being a reactive to a preventive practice, because there will be a 'cure' for each defective gene even before its effects become manifest. Additionally, great benefits to industry are foreseen because it will enable the pharmaceutical industry to develop a large therapeutic repertoire to treat human diseases (Hood 1992: 158).[2]

Generally speaking, the cultural currency of scientific discoveries in American society, and the new genetics in particular, influences people's lives in almost all areas of existence, as has been recognized by numerous scholars from many disciplines (Andrews 1992, 1994, 2001; Andrews et al. 2002; Dolgin 2001; Evans et al. 2001; Everett 2003; Finkler 2003; Finkler, Skrzynia and Evans 2003; Greely 1998; Marteau and Lerman 2001; Wertz 1992; Wolf 1995 and others). In the United States, there are reports in the mass media on some facets of genetics almost daily. We may have now reached what Seabrook (2001) aptly calls 'the age of household genetics'.

But as with all dramatic innovations in human history, while knowledge of our genome creates unprecedented opportunities it also presents profound personal and ethical dilemmas. The enthusi- astic support for the genomics revolution, especially in the realm of pre-symptomatic genetic conditions, requires caution lest we create a new category of asymptomatic *'perpetual patients'* (Finkler 2000a), which is bound eventually to include all of us. Patients may in actu- ality be asymptomatic but they may be treated for diseases that will be predicted to occur in the future (Jonsen 1996). The new genet- ics is redrawing the boundaries between the healthy and unhealthy by regarding all people as possible carriers of malfunctioning genes or genetically predisposed to a multitude of diseases. It may uncover asymptomatic conditions that may remain forever asymptomatic, or reveal susceptibilities or risks for developing common diseases such as breast cancer or diabetes. Its findings may make people feel constantly threatened by the possibility of developing a disease because of their presumed genetic predisposition to it (Finkler 2000a).

Collins believes that by 2020 the impact of genomic medicine will be felt at all levels of society, including medical treatments of the future, which will include drug therapy (pharmacogenomics) tailored to specific individuals or ethnic groups in order to maximize drug efficacy and minimize adverse reactions (Kahn 2007; Wailoo and Pemberton 2006).[3] It is anticipated that there will be gene-based designer drugs for diabetes, hypertension, mental illness and many other conditions (Kahn 2007). The medicine of the future will be the medicine of the individual, depending on genomic analysis rather than on a broad epidemiological understanding of disease at the population level.

Recognizing the benefits and drawbacks of beliefs in the new genetics, particularly personalized genetics, in this chapter my central aim is to reflect on some of their fundamental assumptions; explore the concept of risk, essential to an understanding of the new genomics, and consider the ways in which the new genetics may impact on an individual's family and kin relationship, as well as on some basic ethical and ontological issues.

The New Genetics and its Methods of Testing: From Linkage Analysis to Personalized Testing

Gregor Mendel published his paper on genetic inheritance in 1865, establishing the fundamentals of genetics (Kevles 1992), though his work was rediscovered only in the early part of the twentieth century. Though it was poorly understood, the hereditarian concept of disease first appeared in 1885 when Weismann asserted that only germ cells (sperm and egg) transmit hereditary materials to the next generation (Griesemer 1994; Fox Keller 2000). The new genetics, however, refers to a body of knowledge and procedures that are based on recombinant DNA technology (Richards 1993). This new genetics is represented as information-processing, with messages encoded in DNA – a protein that reproduces itself and is transmitted between parent and offspring (Rose 1993: 189) – programmed and stored in a memory (Kay 2000). Methodologically, the creation of genomic knowledge about ourselves is contingent on contemporary computer technology by converting biology into an information science (Fujimura 2000: 87). The huge volume of information rendered by genomics can be understood, if at all, only by using computers with a variety of software (Fujimura 2000). Prior to the 1930s, genetic messages did not exist and genes did not transfer information before the 1950s; they were simply biochemical entities with specific functions (Kay 2000: 18).

The new genetics came to the forefront in American society in the 1960s (Allen 1996; Billings, Beckwitch and Alper 1992; Fox Keller 1992, 2000).[4] Unlike in the past when ideas about heredity may have been understood in terms of 'like begets like', the new genetics engenders the idea of causation.[5] Additionally, belief in genetic inheritance has gained a new meaning such that families beget the abnormal individual (Lloyd 1994). While all humans are comprised of like DNA molecules, it is the rearrangement of some molecules that results in 'abnormality' and disease. The pendulum has swung from the 1950s and1960s when social and psychological disease causality ruled, to the 1980s when there was a gradual renewed interest in genetic causes of crime, alcoholism, mental illness (Wertz 1992) and other diseases. Actually, the new genetics took off with the Human Genome Project (HGP) that was conceived in the late 1980s and formally instituted in October 1990, with the optimistic goal of identifying, mapping and sequencing all human genes to make them accessible for microbiological study and to unlock the secrets of all diseases and life itself.

Contemporary biomedicine is redefining disease aetiology in genetic terms (Pollack 2008). The medicine of the future will likely classify diseases based on their genetic components along with the traditional metrics of anatomy and physiology. Researchers are currently suggesting that 'in the not too distant future, we will think about these diseases (e.g. breast cancer) based on the molecular pathways that are aberrant rather than the anatomical origin of the tumor' (Pollack 2008: D3). Concurrently, the number of genes linked to diseases is increasing because 'gene chips' or SNPS – single nucleotide polymorphism marker sets, where a single unit of DNA is changed – more or less spaced on the genome, are used to search for differences between the genomes of people with a disease and those without (Pollack 2008: D3). All of this is to point to the current meaning of the new genetics and its methods, which leads me here to examine their implications from an anthropological perspective.

Personal Genetics

The new personalized genetic testing, an offshoot testing technique of the new genetics, opens the way for people to live out the theoretical assertions made by the HGP and the promises of the new genetics for a healthier future. All a client needs to do is to submit a swab of spit from the cheek, deposit it in a kit supplied by the commercialized genetic company, and send it to the company for analysis. No referral by a physician or a biomedical authority is usually required. Occasionally a blood sample may also be requested, as described in Table 6.1.

From early times human beings could be bought and sold, but a hallmark of the contemporary age has been the conversion of separate body parts into tradable goods, including genetic material (Andrews and Nelkin 2001; Sharp 2000). What is currently identified as personal genetics testing has most recently become a business: searching the World Wide Web in 2016, one can find thirty-seven such companies cross-culturally and thirteen in the United States, of which, most notably, are the top two: 23andme and Myriad genetics, displayed in Table 6.1. along with some others. They offer a spectrum of genetic information for a fee, with prices being market driven (Angrist 2010). These companies together sell a large number of different genetic tests (Wilde Mathews 2008). In the United States, the federal regulation of such companies is controversial and in a state of flux; it may vary from state to state.

These enterprises variously promise to assess a person's risk susceptibility to numerous diseases; they provide a description of the individual's personality and predisposition to addictive behaviour (Harmon 2007b) and can offer to connect the client to his or her past or track inheritance of specific genes in one's family.[6] Myriad Genetics, one of the first of such companies, founded in 1991, markets patented tests that analyse the BRCA1 and BRCA2 gene (hereditary breast cancer genes) and colon cancer genes. Significantly, it increased its sales by over 50 per cent after launching an advertising campaign on radio and television, pitching the tests directly to the public, especially to women with a family history of breast cancer (Chase 2008), notwithstanding the fact that the test may be useful for less than 5 per cent of the female population (Patsner 2008). Other companies, including 23andme, were founded between 1987 and 2007, as shown in Table 6.1.

The most prominent of these companies, and the most frequently mentioned in the print media, is 23andme. It is said to look at genetics 'holistically', with information on non-disease traits and ancestry being part of the big picture that customers want (Angrist 2010: 76), by offering the widest breadth of services, including testing for ninety-seven diseases, and ancestry analysis comparisons with 'family, friends and people around the world' as part of the company's 'sharing and community' feature (23andme.com 2011). It also reports on forty-seven risk estimates of clinical traits, food preferences

Table 6.1 Descriptions of selected commercial personal genetic companies

Company	Need doctor?	Blood sample required?	Lab/Internet/ Mail?	Cost	When established?	What is promised?	Steps for submitting sample
23andMe	No	No	Internet	$199	Apr 2006	Risk factors for ninety-seven diseases. Assesses ancestry and non-disease traits. Reports on forty-seven risk estimates of clinical traits. Founded to empower the individual. Helps others attain self-knowledge. Looks at genetics holistically.	Order kit, spit in tube, send to labs, receive results in six to eight weeks.
Myriad	Yes	Depends	Doctor visit, results by mail or electronically	Varies	May 1991	Permits doctors and patients to understand the genetic basis of human disease. Assesses risk for developing disease later in life, and identify a patient's likelihood of responding to certain drug therapies.	Blood or saliva sample must be taken by doctor. Sample is shipped to lab, and results are sent electronically to healthcare professional.
HealthCheck USA	No	Yes	Lab	Varies	1987	Offers you control, allowing you to order only the tests you want. Deeply discounted prices.	Order test online. Visit lab to give blood sample. Receive results online.

Company						Features	Process
Kimball Genetics	Only to send results to	Depends	Must have doctor to send results to	Varies	1994	Expert genetic consultation. Detailed reports with interpretation, recommendations and education. A personal approach.	Call lab to talk with genetic counsellor. Receive kit in mail. Some tests require blood sample, some saliva. Results are reported to you and your physician.
Illumina	Yes	Yes	Doctor visit	Varies	Apr 1998	Obtain vast amount of DNA data that is your genome story decoded. Identify important information about your health, like underlying diagnoses, risk for inherited diseases and genetic changes within a cancer.	Doctor must request sample. Collect blood and saliva sample, then sent to lab. Results are sent to your doctor.
Counsyl	Yes	Depends	Results available online	Varies and is covered by most insurers	2007	Through testing, twenty-two different genes associated with an increased risk of certain cancers are analysed. Getting checked earlier, preventative surgery and medication are listed as next steps if irregularities are found by the test.	Make an account online. Counsellor gets in touch with your doctor for approval. Samples are collected at home for saliva or with doctor for blood and then sent off for analysis. Results available in two weeks online and experts available for consultation.

Table 6.1 Descriptions of selected commercial personal genetic companies

Company	Need doctor?	Blood sample required?	Lab/Internet/Mail?	Cost	When established?	What is promised?	Steps for submitting sample
GenebyGene	Yes	Yes	Mail	Varies	2000	Offers clinical, research, ancestry and carrier screening. Clinical testing for a multitude of genes. Very detailed reports of variants and likelihood of a certain disease or trait like BRCA1/2.	Select the test online, contact your clinician for them to order, submit buccal swab. Results are sent to clinician for them to discuss with you.
Interleukin Genetics	Yes	No	Lab	$150 and some insurance covers it	1999	This genetic test looks for a genetic variation that increases risk for severe periodontal disease.	Buccal swab performed by dentist or dental hygienist, sent to lab for processing. Results go to dentist's office.
Invitae	Yes	Yes	Internet	$475	2010	Brings comprehensive genetic information to mainstream medicine. Provides counselling after results are revealed and helps planning should results pertain to the family. They also confirm pathogenic variants.	Order test with healthcare provider, submit blood sample, and results will be available online in three weeks approximately.
Kailos	Yes	No	Internet	Varies	2010	An effort to bring knowledge about the consumer's genetics to them. Includes risk for breast and ovarian cancer.	Order test online, kit delivered to house, saliva sample collected and sent off to lab. Results available online in ten days to you and to your doctor.

or hair colour (Angrist 2010: 57). According to its website (23andme. com, August 2011), it was

> founded to *empower* individuals and develop new ways of accelerating research. The members of 23andme have come together because we believe in the combined potential of genetics and the Internet to have a significant, positive impact. These Core Values represent what motivates us at 23andme. For more than a century scientists have been learning *how our genes help make us the way we are*, operating in conjunction with diet, environment and other factors to influence aspects of our appearance, behavior, and physiology. Yet until now it has been impossible to see more than a tiny fragment of the DNA code that lies inside each of us. At 23andme we believe genetic research tools can and should be used to give us a deeper understanding of the role genes play in our individual lives. By tapping into advances in DNA analysis and offering education, tools, and expertise, we at 23andme want to help others take a bold, informed *step toward self-knowledge*. (23andme. com 2011, Core Values section, emphasis added)

The website also states that 23andme wishes to 'help you connect to and create communities around existing common interests and newfound affinities' (23andme.com 2011). In its search for ancestry, 23andme potentially offers its clients information about their relationship to historical figures and celebrities 'plus people you share data with' (23andme.com 2011), which refers to social networks. This company has been so successful in its publicity that people have organized 'saliva collection parties' (Salkin 2008), and persons with a family history of any disease are especially encouraged to avail themselves of their tests Salkin (2008).

All the companies claim to predict risk not only for single gene diseases (e.g., cystic fibrosis or Huntington's disease) but also furnish risk information for genetically complex diseases such as diabetes, Alzheimer's and other widespread chronic diseases (Kalb 2008) whose causes remain unexplained (Angrist 2010; Khoury et al. 2009). Some companies may require physicians' referral, or some form of medical participation; with some exception, most do not have personal contact with the client.

Unlike companies that had patented genes (e.g., Myriad genetics) and could trade in them (Andrews and Nelkin 2001), almost all others stress on their websites that the genetic material remains the client's. But they trade in the genetic information produced by these tests, using it for research. Through the emergence of personalized genetics, a person's individual genetic information now may have not only medical but also material value. People may order these tests regardless of whether there is any clear utility stemming from them, and indeed most critics claim that not only is heritability of most diseases unexplained, but that these tests are also simply inaccurate (Angrist 2010; National Institutes of Health 2009, ncbi.nim.nih.gov). It is noteworthy that the medical profession has been highly critical of the personal genetics enterprise, asserting that the medical information such tests offer is useless, imprecise and mildly anxiety-provoking (Bloss, Schorck and Topol 2011), with one geneticist characterizing them as equivalent to astrology (Angrist 2010; also Brody 2009). Every new genetic discovery feeds the current craze of personalized genomic medicine. Complicating the situation, physicians are not well prepared to 'explain complex statistical risk information to healthy individuals who are seeking to enhance their chances of staying well' (Andrews, Mehlman and Rothstein 2002: 10). The data obtained from these analyses are most difficult to interpret. Angrist cites one researcher, noting that he has not the vaguest clue what the genome means or what it does (2010: 283; also Winslow and Wang 2012).

Indeed, there is legitimate concern that people do not understand the genetic information they may glean from personalized genetic tests (Soares 2007). Moreover, as Andrews observes, referring to genetic studies in general, 'the development of genetic data carries with it a margin of error; some information communicated to subjects will, in the end, prove to be wrong' (Andrews, Mehlman and Rothstein 2002: 96). This is especially so with personalized genomics, which offers genotyping at 500,000 to 1,000,000 loci (e.g., 23andme). There is a very high risk of spurious associations in such studies (Evans 2008) and their accuracy has been questioned (Begley 2008; Evans 2008; also Wade 2007). Nevertheless, almost all the commercial companies emphasize on their websites that by having such a test one becomes, in their word, 'empowered' by the knowledge of one's predisposition to or inheritance of a disorder, suggesting that something could be done to prevent the inevitable, if only by avoiding identified risk factors. Ultimately, then, contemporary humans' ideology of control of the future through controlling the risk of inheriting a genetic disease is 'empowering' and comforting, especially in an age of uncertainty and flux. Paradoxically, personalized genetics, riddled with uncertainties, telescopes further the uncertainty, with its provisional diagnoses of predisposition to a particular disease that may never materialize. And yet, remarkably, despite the uncertain knowledge produced by the new genetics, it is nevertheless promulgated and pitched as 'empowering' us in the present and future, a point to which I will return shortly. Consider that for many contemporary people beliefs in the essence of scientific truths tends to lead them to discount the contingencies of such knowledge by ignoring the inherent contradiction of an 'empowering' uncertainty.

Concept of Risk

Empowering uncertainty is further promoted in the new genetics by the concept of risk, since undergirding genetic knowledge are notions of probability and risk, which lack certainty and are ultimately probabilistic (Finkler, Skrzynia and Evans 2003; Khoury 2003). Genetic information, genetic testing and screening rely on historically produced notions of probability and risk that arguably came into Western thought to alleviate the uncertainties that were created by the Scientific Revolution (Finkler 2003). By and large, contemporary humans have lost their sure footing in the world, especially following the scientific revolution of the seventeenth century and the Enlightenment of the eighteenth century, which championed human rationality and freedom from religious authority, promoting a new consciousness that led to the secularization of society by removing the 'domination of religious institutions and symbols' (Berger and Luckmann 1966: 107). But even as the Enlightenment envisioned the control of nature as part of humans' ability to understand the world, the new consciousness led to a new insecurity and a loss of a sense of certainty in a world no longer determined and ordered by God, or as in antiquity, by Fortuna[7] and Fate. Gilkey (1968: 66–67) defines Fate as: 'blind forces of nature, of genetic inheritance, of disease and uncontrolled scarcity of social structure and tradition of local or family custom and most important, of the inner psyche, all those forces that shape human existence in directions antithetical to or destructive of conscious human goals and purposes'.

It may be difficult for modern humans to imagine that the notion of chance and probability were relatively recent developments in Western thought. In actuality, these revolutionary concepts, having had their beginnings in the seventeenth century, introduced the novel notion of probability[8] that had not existed in Western thought prior to 1654 (Hacking 1975). In the context of gambling, the concept of probability is ancient, but the notion that random chance conforms to rules of probability has its origins in the seventeenth century.[9] Whereas notions of probability had their beginning in the seventeenth century, the concept of risk became firmly fixed in Western European culture only in the nineteenth century,[10] when the mathematical theory of risk became widespread and with it the belief that whole classes of phenomena previously taken to be the very model of the unpredictable, from hail storms to suicides, were in fact governed by statistical regularities (Daston 1988: 164). The notion of risk shifts human fate from the caprices of the gods to the whims of mathematical probability.

We now live with the notion that we can control risk and dominate the future,[11] what Beck describes as a 'risk society' (Beck 1992, 1998), where we cannot take 'traditional certainties for granted' (Beck 1998: 10). Managing risk is, in his words, 'colonizing the future' for 'events that do not exist (yet) strongly influence our present affairs and activities' (Beck 1998: 11; see also Giddens 1991: 109; Strathern 2005). The notion of risk assessment makes the 'unforeseeable foreseeable or promises to do so' (Beck 1998:12). The idea of risk factors affecting health was introduced by Framingham researches in 1961, a three generational health study on a large population that now permeates almost all contemporary Western awareness (Rockhill 2001). Importantly, traditional concepts of risk referred to the statistical profiles for aggregate population. But in today's collective consciousness the notion of risk has become privatized (ibid.), meaning that it is applied to individuals and not to groups. The prevailing belief is that the individual is at risk rather than the population of which he or she forms a part.

As every person who is treated medically, or is exposed to the mass media in the United States, knows, myriad risk factors, genetic or otherwise, including obesity, drinking, smoking, and poor diet, must be avoided to maintain good health. Failure to avoid all such risks will result in the person being blamed for his or her sickness; potential for affliction with such disease could be revealed by a genetic test. In effect, modern concepts of choice and decision theory, as well as risk analysis, are anchored in culturally constructed notions of probability and are historically produced, leading to statistical thinking and subsequently applied to medical events. Today, contemporary life continues to be dominated by statistical modes of thought, creating new realities.

Though belief in the genetic inheritance of disease puts at risk every person with a family history of a disease, we cannot, alas, undo our family medical histories, no matter how much we may wish to. An adverse genetic medical history may lead people to experience both a sense of predestination, fostered to some degree by genetic determinism, and a sense of having control over their health. Personalized genetic commercial companies remind clients that human beings can control the risk of inheriting a genetic disease and influence their present and future health by knowing their genome. Indeed, if we accept that genetic inheritance foretells our future health state and determines our being, we are, paradoxically, firmly back to the idea of predestination.[12] In Cole's words, 'it is humbling, then, to regard our genome and recognize how much it determines who we are' (Cole 1994: 20), including human spirituality. The notion of risk and risk factors cloak uncertainty in degrees and percentages of certainty, thus mediating the ambiguities of living in a postmodern age that Harvey (1989) has characterized as one that, because of its uncertainty, places the future in chaos.

Paradoxically, molecular biology and the genetic model of family and kinship inheritance bridge the essentialism of modern science with postmodern ideologies and experience. Genetic ideology suggests that DNA from the past inexorably repeats itself in the future, and thus the belief in genetic inheritance promises immortality and rebirth. This promise may also help to explain why the reduction of the human essence to a gene could be so willingly accepted and why empowerment of uncertainties is acceded to. In a secular world where we may live with the notion of being reduced to nothingness, nothingness can now be transcended by belief in genetic inheritance. It could even be said that the notion of genetic inheritance promises contemporary humans immortality within the flux of the postmodern world. The individual exists in a transient world but is fastened biologically to the past and future through genetic inheritance and transmission.

Medicalization of Family and Kinship

Among the numerous risks individuals must confront is that of inheriting a disease from their family (Finkler 2000a, 2001), thereby medicalizing their kin. Consider this: embedded in concepts of genetic inheritance is the notion that family and kin are the medium through which inheritance flows. Family and kin connections are framed in terms of genetic inheritance from parents, grandparents and other relatives.[13] One's ancestors may be toxic.

And yet, generally speaking, biological processes are contingent and dependent on chance events. In fact, 'chance, or contingency, is the defining characteristic of evolution, and possibly even its driving force' (Fox Keller 2000: 104). Changes in the genotype may not necessarily become expressed in phenotype owing to functional redundancies built into the DNA replication process (Fox Keller 2000: 113), suggesting that many genetic mutations may never be expressed (ibid.). Additionally, the original DNA transmitted from parent to offspring is diluted millions of times over by the newly synthesized molecules resulting from cell division (Fox Keller 2000: 212).[14]

Moreover, and most importantly, it may sometimes be ignored that while humans, as all living creatures, inherit predictable character-istics for their species, the variation within their species, including disease, is inherited by random chance (Finkler, Skrzynia and Evans 2003; Hadler and Evans 2001; Monod 1971) and shaped by intracel-lular, intrasomatic and external processes (Hubbard and Wald 1997; Rose 1997). Sadly, no matter how fervently humans may wish to leave nothing to chance, in the domain of genetic inheritance chance and randomness govern, be it eye colour or a disease (Hubbard and Wald 1997; Rose 1997; Hadler and Evans 2001). In the words of the physi-cian Hadler and geneticist Evans,

> In our deterministic fervor, we often forget that whether one develops any disease has less to do with "nature or nurture" than with chance. Random stochastic mechanism is the most important determinant of disease occurrence and progression. It is a fool's hope [or perhaps bless-ing] to believe that we will be able to sort out the interactions of envi-ronment, 100,000 human genes, and the role of chance to provide a crystal ball that is anything but murky. (Hadler and Evans 2001: 253)

Yes – unless one resorts to genetic engineering. By avoiding identified genetic risk factors humans may not be able to protect themselves from randomness or 'tame chance' (Hacking 1990), even though they may have attempted to control their existence by supernatural means from their earliest beginnings. Arguably, most diseases, including cancer, result largely from poorly understood mutations, often induced by external environmental and other exogenous factors or dietary defi-cits, rather than from genetic inheritance (Hubbard and Wald 1997). Still, our kinship relations have been given a new dimension by stress-ing faulty genes, and by leaving us a toxic legacy. In earlier times and in premodern Anglo-American society, people inherited their status, rights and duties, property and power as well as poverty from their kin (Giddens 1991; Finkler 2000a: Chapter 2 and 3; Holy 1996). In contemporary times, kinship relations in the United States usually do not confer on people any particular status among the population.[15] In fact, the majority of middle and lower class families may have little property to transmit to their descendants other than ephemeral moral values (Finkler 1994). Instead, cultural significance is given to genetic transmission, for better or for worse, re-emphasizing, too, the tradi-tional biogenetic family, which goes against the lived experience of postmodern and recombinant families that are established by choice rather than biology (Finkler 2000a).

The medicalization of family and kin is a two-edged sword and may not necessarily affect all people adversely. The medicalizing of our kin may give an affliction meaning by addressing the question of 'why me' and 'why not others' in the community, since the risk of inheriting the affliction is predicted by the family history and explains the aetiology of the disease for which biomedicine lacks an explanation. For example, the senselessness and randomness of breast cancer can become meaningful because it afflicted another in the family, and also establishes for a woman a connection with her kin and ancestors (Finkler 2000a). As I have suggested elsewhere (Finkler 2000a; Finkler, Skrzynia and Evans 2003), in the United States, where cultural awareness of genetics is fomented every time a physician requires a family medical history, and by the mass media, the new genetics and its testing methods may promote closeness among biologically related persons, where such closeness may not have existed previously, and open the way for new, if only sporadic, interaction with individuals sharing the same genetic inheritance. People may even take pride in the genetic inheritance of favourable characteristics. It may reassure some people that if no one in the family, past or present, has suffered from a particular disease they too are protected from becoming afflicted. It may furnish the person with a feeling of security, notwithstanding the fact that this sense of protection may be nothing more than an illusion.

Conversely, knowing that one is at risk because other members of the family have been afflicted by a particular disease may create for healthy people a fear of falling ill (Finkler 2000a) that may even be transmitted to the next generation.[16] People's reality encompasses a future that may be incessantly punctuated by worry. The notion of genetic risk for a disease has now become almost a disease in and of itself (Nelkin 1992: 188).

Significantly, prior to the development of modern genetic testing techniques, the most useful tool in assessments of genetic risk for a disease was family history, usually about three generations deep and including lineal and collateral relatives (Berkow, Beers and Fletcher 1997). Until the beginning of the twenty-first century, linkage analysis was the prevailing genetic testing method used in biomedicine to evaluate a genetic risk profile, whereas personalized genetics has radically changed genetic testing techniques, creating fresh ramifications, above all for family and kin interaction. While linkage analysis required the active participation of relatives, through the provision of blood samples and their consent, the new technology requires minimal or no family involvement and/or even minimal family interaction.

These recent innovations in genomic analysis are profound and therefore call for a reconsideration of the medicalization of kinship (Finkler
2000a, 2001).

Current personal genetic testing techniques may change biomedical practice in the future by eschewing the family medical history and
concentrating instead on the autonomous individual. A single individual's saliva sample provides a great deal of information without
the need for family data or the necessity of participation by family
members in any form. While the family history remains a useful tool,
the need for specimen collection and analysis from an individual's kin
is disappearing, rendering cooperation of family members increasingly irrelevant to the process of genetic analysis and risk prediction.
As I noted earlier, the individual needs only to order the test through
the World Wide Web and send a saliva sample through the mail. The
contemporary ease of DNA collection and analysis means that one
may readily obtain a sample of another's DNA unbeknownst to that
person; for example, by simply swabbing a toothbrush, containing
plentiful DNA given the sensitivity of modern analytic techniques.
Such a sample can then be subjected to truly stunning levels of analysis, with evaluation 'SNPs' within an individual's genome. These SNPs
can provide information that relates to everything from psychological
proclivities to the risk of glaucoma.

In short, the medicalization of family and kinship may have benefits and drawbacks for the individual, especially within the realm
of health matters. The new personalized genetic testing techniques
alter the family and kin interactions facilitated by earlier techniques;
requests to execute the test need not create a new connection among
persons sharing a family genome, since the individual may only
require electronic interaction with a website. The person remains on
her own, or just 'alone'.

I hasten to emphasize here that my analysis of the medicalization
of kinship and its possible consequences for people's lives is based on
empirical research in the United States, chiefly with women who have
family histories of a life-threatening disease, such as breast cancer, or
persons with a family history of colon cancer. The degree to which
beliefs in genetics and genetic testing of any type may influence family
and kinship interactions may depend on various factors, including
the following: people's awareness promoted by biomedical practice
and by the exposure to a genetically partisan mass media; their experience of a specific disease and its treatability – whether, for example,
it is life-threatening, such as cancer, or easily controllable, such as
high cholesterol – and the role that kinship relations play in specific

societies. Moreover, while we know that education and class position influence the degree to which people accept biomedicine and its practices in general, we still need to explore to what degree a person's class position and ethnicity may lead to acceptance or rejection of genetics and genetic testing, including commercialized personal genetic testing.

Reflections on Issues Raised by Personal Genetics: The Individual, Biomedicine and Ethics

Writing about genetic information in general, Strathern (2005: 35) observes that,

> One of the products of genetic knowledge acquired for clinical purposes is widely understood to be information on a whole range of matters about life-circumstances of great interest to the person in question. The issue is that many of them could also be of great interest to third parties. In this light, it has become a truism to say that genetic knowledge is frequently regarded as at once full of promise and full of danger.

If, as I believe, Strathern is right, what are these dangers, and what are the implications of the knowledge personal genetics produces, not only for familial history of disease but for personhood, or self and others in one's kin group? The personal genetics phenomenon in the United States, and presumably also internationally, as advanced by commercial companies on their websites,[17] prompts me to reflect on its potential effect on several issues bearing on the individual, biomedical practice and bioethics.

But it is necessary first to pose a question: Do genetic test results yield an exceptional type of knowledge, providing new insights about ourselves, if not about the world, or are they simply like any type of routine test, such as for diabetes or cholesterol? Currently the potential effects of these tests on the populations in general are not known (Bloss, Schorck and Topol 2011). Although genes are proteins, we can nevertheless hypothesize that the information gathered by personal genetic tests is not just knowledge of any kind, because, unlike prior to the 1950s when they were just biochemical entities, we have now attributed to these particular chemicals values above and beyond concern over diagnostic examinations such as standard cholesterol tests.[18] Genes conjure up feeling-tones and thoughts about ourselves, our kin and our identities; of course, they may also occasion relief that one is not afflicted by some terrible disease.

The supporters of personal genetics (especially company officials) claim that in addition to attempts to predict a person's predisposition to disease, personal genetics also purport to address the ancient and by now clichéd adage 'know thyself' (Angrist 2010: 76), suggesting that genetic tests are unique in their aims (see also Everett 2003, 2004). After all, a basic assumption by many about the overall emerging genetic landscape is that genetic analysis encapsulates one's personhood, with individual human essence residing in the gene (Dolgin 2001; Everett 2003, 2004; Pinker 2009). Rabinow goes as far as to say that this knowledge bears on the very soul of a person. He claims that 'the identification of DNA with the "human person" [is] a self-evident synecdochical relationship – the part literally stands for the whole – [thus] constitutes a "spiritual" identification' (Rabinow 1999: 16; see also Finkler 2005), joining the essence of the person with his or her prospect of affliction. In this view, the site of knowledge production of the self, of one's personhood, rests at the level of the biotechnology industry. Whereas in pre-Enlightenment times the site of one's personhood could have rested in a soul, in spirituality, and in the post Enlightenment modern period in rationality, now the self may be embodied in genomic information lacking a person's creative input of what came before.

The individual and the reflexive self is the hallmark of modernity, according to Giddens (1991: 77, 196). Indeed, what can be described as the 'age of personalized genetics' reflects the age of individualism par excellence coupled with the florescence of computer technology, having its origin in the ethos of American individualism (Bellah et al. 1985; Tocqueville 1980). According to Giddens (1991), the notion that one has a unique character is a modern phenomenon, and in genetics it is asserted that every person has a unique genome; by extension, the modern individual may seek to find a secular static self in his or her genetic make-up.[19] But does the knowledge of the self through genetics offer a new kind of knowledge, or is it old knowledge repackaged in microbiological terms? Does it add any new insights to enhance or detract from our existence?

Personalized genetics is at the vanguard of postmodern society because it echoes and further bolsters the contemporary autonomous individual. In an extensive article titled 'My Genome, My Self' in the Sunday *New York Times Magazine*, Pinker (2009) describes what he calls 'consumer genetics', which provides information about health, physique and personality. Yet significantly he makes no reference to his family or familial relationships; he stands alone. We are not told what the genetic 'my self' tells us about other members of his family with regard to the traits he lists. Pinker's article seems to suggest (as do the, for example, names of personalized genetic companies, such as 23andme) that the new techniques are pushing us further and further into seeing ourselves as the 'me', the autonomous individual we are not, and thus promoting the bioethical principle of autonomy (Finkler 2008), especially when faced with important decisions about matters of health, and health prevention by knowing one's genetic predisposition through genetic testing.

Notwithstanding Pinker's (2009) enthusiasm for the results of his test, knowledge produced about the 'self' by current personal genetic testing techniques reverberates on our deeply held cultural under-standing of an autonomous, unchanging 'self' lodged in an interior space in our bodies, in our DNA, as constructed in a laboratory, and on the health risks it purports to divulge. Such knowledge challenges the notion of a processual 'self', one that 'becomes' out of shared experience and is engaged with the world; an ongoing emergent self, which in large measure is uncertain, tentative and contingent (see endnote 17). And while it may afford us knowledge about our ancestry, it fails to furnish knowledge about our families' or kin's likes and dislikes, their angers and pleasures, or the richness of knowing their heritage. Strathern (2005: 21) put it well when she noted that 'heredity has become heritage', but a heritage devoid of its humanity.

As I noted earlier, a family member's cooperation in the form of contribution of blood samples and medical information to assess a person's genetic profile gives way to an individual's saliva test. Does this suggest that personalized genetics has 'de-medicalized' family and kinship? After all, individuals may bypass the medical establishment by turning to the commercial sector for a glimpse of their possible disease profile, and future health. Actually, personalized genetics teeters between medicalization and commodification, as suggested by the recent controversy between the State of California and its Public Health Department. The issue at hand was whether personalized genetics companies are offering medical information requiring inter-pretations by physicians, or are instead offering a service to provide knowledge about 'oneself' to which every person has a right (Pollack 2008). Increasingly, with the movement towards commodification of family and kinship, a person's decision-making about genetic testing is being removed from the medical professionals and transferred to a commercial entity, converting the individual from a patient to a consumer. The person thus enters into a contractual relationship within the commercial sector of society, leaving a presumed trusting relationship between doctor and patient. In bypassing the need for a physician's recommendations the person is liberated from a dependence on his or her family and the traditional medical profession in the process of obtaining genetic information for medical purposes. The domain of medicine is replaced by the world of commerce; giving new control to the person and allowing for anonymity to circumvent one's medical record. However, de-medicalization only goes so far: once an individual has acquired such information, its sheer complexity may prompt her to seek expert advice in the form of a knowledgeable genetic practitioner. Either way, personalized genetics shifts a person from the domain of authoritative knowledge of medicine to commodified knowledge of the marketplace, with the interior of the body becoming commodified in a new way.

Ironically, but significantly, the person being tested may garner much information about the rest of the family members, with or without their knowledge or permission, thereby raising ethical dilemmas, especially concerning privacy, confidentiality and informed consent. In Dyson's words (2008: 52) 'A genome does indeed carry a fair amount of information; it can uniquely identify anyone, except an identical twin, and it can reveal family relationships that may have been hidden'. In the coming age of personal genetic testing, the autonomous individual, and his or her rights, may hence be pitted against the rest of the family. In one study that used linkage analysis, the suggestion is made that women more than men assume the responsibility of informing other family members about genetic test findings (d'Agnicourt-Canning 2001), but irrespective of the gendered nature of transmitting such information, it has been observed that not all members wish to know their presumed genetic status (Andrews 2001; Andrews, Mehlman and Rothstein 2002), or that some may wish it to be kept secret, or just not know.

With these new personalized genetic techniques one can now know not only oneself, but also 'themselves' – with one person having the power to know the many in the family; a new family dynamic and kin interaction may come into play with commodified genetic information. While genes as protein entities in themselves make no requirements of the individual, the revealed knowledge we attribute to them creates a moral universe of responsibility to other members of the family – or does it? Since the decision whether or not to pursue personalized genetic analysis rests only with one sole person, such tests raise the stakes of the ethical principle of privacy and confidentiality more than ever (Finkler 2008). Does the autonomous individual, then, have a moral obligation to warn all other family members of possible disease risks, and inform other relatives of a 'diseased heritage' (e.g., see Finkler 2000a) if breast or colon cancer is found in the genetic history of a family. In my earlier study of women with family histories of breast cancer, assessed by linkage analysis (Finkler 2000a), I found that, with one exception, all women unquestioningly accepted a moral responsibility to forewarn others in their families that they should take preventive measures. However, other studies suggest that the sharing of genetic knowledge among family members may lead to dissension rather than gratitude (Andrews 2001).

In short, personal genetics is only personal in name; true, it leaves to the individual the decision whether or not to have the test done, but the new information may give a special power to that person within the family; it is not personal because the results often contain information about other members of the family that individual members may or may not wish to know, or have revealed.

Significantly, the fact that personal genetics is not personal comes into bold relief in a recent report that even the new legislation protecting individuals from health insurance companies' uses of medical genetic information stops short at the threshold of the legal system.[20] Dyson (2008: 52) is concerned that the 'flood of medical and genetic information' may lead insurance companies to make predictions on the basis of statistical studies that track the effects of treatments, and diseases of a given population that may be assigned to individual risk. Or, in another instance, California officials have announced that they will draw on the state's official databases to utilize 'familial searching', used also in Britain, which allows them to track down a suspect by analysing the DNA of his or her relatives already found in these databases, even though the relatives are not suspected of any crime, as reported by *The Economist* ('Genetics and Lung Cancer' 2008: 83).

With genetic knowledge represented by strings of letters (G, C, T, As) and stored in databases 'accessed through computerized information networks crossing the globe' (Fujimura 2000: 88), yet another major ethical debate emerges on a societal level revolving around ownership of these databases. While people may believe that genetic information is their private property, the commodification of genetic testing opens an avenue for these companies and other multinationals to use the information for their own commercial purposes (see the famous Moore case in Rabinow 1999). Who, then, has a right to knowledge of our souls, especially if one's genome may possess some unique characteristics and become a valuable property (e.g., Rabinow 1999).

In the final analysis, knowledge produced by the new genetic technologies has many limits due to its complexity and the risk of false outcomes (Evans 2008). More and more the complexity of gene-environment interactions is being recognized. In Fox Keller's words, 'To focus endlessly on genes keeps us stuck in a linear, unidirectional and two dimensional view of life, in which instructions are read out and dutifully followed' (cited by Angier 2008: D2). Fox Keller adds that this is a dynamic process that may not always be predicted. Indeed, since by focusing on genetic inheritance as the perpetrator of a person's disorder, insufficient research attention is devoted to the physical, social, cultural and individual life world with all its messiness and moral conundrums that impact on a person's health state, which are embodied by what I have identified elsewhere as 'life's lesions' (Finkler 1994, 2000b, 2007).

Gene-Based Virtual Communities

The commodification of personalized genetics in cyberspace may actually lead to uniting autonomous individuals electronically in a novel way by the creation of gene-type virtual communities comprised of people sharing a common ancestry and affliction. When researching the personal genetics companies' websites, I was particularly intrigued by 23andme's idea to form such groupings (Wojcicki cited in Weiss 2008). In the words of the founder of 23andme, Wojcicki, 'We envision a new type of community where people will come together around specific genotypes, and these artificial barriers of country and race will start to break down' (cited in Weiss 2008; see also Rubin 2008; Shute 2008). Such genotype communities will connect people sharing a common genetic legacy (see also Rabinow 1999) and common ancestral DNA rather than heritage based on beliefs, language and practices. Such gene-based virtual communities will fashion genetic invisible identities, constructed around, say, high cholesterol, depression or other hereditary predispositions that may shape a person's future, while destigmatizing conditions, especially those associated with behavioural or mental states. Such communities may also facilitate finding long-lost relatives; create new ways of social networking by fostering the experience of discovering similarities with an extensive number of people (Shute 2008);[21] thereby producing a virtual kinship where one need not physically see or touch anyone.

Interestingly, gene-based virtual communities may be arranged by pharmaceutical companies (Rose and Novas 2005: 447) to promote direct-to-consumer advertising and consumption of medicines produced for individuals with specific medical conditions (cf. Winslow and Wang 2012). To sort people around shared genetic predisposi- tions for a particular disease would be of great advantage to pharma- ceutical companies, whose products may in reality have toxic effects, as for example cigarettes, alcohol, junk foods. Persons assessed as having genetic predispositions to such behaviours could be isolated from the rest of the population, which would not need to worry about falling ill and could continue to smoke, drink and enjoy a junk food diet (e.g., see Pollack 2009) without fear of developing a disease asso- ciated with such behaviours. 23andme could fashion a world with gene-based virtual communities founded on common genotypes that, arguably, may bestow on a person an identity, possibly even an ethnic or invisible racial identity in lieu of the presumed visible traits that rule our folk racialized categorizations (see also Glasner and Rothman 2001; Simpson 2004).

But how different would communities founded on invisible genetic traits really be from communities based on visible characteristics, such as skin colour or other surface differences? Communities of this type could potentially establish new hierarchies comprised of 'genetically rich', or healthy, and 'genetically poor' or sick persons, or what Silver (1998) calls 'genrich' and 'naturals'. Silver foresees a time when the world may be divided, especially with genetic engineering, between the 'genrich' and the 'naturals', with the former having all the advan- tages attained not only through education and economic position, but also acquired genetically.[22]

If indeed we live in a multicultural society, some people may find communities arranged around genotypes to be acceptable and satisfy- ing. But such 'communities' lacking a shared physical space or face-to- face contact, and lacking a common heritage and responsibility to one another, may become fraught with more danger than before. What the founder of 23andme may fail to recognize is that such virtual commu- nities may create new racial groups that rest, once again, on solely biological features, substituting discrimination based on genetic anal- ysis for that of visible racial type (see also Harmon 2007a). There may, of course, be an advantage to attaining a degree of equality when we create classes of people based on invisible distinctions. Visible bodily attributes, especially physical features such as obesity, may often be markers of class (in the famous widely quoted saying by the Duchess of Windsor, 'one cannot be too rich and too thin'), conjuring up an image of a person lacking self-control. Interior bodily markers could be classless, telling nothing about one's moral sense, but it may tell us about our ancestry, which actually cannot be fudged, for example, by claiming ancestors who arrived in the Americas on the Mayflower.[23]

We can attempt to alter external features and have some control of the visible characteristics by makeovers, including nose jobs, facial uplifts and attempts to control the appetite, but we have no control over what the genetic test will tell us about ourselves.

Summary and Conclusion

A historical overview, like cross-cultural studies, points to the cultural nature of human beliefs and actions, including Western notions of probability, risk and genetic knowledge. I must stress, however, that the truth or falsity of the entire corpus of genetic knowledge developed by Western science is not being questioned.[24] Nonetheless, I hasten to add that genetic knowledge, like biomedicine, or any medical system, is a cultural system (Finkler 2001; Hahn and Kleinman 1983; Ingleby 1982; Krieger and Fee 1994; Lock and Gordon 1988; Martin 1997; Wright and Treacher 1982; Young 1981). Biomedicine, like science itself, is not an acultural form of intellectual endeavour, but one that has emerged during a particular historical moment in the social formation of Western society (Brandt 1997; Fujimura 1996; Haraway 1991; Hess 1997; Latour and Woolgar 1979; Martin 1997; Richter 1972; Turner 1987, 1992). According to Bowler,

> Without denying the important factual consequences that have flowed from the development of genetics, the history of the field will show that the new science was invented to serve human purposes – it did not grow automatically as a consequence of factual observations. (Bowler 1989: 12)

Thus, 'theories are invented rather than discovered' (ibid.: 13). From Bowler's perspective, genetic models are constructed to 'reflect the values of the social groups whose interests are best served by the promotion of these particular models' (ibid.: 17). Fujimura (1996) makes a compelling case for how genetic knowledge is constructed by demonstrating that, in the late 1980s, the view of cancer changed from a 'set of heterogeneous diseases marked by the common property of uncontrolled cell growth to a disease of human genes' (Fujimura 1996: 1). This change was brought about not by new discoveries or new epistemic advances, but rather by negotiated social processes (see also Latour 1987).

One of the dangers of personalized genetics is that it may distance people even further from their kin; as kin may become less necessary or irrelevant in the quest of self-knowledge or knowledge about potential health hazards. Personalized genetic test results may lead to a new way of knowing and talking about the self: a concrete poetics, but is there an imaginative longing embodied in our genes? Ironically and contradictorily, knowledge garnered from personalized genetic tests is personal and objectified: personal genetics gives us an impersonal glimpse of ourselves by technological analytical means, ignoring our experiential selves – the self of imagination, of intentions – and the life world, which also influences our state of health (cf. Finkler 1994, 2000b, 2007).

The human genome writes the evolution and history of all humanity and can reveal the ethnicity and kinship of individuals. The knowledge we acquire from genetic analyses is about the human past, possibly as far back as the Neanderthals; it can also take us back to our ancestral heritage, reminding us of who our ancestors were, although lacking accuracy.[25] Genes become our memory banks, storing a record of our kin who came before us that in contemporary society we tend to forget. Our genetic inheritance, understood in terms of DNA transmission, is not simply a condensed symbol but a physical trace that may stand in for our ancestor, forecasting our future health. Knowledge of our genetic inheritance traced through the DNA can stand as a proxy for memory by connecting people to their ancestors and reinforcing continuity with them that may be absent in postmodern life. Minicuci (1995) describes how memory was once 'activated by the construction of genealogies', passed down from parents, grandparents and other family members. It stirred up powerful feelings and associations, and may have contributed to defining one's identity. Individual memories of ancestors recorded in faded photographs and other artifacts – or embedded in the consciousness of sounds, smells, affect and tales, comprised of sensations, thoughts, feelings and emotions – genealogical memories – evoked traditions of what ancestors believed and did, creating and reinforcing a shared history. Nowadays the focus is on a present that lacks any time depth, and genetic memory may become a unifying force among kin that is captured by the DNA but is devoid of such sensations. Knowledge of shared DNA may substitute for our fragile memories by keeping a record of persons who may have been long forgotten, but does not permit the reinvention of the self or the embellishment of one's ancestry. The work of memory is both to remember and to forget some genealogical ties, but our genetic record in its personalized DNA form may not permit such memory lapses, and disallows secrets, preventing the creation of a past that may never have happened (see Finkler 2000a).

Memory is the subjective experience of time that also transcends linearity. Genetic knowledge transforms subjective time into objectively measurable time by DNA transmission, converting an ambiguous postmodern reality into a modern positivist one. Generally speaking, time in the West is reckoned linearly. Despite its uncertainties, the new genetics creates both a sense of linear and cyclical time. Our personalized genetics, encapsulated in our DNA, crystallizes the past and the future in the present; the now compresses time into an everlasting presumed 'empowered' present that is nevertheless potentially fraught with the fear of falling ill in the future (Finkler 2000a). Concurrently, new genetic knowledge ordinarily introduces a sense of cyclicality to postmodern life, with the genes of the past being reborn in the future. Farriss, discussing the ancient Maya of Mesoamerica, observes that their time served 'both history and prophecy, a guide to the future as well as a record of the past' (1995: 110), in much the same way as a genetic test of any type and analysis of one's DNA purports to tell about one's past and forecast one's future health, a profound aspect of our existence, possibly calming the turmoil of a postmodern world; despite its underlying uncertainties with promises of 'empowerment'.

In postmodern globalized society time and space are compressed, as they are on the genetic map that summarizes generations of history; personalized genetic testing gives us 'instant messaging' from the past and promises glimpses of future time, particularly as it pertains to our health status, which can become a mixed blessing. Such messages may give rise to new a moral obligation to alert members of the family of a potential disease, or create ethical quandaries and a sense of control over our future health, although it may not alter our behaviour (Bloss, Schorck and Topol 2011), but, of course, not everyone may wish to know the future prophesized by genetic tests. To summarize: belief in genetic inheritance, assessed by personal genetic tests, could create depth and continuity with previous generations that may be lacking in postmodern society and may link people with their biological past that may be considered the source of their true personhood, or even their soul, as Rabinow suggests.

According to the websites of personal genetics companies, their services are available internationally. But the role genetics plays in people's lives will obviously be diverse in different parts of the world. It will vary within each Western society and among Western societies, where a scientific ethos prevails; in non-Western societies, arguably, sensibilities are rooted in other cultural traditions. Based on previous research, I present here the sensibilities emerging out of American society that provide a fertile ground for propagating an epistemological 'self' that is rooted in physicality and microbiology. It remains to be seen whether beliefs about genetics, and personalized genetics, will travel equally well across the world as the iPad, iPhone and other such twenty-first century technological marvels do, seducing it. Will personalized genetics become a globalized project? Do people the world over wish to gain knowledge about themselves that is produced in microbiological laboratories? This question remains to be explored by other scholars, or to be seen as it unfolds in real life. In the end, what is most significant is how human beings experience new knowledge produced by science.

My aim in this chapter has been to theorize about a widespread phenomenon that purports to produce new knowledge about ourselves, our personhood, and what our futures may hold for us, especially in the realm of health and sickness, and the ethical dilemmas such knowledge may engender. I raised here more questions than I am able to answer, but since personalized genetic techniques are a relatively new aspect of genomic knowledge, it is my hope that other scholars will address some of these issues. For example, they may consider the phenomenology of experiencing personal genomics; the ways it may alter a person, from the moment a person sits down at the computer, contacts one of the personalized companies and submits their saliva, to the moment the results arrive at their doorstep, to attempts to decipher them and make sense of the outcome.

By way of closing, Cranor (1994: 138) suggests that in two decades from the time of his writing the focus will be only on genetics, closing the door to serious investigation of other causes of disease. The focus on genetic causation reflects the more general view of biological causation rather than environmental causality. Science possesses prodigious authority the world over and concepts of genetic inheritance are wrapped in its cloak. No matter how persuasive the arguments against the genetic inheritance of most genetic diseases (Fox Keller 1992; Hubbard and Wald 1997; Lewontin, Rose and Kamin1984, 1992; Nelkin and Lindee 1995; Spanier 1995 and others), still, generally speaking, the prevailing view in the United States is that we are largely defined by DNA and that most diseases could be inherited.

Genetic determinism is not yet accepted by many geneticists (e.g., J. Evans, personal communication, 2004) nor has it penetrated in full force all segments of contemporary society, but much of the research effort turns on genetics rather than external causes. Directing attention towards genetically inherited disease causality, and away from environmental disease aetiologies, tends to eliminate the need to seek other sources of, say, behaviour, or healthful nutrition. As we saw, these companies claim to be able to predict multiple diseases, ignoring that a person's health is shaped not only by microbiology but also by the context of his or her life (Finkler 1994, 2000b, 2007).

One last point merits consideration. In this chapter I reflected on genetic knowledge production, with some emphasis on current practices of personal genetics from various dimensions. Rabinow (2011), discussing his research at a scientific research centre, [26] emphasizes his outsider status among this community of scientists. This is not a novel revelation. From its inception the anthropological enterprise was predicated on the outsider looking in; and by so doing he or she attempts to capture the cultural ways and their implications that are unselfconsciously taken for granted by the insider. As an non-physician but one who has observed and written extensively on bio-medicine, and other healing systems cross-culturally, and the science of genetics from an anthropological perspective, my enquiry into the relatively new data created by personal genetics reveals a multi-edged sword, so to speak, that its practitioners may not always recognize. As the outsider to geneticists' endeavours, my aim here, as mentioned previously, is not to question the validity of the science of genetics, or its numerous usages, including personalized genetics,[27] but to consider its effects for the receivers of this knowledge. Thirty seven personal genetics testing companies, cited earlier, are currently distributed the world over, with the exception of Latin America, Africa and the Middle East (not including Dubai), which is in and of itself significant from an anthropological outlook. Future research should further illuminate the many aspects of personal genetics cross-culturally that will benefit all humankind.

Kaja Finkler is Professor of Anthropology (Emerita), University of North Carolina, Chapel Hill. Her specialties include medical anthropology, gender, health and illness, new genetics and reproductive technologies, family and kinship, bioethics, and globalization. She has published numerous articles and five books, including *Experiencing the New Genetics. Family and Kinship on the Medical Frontier* (2000).

Notes

1. National Human Genome Research Institute (2011). See also the special 11 January 1999 issue of *Time Magazine*, which heralds a future of medicine that rests in genetics and genetic engineering.

2. At the time of the inception of the HGP in 1988 its budget was 27.9 million dollars, progressively increasing till in 1998 it had grown to 302.6 million dollars. See National Human Genome Research Institute (1998). The 2011 budget request for the National Human Genome Research Institute (NHGRI) was $533,959,000, an increase of $18,083,000 from the 2010 comparable fiscal year enacted level of $515,876,000 (see http://www.genome.gov/27539063, retrieved 3 November 2016).

3. See especially the case of BiDil (Kahn 2007; and also Wailoo and Pemberton 2006), a medication claimed to be effective only for African Americans.

4. A 1962 article in *Time* refers to the '*baby* science of molecular medicine' ('Inheriting Bad Health' 1962, emphasis added).

5. To quote one geneticist, the major differences between the new genetics and previous beliefs about heredity are 'in our perceptions regarding cause and effect in disease. We have been used to a naïve and incomplete model of causation in which diseases were "caused" by rather simple agents. What we now realize that while external agents are very important in causation, so too are underlying host predispositions' (Evans 2004).

6. One company also provides DNA Infidelity Testing Services (www.gtldna.com.au) if 'your spouse is cheating on you' and you 'find a suspicious article of clothing such as a stained undergarment or other object that could be submitted for testing' (see also Friedman 2015).

7. The ancient Roman goddess of fortune.

8. Following Hacking, probability refers both to a tendency displayed by some chance occurrences to produce stable relative frequencies, and a degree of belief that is supported by evidence from nature and material things rather than by people's testimonies (Hacking 1975). Additionally, according to Daston 'mathematical probability theory was to be the codification of a new brand of rationality that emerged approximately the same time as the theory itself, or rather of a more modest reasonableness that solved everyday dilemmas on the basis of incomplete knowledge, in contrast to the traditional rationality of demonstrative certainty' (1988: xi).

9. While prior to the seventeenth century ideas about determinism prevailed, human beings attempted to control and even predict the future prior to the development of the laws of probability by acts of randomization; for example, when they cut up fowls or by practices such as scapulimancy (Moore 1957). Humans used divination throughout history to help them make decisions about matters for which they lacked information (Wallace 1966). Divination supplied people with the missing information by 'direct, if apparently arbitrary, advice from supernatural authority' (Wallace 1966: 108). Azande oracles, as described by Evans Pritchard (1937), weighted probabilities by consulting a poison oracle, which instructed a person on which actions to take. In the ancient art

of astrology, which was based on the study of movements of the heavenly bodies, the astrologer could 'construct a horoscope for some future point of time, and thus predict the influence the heavens would exert on that occasion' (Thomas 1971: 285). But the astrologers were always at the mercy of the heavens, which ultimately controlled future events (Thomas 1971).

10. The notion of avoiding risk dates back as far as the thirteenth century (Daston 1988), when the medieval church riled against usury and the taking of interest. However, the church accepted the right of an individual to be compensated for the risk of time and distance involved in an exchange transaction. Gradually the church accepted risk as a legitimate basis for charging interest on loans (Daston 1988).

11. See Finkler (2003) for a discussion of the history of probability and risk.

12. It is important to stress that there are numerous interpretations of the notion of predestination. Calvinism, arguably, made the most use of the notion of predestination (Martin 1919). He defined predestination as 'the eternal decree by God, by which he determined with himself whatever he wished to happen with regard to every person' (McIntire 1987: 429).

13. The BRC-1 gene for breast cancer was discovered by dependence on blood samples and family histories from numerous extended families.

14. Most recently researchers are finding that a person may have multiple genomes (Zimmer 2013); and another article about genetic tests reports that numerous mutations are found in an individual that are 'variants of unknown significance' (Grady and Pollack 2014: A1–A19).

15. Except, arguably, among elites in America. See Bellah et al. 1985; Marcus and Hall 1992.

16. This became especially clear to me in a recent as yet unpublished study of colon cancer patients and healthy individuals with a family history of colon cancer. One of the subjects and his wife reported that his young daughter lives with great fear that she has inherited the disease from her father and will similarly become afflicted.

17. As Herzfeld (2007) points out, the Internet may serve as ethnographic analysis.

18. See, for example, Silverman (2015), who describes employers offering free genetic tests to workers, who might fear this on the grounds that they might wish to keep information about themselves secret. No such fears are associated with other tests.

19. There is an extensive literature advancing a theory of the 'self' as usually embedded in a larger group (Giddens 1991: 74). 'The self is something which has a development, it is not initially there at birth but arises in the process of social experience and activity that is, develops in the given individual as a result of his relations to that process ...'; that is, it results from relations with others (Mead 1964: 199, 204; also Finkler 1994). See also Josephides' sophisticated analysis of the literature on the self

and how the 'self' is played out, for example, in traditional Melanesian societies (2008).

20. Until 1 May 2008 people feared genetic testing of any kind in the United States (Harmon 2008c) because they could lose their insurance if, for example, they had a breast cancer gene. On 21 May 2008 the U.S. Congress enacted a law banning bias based on genetic testing (Harmon 2008a: A1–A17; Prainsack 2008) and thus insurance companies and employers can no longer discriminate against a person on the basis of genetic testing. Presumably this law allays fears (Harmon 2008b) about having a genetic test done, a fear that is probably greater in the United States than in other countries with laws of guaranteed healthcare (ibid.). However, insurance companies may still deny life insurance, long-term care insurance or disability insurance without penalty (Harmon 2008c), and the law does not apply to people who have already been diagnosed (Prainsack 2008).

21. The article points out that these networks constructing family trees and family medical histories become medical data useful to researchers.

22. We may already be moving in this direction. On 12 February 2009, *The Wall Street Journal* reported that new laboratory techniques are now moving in the direction of offering 'designer children' (Naik 2009).

23. Witness the exhumation of the 'Unknown Soldier'. Presumably nothing remains unknown (Myers 1998).

24. Writing about post-traumatic stress a similar point is made by Young, who argues correctly that it is not for him to deny or affirm the reality of this phenomenon, but to examine the ways in which ideas of post-traumatic stress enters people's lives (Young 1995).

25. Prominent individuals, such as Henry Louis Gates Jr, have searched for their ethnic heritage, as was reported by Nixon (2007), who points out that Gates submitted his genetic sample to several companies but received conflicting evidence about his roots. See also Peikoff (2013).

26. Synthetic Biology Engineering Research Center (Synberc).

27. See an insightful discussion of revolutionary gene editing techniques that open yet fresh avenues for manipulation of the genetic data (Specter 2015).

References

Allen, G. 1996. 'Science Misapplied: Eugenics Age Revisited', *Technological Review*, August/September, 23–31.

Andrews, L. 1992. 'Torts and the Double Helix: Malpractice Liability for Failure to Warn of Genetic Risks', *Houston Law Review* 29: 150–84.

———. 1994. *Assessing Genetic Risks*. Washington, DC: National Academy Press.

———. 2001. *Future Perfect*. New York: Columbia University Press.

Andrews, L., M. Mehlman and M. Rothstein. 2002. *Genetics: Ethics, Law and Policy*. St. Paul: West Group, American Casebook Series.

Andrews, L. and D. Nelkin. 2001. *Body Bazaar: The Market for Human Tissue in the Biotechnology Age*. New York: Crown Publishers.

Angier, N. 2008. 'Scientists and Philosophers Find that 'Gene' has a Multitude of Meanings', *New York Times*, 11 November, D2.

Angrist, M. 2010. *Here is a Human Being: The Dawn of Personal Genomics*. New York: Harper Collins.

Beck, U. 1992. *The Risk Society*. London: Sage.

———. 1998. 'Politics of Risk Society', in J. Franklin (ed.), *The Politics of Risk Society*. Cambridge: Polity Press.

Begley, S. 2008. 'Lies, Damned Lies and...', *Newsweek*, 21 July, 51.

Bellah, R. et al. 1985. *Habits of the Heart*. Berkeley: University of California Press.

Berger, P. and T. Luckmann. 1966. *The Social Construction of Reality*. Garden City, NY: Anchor Books.

Berkow, R., M. Beers and A. Fletcher. 1997. 'Tests for Genetic Disorders', *Merck Manual Home Edition*, 1129–31.

Billings, P., J. Beckwith and J. Alper. 1992. 'The Genetic Analysis of Human Behavior: A New Era', *Social Science and Medicine* 35: 227–38.

Bloss, C., N. Schorck and E. Topol. 2011. 'Effect of Direct-to-Consumer Genomewide Profiling to Assess Disease Risk', *English Journal of Medicine* 364: 524–34.

Bowler, P. 1989. *The Mendelian Revolution: The Emergence of Hereditarian Concepts in Modern Science and Society*. Baltimore: Johns Hopkins University Press.

Brandt, A. 1997. 'Behavior, Disease, and Health in the Twentieth-Century United States: The Moral Valence of the Individual Risk', in A. Brandt and P. Rozin (eds), *Morality and Health: Interdisciplinary Perspectives*. New York: Routledge, pp. 53–79.

Brody, J. 2009. 'Buyer Beware of At-Home Genetic Tests', *New York Times*, 1 September.

Chase, M. 2008. 'New Gene Links to Breast Cancer Found', *The Wall Street Journal*, 28 April, B11.

Cole, D. 1994. 'Genetic Predestination?', *Dialog* 33: 17–22.

Collins, F. 1999a. 'Designer Genes: The Ethical and Social Implications of Genetic Research', *Key Note Address, James M. Johnson Scholars Issues Forum*, April 15. Chapel Hill: University of North Carolina.

———. 1999b. 'Genetics and Faith', *Lecture to the Christian Physician Association of North Carolina*. Chapel Hill: University of North Carolina.

Cranor, C. 1994. 'Genetic Causation', in C. Cranor (ed.), *Are Genes Us? The Social Consequences of the New Genetics*. New Brunswick, NJ: Rutgers University Press, pp. 125–41.

D'Agincourt-Canning, L. 2001. 'Experiences of Genetic Risk: Disclosure and the Gendering of Responsibility', *Bioethics* 15: 231–47.

Daston, L. 1988. *Classical Probability in the Enlightenment*. Princeton, NJ: Princeton University Press.

Dolgin, J. 2001. 'Ideologies of Discrimination: Personhood and the "Genetic Group"', *Studies in History and Philosophy of Biological and Biomedical Sciences* 32: 705–21.

Dyson, E. 2008. 'Reflections On Privacy 2.0', *Scientific American*, September, 50–55.

Evans, J. 2004. Personal Communication. University Hospital, University of North Carolina, Chapel Hill.

———. 2008. 'Recreational Genomics: What's In It for You', *Genetics in Medicine* 10(10): 709–10.

Evans, J., C. Skrynia and W. Burke. 2001. 'The Complexities of Predictive Genetic Testing', *British Medical Journal* 322: 1052–56.

Evans Pritchard, E.E. 1937. *Witchcraft, Oracles and Magic among the Azande*. Oxford: Oxford University Press.

Everett, M. 2003. 'The Social Life of Genes: Privacy, Property and the New Genetics', *Social Science & Medicine* 56: 53–65.

———. 2004. 'Can You Keep a Genetic Secret? The Genetic Privacy Movement', *Journal of Genetic Counseling* 13: 273–91.

Farriss, N. 1995. 'Remembering the Future, Anticipating the Past: History, Time and Cosmology among the Maya of Yucatan', in D. Hughes and T. Trautmann (eds), *Time: Histories and Ethnologies*. Ann Arbor: University of Michigan Press, pp. 107–38.

Finkler, K. 1994. *Women in Pain*. Philadelphia: University of Pennsylvania Press.

———. 2000a. *Experiencing the New Genetics: Family and Kinship on the Medical Frontier*. Philadelphia: University of Pennsylvania Press.

———. 2000b. 'Living with the New Genetics and Fearing the Future', paper presented at the 2000 American Ethnological Society Meeting, 23–25 March. Tampa, Florida.

———. 2001. 'The Kin in the Gene: The Medicalization of Family and Kinship', *Current Anthropology* 42(2): 235–63.

———. 2003. 'Illusion of Controlling the Future: Risk and Genetic Inheritance', *Anthropology & Medicine* 10(1): 51–70.

———. 2005. 'Family, Kinship, Memory and Temporality in the Age of the New Genetics', *Social Science and Medicine* 61: 1059–71.

———. 2007. 'The Application of the Theory of Life's Lesions to the Study of the Menopausal Transition', *Journal of the North American Menopause Society* 14(4): 769–76.

———. 2008. 'Can Bioethics be Global or Local, or Must it be Both?', *Journal of Contemporary Ethnography* 37(2): 155–79.

Finkler, K., C. Skrzynia and J. Evans. 2003. 'The New Genetics and its Consequences for Family, Kinship, Medicine and Medical Genetics', *Social Science & Medicine* 57(3): 403–12.

Fox Keller, E. 1986. 'Making Gender Visible in the Pursuit of Nature's Secrets',
    in T. de Lauretis (ed.), *Feminist Studies/Critical Studies*. Bloomington:
    Indiana University Press, pp. 67–77.
———. 1992. 'Nature, Nurture, and the Human Genome Project', in
    J. Kevles and L. Hood (eds), *The Code of Codes: Scientific and Social Issues
    in the Human Genome Project*. Cambridge, MA: Harvard University Press,
    pp. 281–99.
———. 1994. 'Master Molecules', in C. Cranor (ed.), *Are Genes Us? The Social
    Consequences of the New Genetics*. New Brunswick, NJ: Rutgers University
    Press, pp. 89–98.
———. 2000. *The Century of the Gene*. Cambridge, MA: Harvard University
    Press.
Friedman, R. 2015. 'Infidelity Lurks in Your Genes', *The New York Times*, 24
    May (Sunday Review), 1–4.
Fujimura, J. 1996. *Crafting Science: A Sociohistory of the Quest for the Genetics
    of Cancer*. Cambridge, MA: Harvard University Press.
———. 2000. 'Translational Genetics: Transgressing the Boundary
    between the "Modern/West" and the "Premodern/East"', in R. Reid
    and S. Traweek (eds), *Doing Science + Culture*. New York: Routledge,
    pp. 71–94.
'Genetics and Lung Cancer: Smoking Out the Smoking Gene'. 2008. *The
    Economist*, 5 April, 83.
Giddens, A. 1991. *Modernity and Self Identity*. Stanford: Stanford University
    Press.
Gilkey, L. 1968. 'Evolutionary Science and the Dilemma of Freedom and
    Determinism', in K. Haselden and P. Hefner (eds), *Changing Man*. Garden
    City, NY: Doubleday & Co.
Glasner, P. and H. Rothman. 2001. 'New Genetics, New Ethics? Globalization
    and its Discontents', *Health, Risk and Society* 3: 245–59.
Grady, D. and A. Pollak. 2014. 'Finding Risks Not Answers, in Gene Tests', *The
    New York Times*, A1–A19.
Greely, H. 1998. 'Legal, Ethical and Social Issues in Human Genome Research',
    Annual Reviews of Anthropology 27: 473–502.
Griesemer, J. 1994. 'Tools for Talking: Human Nature, Weismannism, and the
    Interpretation of Genetic Information', in C. Cranor (ed.), *Are Genes Us?
    The Social Consequences of the New Genetics*. New Brunswick, NJ: Rutgers
    University Press, pp. 69–88.
Hacking, I. 1975. *The Emergence of Probability*. Cambridge: Cambridge
    University Press.
———. 1990. *The Taming of Chance*. Cambridge: Cambridge University Press.
Hadler, N. and J. Evans. 2001. 'Comments', *Current Anthropology* 42(2):
    252–53.
Hahn, R. and A.R. Kleinman. 1983. 'Biomedical Practice and Anthropological
    Theory: Frameworks and Directions', *Annual Review of Anthropology* 12:
    305–33.

Haraway, D.J. 1991. *Simians, Cyborgs, and Women: The Reinvention of Nature*. New York: Routledge.

Harmon, A. 2007a. 'In DNA Era, New Worries about Prejudice Surface', *New York Times*, 11 November.

———. 2007b. 'Learning My Genome, Learning About Myself', *New York Times*, 17 November, A1–A14.

———. 2008a 'Congress Clears Bill to Bar Bias Based on Genes', *New York Times*, 3 May, A1–A17.

———. 2008b. 'Fear of Insurance Trouble Leads Many to Shun or Hide DNA Tests', *The New York Times (National)*, 24 February, 1–19.

———. 2008c. 'Personal Genomes Going Public on Web, for the Sake of Research', *The New York Times*, 20 October, A1–A17.

Harvey, D. 1989. *The Condition of Postmodernity*. Cambridge: Basil Blackwell.

Herzfeld, M. 2007. 'Deskilling, "Dumbing Down" and the Auditing of Knowledge in the Practical Mastery of Artisans and Academics: An Ethnographer's Response to a Global Problem', in M. Harris (ed.), *Ways of Knowing: New Approaches in the Anthropology of Experience and Learning*. New York and Oxford: Berghahn Books, pp. 91–112.

Hess, D. 1997. *Science Studies*. New York: New York University Press.

Holy, L. 1996. *Anthropological Perspectives on Kinship*. Chicago: Pluto Press.

Hood, L. 1992. 'Biology and Medicine in the Twenty-First Century', in J. Kevles and L. Hood (eds), *The Code of Codes: Scientific and Social Issues in the Human Genome Project*. Cambridge, MA: Harvard University Press, pp. 136–63.

Hubbard, R. and E. Wald. 1997. *Exploding the Gene Myth*. Boston, MA: Beacon Press.

Ingleby, D. 1982. 'The Social Construction of Mental Illness', in P. Wright and A. Treacher (eds), *The Problem of Medical Knowledge: Examining the Social Construction of Medicine*. Edinburgh: Edinburgh University Press, pp. 123–44. 'Inheriting Bad Health'. 1962. *Time*, 2 February, 37.

Jonsen, A.R. 1996. 'The Impact of Mapping the Human Genome on the Patient-Physician Relationship', in T.H. Murray, M.A. Rothstein and R.F. Murray (eds), *The Human Genome Project and the Future of Health Care*. Indianapolis: Indiana University Press, pp. 1–20.

Josephides, L. 2008. *Melanesian Odysseys: Negotiating the Self, Narrative, and Modernity*. New York and Oxford: Berghahn Books.

Kahn, J. 2007. 'Race in a Bottle', *Scientific American*, August, 40–45.

Kalb, C. 2008. 'May We Scan Your Genome?', *Newsweek*, 21 April, 44.

Kay, L. 2000. *Who Wrote the Book of Life? A History of the Genetic Code*. Stanford: Stanford University Press.

Kevles, D. 1992. 'Out of Eugenics: The Historical Politics of the Human Genome', in J. Kevles and L. Hood (eds), *The Code of Codes: Scientific and Social Issues in the Human Genome Project*. Cambridge, MA: Harvard University Press.

Khoury, M. 2003. 'Genetics and Genomics in Practice: The Continuum from Genetic Disease to Genetic Information in Health and Disease', *Genetics in Medicine* 5(4): 261–68.

Khoury, M. et al. 2009. 'The Scientific Foundation for Personal Genomics: Recommendations from National Institutes of Health, Centers for Disease Control and Prevention, Multidisciplinary Workshop'. *Genetic Medicine*, 556–67. Retrieved from https://www.ncbi.nlm.nih.gov.

Krieger, N. and E. Fee. 1994. 'Man-made Medicine and Women's Health: The Biopolitics of Sex/Gender and Race/Ethnicity', *International Journal of Health Services* 24: 265–83.

Latour, B. 1987. *Science and Action*. Cambridge: Harvard University Press.

Latour, B. and S. Woolgar. 1979. *Laboratory Life: The Social Construction of Scientific Fact*. Beverly Hills: Sage.

Lewontin, R.C. 1992. *Biology as Ideology*. New York: Harper Perennial.

Lewontin, R.C., S. Rose and L. Kamin. 1984. *Not in Our Genes: Biology, Ideology and Human Nature*. New York: Pantheon.

Lloyd, E.A. 1994. 'Normality and Variation: The Human Genome Project and the Ideal Human Type', in C. Cranor (ed.), *Are Genes Us? The Social Consequences of the New Genetics*. New Brunswick: Rutgers University Press, pp. 99–112.

Lock, M. and D. Gordon. 1988. *Biomedicine Examined*. Dordrecht: Kluwer Academic.

Marcus, G. and P. Hall. 1992. *Lives in Trust. The Fortunes of Dynastic Families in Late Twentieth-Century America*. Boulder: Westview Press.

Marteau, T. and C. Lerman. 2001. 'Genetic Risk and Behavioral Change', *British Medical Journal* 322: 1056–59.

Martin, A.S. 1919. 'Predestination', in J. Hastings (ed.), *Encyclopedia of Religion and Ethics*. New York: Charles Scribner's Sons.

Martin, E. 1997. 'The Egg and the Sperm', in L. Lamphere, H. Ragone and P. Zavella (eds), *Situated Lives: Gender and Culture in Everyday Life*. New York: Routledge, pp. 85–98.

McIntire, C.T. 1987. 'Free Will and Predestination: Christian Concepts', in M. Eliade (ed.), *The Encyclopedia of Religion*. New York: Macmillan, pp. 427–29.

Mead, G. 1964. *On Social Psychology: Selected Papers*. Chicago: Chicago University Press.

Minicuci, M. 1995. 'Time and Memory: Two Villages in Calabria', in D. Hughes and T. Trautmann (eds), *Time: Histories and Ethnologies*. Ann Arbor: University of Michigan Press, pp. 71–104.

Monod, J. 1971. *Chance and Necessity: An Essay on the Natural Philosophy of Modern Biology*. New York: Knopf.

Moore, O.K. 1957. 'Divination – A New Perspective', *American Anthropologist* 59(1): 69–74.

Myers, S.L. 1998. 'Laying to Rest the Last of the Unknown Soldiers', *New York Times*, 2 September, 2.

Naik, G. 2009. 'A Baby, Please: Blond, Freckles – Hold the Colic', *The Wall Street Journal*, 12 February, A10.

Nash, M. 1994. 'Riding the DNA Trail', *Time* 143(3): 154.

National Human Genome Research Institute. 2011. Retrieved from https://www.genome.gov/11007524/nhgris-vision-for-the-future-of-genomic-research.

Nelkin, D. 1992. 'The Social Power of Genetic Information', in D. Kevles and L. Hood (eds), *The Code of Codes: Scientific and Social Issues in the Human Genome Project*. Cambridge, MA: Harvard University Press.

Nelkin, D. and M.S. Lindee. 1995. *The DNA Mystique*. New York: Freeman.

Nixon, R. 2007. 'DNA Tests Find Branches but Few Roots', *New York Times*, 25 November, 1.

Palsson, G. and K. Haroardottir. 2002. 'For Whom the Cell Tolls. Debates about Biomedicine', *Current Anthropology* 43(2): 271–301.

Patsner, B. 2008. 'Direct to Consumer Genetic Testing: Think Before You Spit'. Retrieved 4 November 2016 https://www.law.uh.edu/healthlaw/perspectives/2008/(BP)%20spit.pdf

Peikoff, K. 2013. 'I Had My DNA Picture Taken'. *New York Times*, 31 December, D1–D6.

Pinker, S. 2009. 'My Genome, My Self', *New York Times Magazine*, 11 January, 24–50.

Pollack, A. 2008. 'Redefining Disease, Genes and All', *New York Times*, 6 May, D1–D4.

———. 2009. 'Questioning a Test for Cancer', *New York Times*, 7 November, B1–B2.

———. 2010. 'Outlook Uncertain: Consumers are Slow to Embrace DNA Scanning for Health Risks', *New York Times*, 20 March, B1.

Prainsack, B. 2008. 'What are the Stakes? Genetic Nondiscrimination Legislation and Personal Genomics', *Personalized Medicine* 5(5): 415–18.

Rabinow, P. 1999. *French DNA: Trouble in Purgatory*. Chicago: Chicago University Press.

———. 2011. *The Accompaniment*. Chicago: Chicago University Press.

Richards, M. 1993. 'The New Genetics: Some Issues for Social Scientists', *Sociology of Health & Illness* 15: 567–86.

Richter, M.N. 1972. *Science as a Cultural Process*. Cambridge: Schenkman.

Rockhill, B. 2001. 'The Privatization of Risk', *American Journal of Public Health* 91(3): 365–68.

Rose, S. 1993. *The Making of Memory*. New York: Anchor Books Doubleday.

———. 1997. *Lifelines*. Oxford: Oxford University Press.

Rose, N. and C. Novas. 2005 'Biological Citizenship', in A. Ong and S. Collier (eds), *Global Assemblages: Technology, Politics and Ethics as Anthropological Problems*. Malden, MA: Blackwell Publishing, pp. 439–463.

Rubin, R. 2008. 'Are You My Cousin?', *AARP Magazine*, November/December, 43–69.

Salkin, A. 2008. 'When in Doubt, Spit it Out', *New York Times*, 14 September, Sunday Styles, 1–10.

Seabrook, J. 2001. 'The Tree of Me', *The New Yorker*, 26 March, 58–71.

Sharp, L. 2000. 'The Commodification of the Body and its Parts', *Annual Review of Anthropology* 29: 287–328.

Shute, N. 2008. 'A High-Tech Family Tree', *U.S. News & World Report*, 14 January, 41–43.

Silver, L. 1998. *Remaking Eden*. New York: Avon Books.

Silverman, R.E. 2015. 'Genetic Testing May Be Coming to Your Office', *The Wall Street Journal*, 16 December, B1–B6.

Simpson, B. 2004. 'Acting Ethically, Responding Culturally', *Journal of Asian Pacific Anthropology* 5: 227–43.

Soares, C. 2007. Genetics: Attitude Screen', *Scientific American*, August, 25–26.

Spanier, B. 1995. *Im/Partial Science*. Bloomington: Indiana University Press.

Specter, M. 2015. 'The Gene Hackers. The Promise of CRISPR Technology', *The New Yorker*, 16 September, 52–61.

Strathern, M. 2005. *Kinship, Law and the Unexpected: Relatives Are Always a Surprise*. New York: Cambridge University Press.

Thomas, K. 1971. *Religion and the Decline of Magic*. New York: Scribner.

Tocqueville, A. 1980 [1835]. *Democracy in America*, P. Bradley (ed.). New York: Knopf.

Turner, B. 1987. *Medical Power and Social Knowledge*. London: Sage.

———. 1992. *Regulating Bodies: Essays in Medical Sociology*. London: Routledge.

Wade, N. 2007 'Experts Advise a Grain of Salt with Mail-Order Genomes, at $1,000 a Pop', *New York Times*, 17 November, A14.

———. 2009. 'DeCode Genetics is Bankrupt, a Victim of its Research', *New York Times*, 18 November.

———. 2010. 'A Decade Later, Gene Map Yields Few New Cures', *New York Times*, 13 June, 1.

Wailoo, K. and S. Pemberton. 2006. *The Troubled Dream of Genetic Medicine*. Baltimore: The Johns Hopkins University Press.

Wallace, A. 1966. *Religion: An Anthropological View*. New York: Random House.

Weiss, R. 2008. 'Genetic Testing Gets Personal', *Washington Post*, 25 March, A1.

Wertz, D. 1992. 'Ethical and Legal Implications of the New Genetics: Issues for Discussion', *Social Science and Medicine* 35: 495–505.

Wilde Mathews, A. 2008. 'Which Genetic Tests are Really Worth Getting?', *The Wall Street Journal*, 1 May, D1–D6.

Winslow, R. and S.S. Wang. 2012. 'Soon, $1,000 Will Map Genes', *The Wall Street Journal*, 10 January, A2.

Wolf, S. 1995. 'Beyond Genetic Discrimination: Toward the Broader Harm of Geneticism', *Journal of Law, Medicine & Ethics* 23: 345–53.

Wright, P. and A. Treacher. 1982. *The Problem of Medical Knowledge: Examining the Social Construction of Medicine.* Edinburgh: Edinburgh University Press.

Young, A. 1981. 'The Creation of Medical Knowledge: Some Problems in Interpretation', *Social Science and Medicine* 15B: 379–86.

———. 1995. *The Harmony of Illusions.* Princeton: Princeton University Press.

Zimmer, C. 2013. 'DNA Double Take', *New York Times* (*Science Times*), 17 September, D1–D4.

Chapter 7

BIOTECHNOLOGY, LAW AND SOME PROBLEMS OF KNOWING

Marit Melhuus

Introduction

Reproductive technologies in Norway, as elsewhere in the world, have had an ambivalent reception. Although there is an acceptance and certain legitimacy for the use and application of reproductive technologies, they continue to be a site of moral indeterminacy and ethical publicity (Cohen 1999). This is articulated in connection with the legislative processes regarding the use of such technologies in Norway, reflected in the parliamentary debates (and documents serving these debates) and, not least, in the media more generally. These debates and documents are the main 'sites' for my discussion. As Simpson (2004) observes, ethical publicity 'invariably draws on the core values of society, culture, and religion to shape the motivation to give in each particular context' (2004: 2). As I hope to show, the motivational grounding of the public debates regarding the application of biotechnology in Norway are revealing of some tensions about core values in Norwegian society. These pivot around issues of kinship, choice, the individual and society. They involve questions of knowledge, secrecy and truth – as well as the implications of knowing or not-knowing.

There is no consensus – among legislators or the public at large – about the regulations of reproductive and associated technologies, as there is no consensus about the potential benefits or harm that these technologies entail. However, there has been a consensus about the need to regulate. The law regulating biotechnology in Norway is based on a precautionary principle. Two dimensions can be discerned in this act of caution. One has to do with the responsibility or obligation legislators have towards society; the other has to do with visions of a good society as well as what is deemed right. Thus a notion of ethics is inscribed in the very making of the legislation; it forms part of its motivational grounding. According to Pottage, the essential premise of the precautionary principle is that 'technologies that have the potential to cause massive and irreversible harm should be subject to regulation even in the absence of the likelihood of such harm ... the precautionary principle effectively becomes the basis for a very specific mode of balancing technological evolution and potential social harm' (Pottage 2007: 333). Although it would be an exaggeration to state that reproductive technologies in Norway are viewed as potentially causing 'massive harm', there is no doubt that an unrestricted application of these technologies has been – and is – considered as implying potential social harm, and that such harm is also, by some, considered irreversible. It has, therefore, been deemed prudent to regulate in a precautionary mode: better safe than sorry.

As I have argued elsewhere, this legislation can be seen as an expression of a particular imagination – perhaps even an act of the imagination (Melhuus 2007, 2012a). This imagination translates biotechnology into a legal framework – a regulatory regime and a precautionary mode. Imagination, then, does moral work: it is imagining what these technologies and/or practices might entail for a society that has informed a restrictive policy. Fuelling this imagination are ideas of society as well as ideas of nature – or 'the natural' – as these are articulated through notions of maternity, paternity and filiation. Thus, for example, there has been a consistent prohibition on egg donation, in order to maintain a unitary motherhood; a prolonged tension regarding anonymous sperm donation (as this conceals the 'true' father; see below); and fundamental disagreements about the moral status of the embryo, and hence whether or not to permit research on embryos.

The precautionary principle is not just a legal strategy for managing risk, it is also a political strategy for protecting and promulgating sociocultural values deemed central to Norwegian society. Reproductive and associated technologies have been – and still are by some – seen as not only potentially upsetting fundamental kinship categories in Norway, but also as challenging the very idea of a good society. The preamble to the Biotechnology Act[1] explicitly states that the aim of the law is to ensure that the medical use of biotechnology is used in the best interests of human beings in a society where there is room for all (§ 1–1). The preamble underscores an explicit value of equality, while implicitly refuting the potential dangers that, for example, prenatal diagnosis may imply for the sorting away of undesirable individuals. It is the possible corrosive effects of the technologies cum practices that guide the 'regime of caution' (Pottage 2007: 334). What appears to be at risk is not so much the individual body as the social body (Scheper-Hughes and Lock 1987).

In what follows, my focus is intentionally narrow. My point of departure is the Norwegian Biotechnology Act, and more specifically the debates surrounding certain provisions in this Act. I am interested in how ethics is embedded in the '"politics" of life politics' (Haimes 2002: 105), or to extend Keane's term, in 'the ethical life' of politics (Keane 2015: 128). Thus my focus is how a specific biopolitics is articulated and issued and what role knowledge plays in this process. I draw on two examples. They will serve to illustrate interrelationships between policy, technology and knowledge. The two provisions that concern me in this context are those that (1) regulate the use of donor sperm and (2) regulate the application of prenatal diagnosis, more specifically the debates surrounding what is termed 'early ultrasound' *(tidlig ultralyd)*.[2] Both these provisions have been exceptionally controversial. Both are inscribed in particular (though different) historical trajectories. And in both cases, the controversies have attracted the attention of the media and the public at large. They both constitute and are constitutive of an ethical publicity.

Although these two provisions regulate very different practices – one involves assisted conception, the other ascertains the condition of a foetus – they nevertheless address an overall problematic pertinent to my discussion. Both provisions pivot on the availability of specific biological information, its relevance for particular subjects and, hence, on questions of knowing. In different ways, they also articulate a tension between knowing and 'not-knowing', or knowledge and ignorance (Dilley 2010). Working at the interface between science and politics, this tension is instructive in coming to grips with some of the critical issues that have surfaced in the Norwegian debates, disclosing some underlying values and relational implications. I explore the contrasting attitudes to knowledge and knowing that these two legal provisions imply, indicating that they come with different effects. In this effort I take some inspiration from Marilyn Strathern (1999), drawing on her idea that kinship knowledge has certain built-in effects and about how 'knowledge about how persons are related to one another is acquired from ... information about biological process' (Strathern 1999: 65). It is the meanings of biological information and the role it plays in these two cases that draws my attention. This has to do with how 'knowledge itself imposes an obligation on *the knower*', being the cause of moral action and creating a compulsion to act (Strathern 2005a: 6, my emphasis). At issue is also the question of who 'the knower' is.

However, before turning to these questions, some background information on the legislative process in Norway seems pertinent. This will set a particular context.

Background

Ever since the first attempt to regulate artificial insemination in Norway in the early 1950s, assisted conception has been a public issue. Norway passed its first law regulating what was then called 'artificial procreation' (limiting its provisions to assisted conception) in 1987. In 1994 Norway passed its first biotechnology law incorporating the earlier regulations on assisted conception. Since then the law has been revised twice (2003, 2007), and is currently (in 2016) under evaluation for further revision. The present Biotechnology Act regulates, inter alia, within one and the same act assisted conception, research on embryos, cloning, pre-implantation diagnosis, prenatal diagnosis, postnatal genetic testing and gene therapy. This act is on the whole rather restrictive: for example, it prohibits egg donation; it prescribes the use of known donor sperm; it does not permit surrogacy; it restricts the application of pre-implantation diagnosis and also of prenatal diagnosis; and although it permits research on supernumerary embryos (under certain specifications), this provision was first passed in 2007.[3]

Assisted conception is provided within the public health service. Until the passing of the new gender-neutral marriage act (2008), granting same sex and cross-sex couples the same rights, assisted conception was limited to heterosexual couples. With this act, lesbian married couples have the right to access infertility treatment within the public health services. Male homosexual couples, however, do not have this right, as Norway does not permit surrogacy arrangements (see Melhuus 2011). However, they do have the right to adopt, although in practice this is difficult, as most adoptions in Norway are transnational (few Norwegian children are put up for adoption; see Howell 2006) and most donor countries do not allow adoption to homosexual couples.

A few points regarding the legislative process are pertinent for my further discussion. They concern prevailing attitudes towards the issue of regulation and the issue of knowledge.[4] Obviously, in such a brief exposition, I cannot do justice to the various positions. My intention is to convey some of the dominant ideas that have surfaced in the discussions, as well as a certain feel of the zeitgeist.

At the political level, positions have shifted over time, and varying constellations between the political parties represented in Parliament have ensured majority votes. The main divide runs between those who are pro technology and pro research and those who are much more sceptical. In general terms, the Labour Party has consistently responded positively to developments in biotechnology and proposed the most liberal regulations (with support from the Progress Party) whereas the Christian Democratic Party has been most restrictive. The latter have had varying support from the Conservative Party and the Liberal Party. The Socialist Left Party has shifted its position from a more restrictive one earlier on, to a more liberal one. However, an interesting datum is that positions within each party have varied and alliances have cut across party lines.[5] Moreover, except for the last revision in 2007, permitting research on supernumerary embryos, those holding a more restrictive attitude have held the majority.[6]

The 1987 legislation came in the wake of the birth of the first so-called test-tube baby in Norway in 1984. At this point, there was a perceived need to regulate assisted conception – lest matters get out of hand. (This was before the global fertility market subverted all attempts at national control.) A fear was articulated concerning the implications of the technologies as well as the uncertainties that these technologies created, especially with respect to maternity (its potential fragmentation), paternity and questions about the 'truth' of filiation (with regard to donor sperm). This fear was expressed as a resistance to 'meddling with nature' *(tukle med naturen)*, an interference with the natural processes of procreation, and as an opposition to making human beings a means rather than an end (e.g., embryo research). The general feeling I gleaned from my interviews (and the parliamentary debates) was that the potentialities of the technologies were awesome – even frightening. A sense of the inevitable was evoked: once such processes were set in motion, they are almost impossible to reverse. Legislation was viewed as a way to contain the developments within the field of reproductive technologies, to ensure that these practices came under public authority, and not least as an effort to control effects that might potentially be harmful to society.[7] A precautionary principle framed this first Act and two overriding concerns were expressed regarding the aim of the legislation: to secure the best interests of the child and to ensure the interests of society, by hindering selective human breeding and the commercialization of reproduction (Innst. O nr 60. 1986–1987: 2).

The attitude that Parliament and government have an obligation to act on behalf of society in these matters was a salient feature of the reflections of all the politicians, no matter what their position on each specific issue. Moreover, I was told, it was their job as legislators to make a law that is congruent with their visions of and obligations to society. Interestingly, the very idea of society was not problematized. The implication is that it is known what kind of society is being invoked. My point, however, is that the very notion of society carries rhetorical weight. And it does so in two ways, articulating or even conflating 'is' and 'ought'. On the one hand, acting on behalf of society implies an idea of representing 'society' as it is. On the other hand, the obligation to society entails an imagining of what society ought to be. It evokes a notion of a good society. (I return to this below.) Moreover, in Norway state and society are often expressed as coterminous. They become one.[8]

At the time of the first legislation of assisted conception, people on the whole – including the politicians – were ignorant of the technologies and practices that were to be regulated. This lack of knowledge on the part of the legislators was explicitly voiced. Although expressing an excitement about being party to the making of a new law ('of making history' as one person said), many nevertheless did not feel sufficiently informed about reproductive technologies and the practices they entailed, yet were well aware that the little they knew was more than their party colleagues knew.[9] The need to know more was balanced against the need to regulate. However, iterated at the same time was scepticism to scientific expertise, especially among those for restricting the application of reproductive technologies. There was a prevailing attitude that it is in the nature of scientists that if left to their own devices will always push to supersede certain limits. Scientists have an innate drive to renew and refine technologies continually, making possible procedures that were unthinkable only a few years earlier. Therefore, I was told, one cannot leave it to the individual practitioner – or scientist – to decide what is right. As new knowledge displaces old it is the task of legislators to keep pace and preferably be ahead of such technological developments. Others who were more positive to research argued to the contrary, saying that it is impossible to be ahead of developments and the best we can do is regulate ex post facto.[10]

Opinions on these matters work at the interface between 'research' in the field of medical biotechnology[11] and government, articulating a process of political negotiation where knowledge is transacted. One argument that implicitly reflects attitudes to science, and by implication ethics, has to do with the relation between expert and lay knowledge with regard to 'knowing what is right'. Keeping in mind that this was a new law, and that the technologies to be regulated were perceived as awesome, it is not surprising that the situation was considered out of the ordinary. In fact, the legislation itself was considered extraordinary and the issues to be treated as beyond ordinary politics. This distinction (between the ordinary and the extraordinary) points to the significance of the matter being regulated and hence to the values that underpin it, and the ethics that frame the legislation. In the view of the legislators, the law was grounded in other values than those represented by expert knowledge (cf. the precautionary principle).[12] In lieu of the extraordinary situation, ethics was not considered a field for experts (alone).[13] On the contrary, sound ethical judgements could just as well be made by non-experts – that is, ordinary people. The legislators placed themselves in this category. Thus with regard to 'knowing what is right', lay knowledge was privileged. This occurred in two senses.

On the one hand, the notion of personal convictions – or conscience – was raised. Matters regarding essential life processes are understood as being, in the last instance, a question of *livssyn*. Livssyn is a Norwegian term that literally translates as 'philosophy of life' or worldview, and alludes to belief, personal conviction/conscience but not necessarily religious. The application of reproductive technologies was – and is – considered vital and hence cannot be reduced to 'ordinary' politics. The exceptional nature of these vital issues appeals to personal conscience and thus any decision rests ultimately on each person's (in this case legislator's) individual values of what is right (whether these are grounded in religion or not). On the other hand, the meaning of 'lay' has to do with common sense *(sunn fornuft)*, which is generally viewed positively in Norway, as it reflects the sound judgements of ordinary people – *folket*. The vernacular term, *folk*, takes on a special meaning in the Nordic languages. Something that is associated with folk is often seen as authentic, inclusive and more trustworthy than its contrary, which is the elite – or in this case, the experts (Lien and Melhuus 2009). Thus common sense, which implicitly rests on personal convictions (livssyn), gains authority.

In such extraordinary matters, a layperson is as entitled, if not more entitled, as the expert in the field to an informed opinion, and common sense may ground such an opinion. In other words, and to repeat a point already made, you do not necessarily need to be an expert to know what is right. This attitude was reflected in the questions related to knowledge/science and competence-building on two counts: it challenged the authority of scientific experts and it located biotechnology within a moral universe. Thus, the legislation was placed squarely within the realm of ethics – and ethics was not considered a matter only for experts. The debates in Parliament were framed as ethical and ethics was at the same time seen as a premise for the same debates. This is borne out by the very application of a precautionary principle and the attempts to limit the extent of and access to reproductive and associated technologies, as well as research to further such practices.

As mentioned, in 1994 the Act regulating assisted conception was incorporated into the Biotechnology Act. In addition to extending the scope of the regulation, some adjustments were made to existing practices (although the Act was still restrictive on the most controversial issues). For example, the permitted period for storing embryos was extended from one to three years, and access to assisted conception was extended to women living in stable partnerships with men (and not just to married couples). However, a proposal to permit IVF with donor sperm (which was not allowed, as the combined technologies made for 'more manipulation') did not pass; nor did a proposal (by the Labour Party) to permit research on embryos under certain conditions. To permit egg donation was not even an issue. With the change in government in 2001 (from Labour to Christian Democrat/Centre/Liberal) there was a significant shift in the legislation. With this government the anonymity clause regarding donor sperm was repealed. Some adjustments to existing practices were also made (e.g., extending the storage of embryos from three to five years, and granting permission, under certain conditions, to store egg cells). Thus in addition to reflecting the contested nature of the technologies, the continual revisions also indicated a gradual normalization, if not naturalization, of these practices.

The revisions also tell us that legislation is seen as a meaningful way of dealing with developments in science and technology. Just as technology is socially informed '[where] specifically desired ends are built into the knowledge and techniques associated with biomedicine, biosciences, and biotechnology' (Franklin and Lock 2005: 5), so also, I suggest, is legislation. Scientific progress is in a sense embodied in the very law that Norwegian legislators propose (and have proposed), as biological facts are incorporated in the legal discourse. However, this incorporation is not unproblematic and the effects are various. I turn now to an illustration.

Sperm Donation and the Question of Anonymity

In 2003, Norway rescinded its anonymity clause with regard to sperm donation. The current Act prescribes the use of known donor sperm, stating that 'Any person who is born as a result of medically assisted reproduction using donated sperm has the right to information on the sperm donor's identity at the age of 18. A donor register shall assist the child in this matter'.[14] However, the law does not oblige the parents to inform the child about the way it was conceived. This move was the culmination of a legal process that had been going on since the early nineteen-fifties. Ever since the first attempt in 1953 to regulate artificial insemination by donor (AID), as it was then called, the question of donor anonymity has been controversial. In what follows, I will trace the shifting arguments regarding the use of anonymous sperm. At issue are meanings of marriage, questions of paternity and filiation and how they turn on the links between biology, identity and the rights of the child. At the heart of the matter lie secrecy and truth and the implications of knowing or not knowing your biological origin. These implications have been variously understood.

In the early nineteen fifties, the question of sperm donation became a public issue. At the same time as the Norwegian government had appointed a committee to evaluate possible legal regulation, articles (and even a book) on AID were being published. It was known that sperm donation was practised (Løvset 1951; Molne 1976). The question was whether this practice should be regulated. Public opinions on the matter were vociferous. The committee submitted its report in 1953,[15] and they were divided in their conclusion. The majority was in favour of a regulation. However, no regulation was passed at that time. I will briefly recapitulate the main arguments for and against.[16]

The institution of marriage was a central reference point for the committee's deliberations. It was taken for granted. Moreover, the committee assumed the principle of pater est (the father of the child is the man married to its mother). In fact, this principle was the basis upon which other arguments rested. The debates for and against AID shifted between biological and psychological arguments, between nature and nurture and the moral connotations these evoke with respect to what is natural, good and right. Arguments on both sides centred on marriage, home and love on the one hand, and women's natural desire to have children and the significance of infertility for male identity on the other. The act of lying and the introduction of a third party in marriage are themes constantly reiterated. For those in favour of permitting AID, nurture was given weight over nature. It was argued that what was important for the psychological development of a child was not its biological relationship to its father, but its home environment. At the same time, the majority underscored the significance of the donor child's biological relatedness to its mother, as an important contributing element towards strengthening the bond between the spouses. Those who were against AID turned the arguments around. They pointed to the fact that homes are not harmonious, and that divorce was increasing. Furthermore, they insisted that a child biologically linked to its mother and not its father could create tensions between the spouses rather than foster unity. Most significantly, they claimed that introducing a third party into a marriage is equivalent to undermining that very institution, 'driving a wedge into the very life principle of the home', a violation of its very sacredness (1953: 50, 54).[17]

Those in favour saw AID as a means for women to realize their natural desire to become 'real mothers'. This desire belongs naturally to marriage and contributes to realizing its full potential. At the same time, it is argued that insemination by donor allows the husband to overcome his feelings of inferiority (attributed to him because of his lack of fertility) in that his wife will bear him a child that in the eyes of society is his (biological child). And this is the crux of the matter.

Donor insemination implied secrecy, creating an 'as if' situation. For the minority, the uncertainty of the child's origin was in itself sufficient to destabilize the marriage; the husband will daily be reminded of his incompetence: 'he has by his side a wife whose motherhood is real, while his fatherhood is false' (1953: 54). Insemination by donor was said 'to conceal the truth and proscribes secrecy about the mutual relations amongst a series of people ... and ... departs from the principle of biological fatherhood' (1953: 56). This argument was linked to the postulate that 'the insemination child will lack true knowledge of its origin and therefore also of itself'. Although this identity argument was not prominent in the 1950s, it is precisely this argument that gained salience in the 1990s. A child's right to know its biological origin is viewed as a precondition for knowing who he or she is. The truth of biological relatedness is upheld – but in favour of the child, not the biological father.[18]

When assisted conception was first regulated in 1987, sperm donation was legalized and anonymous sperm was made the norm. However, already at this time there were voices insisting that it is the right of a child to know its biological origin. There were also those who were against sperm donation altogether (especially members of the Norwegian Church),[19] arguing that this practice would split the biological unity of mother, father and child, by introducing a third party, echoing the earlier arguments. In 1994 the question of donor anonymity was debated in Parliament, and several of the members of Parliament argued for rescinding the anonymity clause, again with reference to a person's right to know its biological origin. Those arguing against (the Labour Party especially) rescinding the anonymity clause stated that doing so would be tantamount to a social experiment, whose consequences are difficult to foresee. To give the child the right to know a father who has never wished to be that child's father was just not tenable. An additional argument for upholding the anonymity clause had to do with the availability of sperm.

At this time, Norway imported most of the sperm used from a sperm bank in Denmark. As Denmark upheld the practice of anonymous sperm, this would no longer be possible, and hence the very offer of AID would not be available in Norway. Those in want of anonymous sperm would then have to travel abroad, and perhaps obtain treatment not regulated by any authority. Moreover, they must pay for it themselves (an argument that challenged the principle of equal access to healthcare services). The proposal to maintain anonymous sperm donation was passed. This changed, however, in 2003.

With the shift in government (from Labour to a Christian Democrat coalition) the anonymity clause was repealed. The Labour party, wanting to uphold the anonymity clause, presented an alternative proposal, but was defeated. Thus a practice, contested since 1953, was overturned. The main argument for revoking the anonymity of sperm donors was that it is in the child's best interest and a child's right to know its biological origin (*opphav* is the Norwegian term used, which connotes descent). The legal introduction of named sperm is based on the assumption that it is essential for a child to know its origins, as this is tantamount to knowing who you are. Hence, sperm is attributed a defining quality: it not only creates identity, it is (in a sense) synonymous with it. Moreover, the majority argued that, 'a legal precondition (for assisted conception) is that biological origin can be clearly defined as one biological mother and one biological father' (Innst. S. nr 238, 2001–2002).[20] Thus a fundamental link between identity, kinship and knowledge of biogenetic origin is established, and concerns about secrecy and the 'truth' of filiation are finally put to rest.

There is no doubt that framing the question of anonymous sperm donation in terms of children's rights and the best interest of the child, with reference to adoption law and international conventions, has been constitutive for the more general change in opinion on this matter (Melhuus and Howell 2009). This has become the ethically correct position, so much so that it is difficult to refute: who can be against what is deemed the best interest of the child? The significance of biology or biogenetics – as articulating a truth about kin relations – has captured the social imagination, shifting the perspective from the parents (and the institution of marriage) to the child.

Pre-natal Diagnosis and the Question of Early Ultrasound

I turn now to another illustration where a question of biological information and knowledge is involved. In contrast to the previous example, which concerns kinship knowledge (filiation), this example is about knowledge of the condition of a foetus. Ultrasound is a technology that is used in pregnancy care to assure the health of the mother and child. However, ultrasound may also reveal abnormalities in the foetus. 'Early ultrasound' (as the term is used in Norway) refers to the administration of this technology to pregnant women between weeks eleven and thirteen of pregnancy – that is, within the period where self-determined abortion is permitted. As mentioned, the Norwegian biotechnology act restricts the use of early ultrasound (within the public health system), but it does not prohibit it. So-called 'routine ultrasound' is carried out as a pregnancy control on all pregnant women around week eighteen.[21]

The discussion about early ultrasound has evolved in relation to whether this technology is classified as pregnancy care (where it is the health of the mother and/or foetus that is in focus) or as prenatal diagnosis *(fosterdiagnostikk)* understood as a risk assessment, including the identification of Down's syndrome.[22] In the early 1980s, ultrasound was seen first and foremost as a novel means to facilitate preventive healthcare for pregnant women, and not as a prenatal diagnostic instrument. The ethical aspects of this technology were not yet an issue (Kvande 2008b). There was as yet no explicit connection between ultrasound and genetics and ultrasound and ethics, and hence the problematic issue of selective abortion.

Although some ethical issues were raised in the mid eighties, these centred on the economical and organizational aspects of ultrasound in the implementation of a possible screening programme, with a focus on competence and standardization, and not on the question of foetal abnormalities (Kvande 2008b). However, with the advent of reproductive technologies questions concerning the ethical challenges and limits to medical practice became a public concern. It was in the wake of these discussions that ultrasound was drawn into a bioethical debate. According to Kvande, the ultrasound debate articulated an incipient lack of confidence in medical doctors and their ethical practice and a demand for public access to and regulation of these practices. The ethical debate was as much about trust and legitimacy for medical expertise as it was about the grounds for selective abortion.

By 2003, and with the revision of the Biotechnology Act, the question of early ultrasound and selective abortion was placed squarely on the political agenda. The government at that time was, as mentioned, a right-centre coalition, with a strong Christian Democratic party. It was this government that rescinded the anonymity clause with regard to sperm donation. However, they were also very much concerned with the practice of early ultrasound. When the law was being debated in Parliament, the then Minister of Health, Dagfinn Høybråten, used his allotted time to argue against early ultrasound, flagging the threat of systematic selection of foetus as a consequence. This would, he claimed, lead to a 'sorting society' *(sorteringssamfunn)*, a term that has been amply used and gained much currency in the bioethical debates in Norway to designate a society 'where there is not room for all'.[23] I will briefly summarize his main points, as these reiterate arguments held more generally. They turn on matters of individual choice and the possibility of selection and, not least, the obligation of the state to prevent the creation of a society that permits systematic elimination of impaired foetuses.

The Minister of Health grounded his arguments in the controversies and public debates that biotechnology had provoked, not least regarding questions tied to notions of human being – that is, views about when human life begins, human reproduction, the moral status of the foetus and the fertilized egg, and questions related to the use of technologies in order to sort away *(sortere bort)* or eliminate undesirable genetic characteristics. Moreover, he framed his speech to Parliament with an explicit reference to ethics and ethical dilemmas, insisting that this law was ultimately about what kind of society we (Norwegians) wish to live in. In this respect, he argued that it is paramount that research and development be controlled and regulated for the benefit of all. He said: 'We cannot let the technologies rule us; we must take hold of the development and direct the technology in the direction we wish to follow'.[24] He refers explicitly to the preamble to the law (§ 1–1). The preamble emphasizes that the medical applications of biotechnology are to be used for the benefit of everyone in a society where there is room for all and in accordance with principles of respect for human dignity, human rights and is without discrimination on the basis of genetic constitution, and based on the ethical norms that form part of our Western cultural heritage. He insisted that 'society has the right and the freedom to set the limits and framework for the practice of the experts in the field'. And he insisted that this debate is not about abortion and 'women's right to determine whether or not she will complete her pregnancy to term', rather it is about denying a woman 'the right to choose what kind of child she wants'. The Minister expressed his satisfaction that there is consensus on the latter despite disagreement about the former.

The Minister's arguments are phrased in terms of society, and not in terms of individual choice or rights. In this vein, selective abortion is framed as something qualitatively different from self-determined abortion; and along the same lines, prenatal diagnosis is defined as something different from routine ultrasound. However, in so far as the application of ultrasound can reveal the same kind of information as prenatal diagnosis, the Minister argued that it should be regulated by the same regulation as PND (prenatal diagnosis). This was the heart of the matter. At issue, then, is not the right to abortion on demand, but whether the Norwegian state should endorse a policy that might lead to a sorting society – that is, a society that, for instance, allows the elimination of a foetus with Down's syndrome. Such elimination would be possible if diagnosis was carried out within the twelve-week limit of self-determined abortion. This would be tantamount to accepting that some lives are unworthy of living, thereby challenging the very notion of human dignity. It would also undermine a fundamental principle of equality in Norwegian society, potentially creating 'completely new classes of difference' (for reference see endnote 25). Such is the thrust of his argument.

However, members of the Labour Party chose a different tack. They were more concerned with choice and not least women's self-determination. As one representative said,

> many have got the impression that this represents a greater limitation on the pregnant woman's self-determination ... The reason for this unease is that the majority of Norwegian women regard ultrasound examination as a routine practice during her pregnancy, not to find abnormalities in her foetus ... Women must have free access to obtain knowledge about the foetus she is carrying ... We have confidence that women themselves can regulate this need.

Or in the words of another Labour Party representative: 'It seems as if fear of new technology overrules freedom of choice, pregnancy care and foetal surgery. But this tightening (*innstramming*) [of the law] also indicates a lack of confidence that women can make responsible ethical choices'. The representatives from the Labour Party and the Progress Party voiced their concerns for the individual's right to choose, for greater trust in both patients and researchers, and, in general, for a more positive view of science and knowledge. Moreover, they would not accept being relegated to an ethically inferior position, just because they have a different view on these vital matters and do not fear a potential sorting society. As one member of the Labour Party said: 'I do not believe that it is only the majority that considers that the individual human being has an autonomous value (*egenverdi*) ... I do not accept being evaluated on a scale, where someone claims that his or her position on restrictions regarding ultrasound are ethically or morally superior'.[25]

It is the conjunction of PND (early ultrasound) and self-determined abortion that is the cause for concern, hence the need for a regulation designed to impede a woman (or couple) from being able to choose the kind of child she wants. However, implicit in this assumption is that left to their own devices, women will sort. Empirically this also seems to be the case. Nine out of ten pregnant women who know they are carrying a foetus with Down's syndrome choose to abort; but very few have this knowledge.[26]

Whether the resistance on the part of the majority to permit early ultrasound is (f)actually an indication of a lack of confidence in pregnant women (as the Labour Party claims) is hard to discern. However, if we are to take the Minister's words at face value, the reticence to permit early ultrasound can be read as an indication of a reluctance (on the part of legislators) to be held responsible for creating a society that may lead to systematic elimination of undesirable foetuses. This could be a possible outcome if early ultra sound is instituted as a routine practice, granting women the choice to access information about the condition of the foetus within the limit of self-determined abortion. Therefore access to such information is withheld, at least as an offer within the public health service. However this is interpreted, the fact remains that, for the majority, value is placed on ignorance regarding some specific condition of the foetus. Yet this ignorance is fictitious, as women have access to private clinics in Norway and abroad that offer early ultrasound – of which many women choose to avail themselves.

Moreover, the Labour Party has early ultrasound on its party platform. Their proposal to allow early ultrasound for all pregnant women spurred a new round of sharp debates, especially in the media.[27] A feature article on early ultrasound in one of Norway's major newspapers, entitled 'Life in the Sorting Society' confirms this trend (Saugstad 2012). Saugstad (Professor of Paediatrics at the University of Oslo) draws attention to the claim by the then Minister of Health (Labour Party) that she is as much concerned about human dignity as are those who are against early ultrasound, while provoking her to consider whether she wants to be part of a tradition that has encouraged racial hygiene. This tradition, he claims, has strong roots in the Norwegian society, not least within the Labour Party.[28] Although debates about biotechnologies, the sorting society and early ultrasound have evoked eugenic practices (and racial hygiene) of the 1930s, rarely have the arguments in the media been that explicit.

Knowing or Not-Knowing: Is That the Question?

Above, I have briefly outlined some of the salient aspects of the issues raised in the debates about anonymous sperm donation and the application of early ultrasound. Both these regulations have been controversial and both have been played out in Norwegian *offentlighet*. Although regulated within the same law, their ethical trajectories have not been the same. Moreover, whereas the question of anonymous sperm donation seems to have been put to rest, the issue of early ultrasound is still unresolved. Both practices have nevertheless formed part of an ethical publicity. Although sperm donation and early ultrasound are very different practices, they both involve biological information. Both also turn on the question of knowledge and the value of knowing or not-knowing. However, they do so in different ways. This difference has to do with the effects of knowing, who 'the knower' is presumed to be, and hence, also, to the level – or scale – that biological information can be made to work. I turn now to these questions.

In the case of sperm donation, the biological information that is made known is that of identity of the sperm donor. The tacit understanding of ignorance contained in anonymity is transformed: it is drawn out of the private (secret) realm, and becomes public and explicit (in that it is recorded) and hence available information. It is presumed that the availability of this information is in the best interests of the child. The information provides a truth about kinship knowledge in that it specifies the biogenetic link between a child and a man who has 'fathered' it, but who for all intents and purposes is not the legal father. This information is seen as constitutive of identity (that is one of its effects), and a child in order 'to know' who she/he is should have access to it at the age of eighteen. The information is lodged with the

state (in the donor register). Nevertheless, the right the child has to
this information is not matched by an obligation of its legal/social
parents to reveal the facts of its conception. Although they know that
there is a genetic father, other than the legal father, they may choose
to withhold that knowledge. Thus, an effect built into the possibility
of knowing may not be realized. The child may remain ignorant of
its biological origin.[29] There is, then, a potential knower, the child,
who may want to find out his or her genetic origin and act upon the
information received. The availability of this information depends on
the family relations in which the child is socially embedded and how
they are expressed and practised. Knowledge of filiation may or may
not be deemed significant, may or may not be revealed. If revelation is
not the practice, there is an unresolved question: does the child then
not really know who he or she is?

However, and perhaps more importantly, there is another 'knower'
– the state. The move to rescind the anonymity clause rests on the
conviction that biological origin represents a truth about a person.
That truth is considered significant, so much so that the state deems
it necessary to supply it and guard it. In the case of sperm donation,
the state privileges the biological connection, irrespective of the
actual lived kinship relations (see Cadoret 2009). At the same time,
the state reveals an ambivalence. Social parenthood is acknowledged.
(Anything else would be to deny Norwegian social reality.) It is left to
the parents' discretion to tell or not to tell. Thus, the legal regulation
contains a contradiction. Seen from the point of view of the state,
the truth now exists. The information is available, and the state is its
guardian. What people choose to do with this information is their
responsibility. The state provides a service (sperm donation) and it sets
the terms under which this service may be had. These terms reflect an
ethical position about kinship relations and the significance of biological information, about children's rights and about society. It also,
albeit indirectly, acknowledges individual autonomy.

The case of early ultrasound is different. More prominently than
in the case of sperm donation, I argue, what is at stake here is society
– that is, the social body and not the individual body. Also in this case
biological information is involved and who should have access to it.
Early ultrasound pivots on the implications of 'knowing' the condition
of a foetus and in contrast to sperm donation the regulation privileges
a principle of 'not-knowing', of ignorance. The legal issue is whether
early ultrasound should be considered a prenatal diagnostic instrument and hence restricted by the law or whether it is a service that is
part of pregnancy care and hence should be offered to all pregnant

women. Again the question is what access to certain biological information might imply. In this case it is the fear of systematic selection of an abnormal foetus (an undesired child) that guides the regulation. Such systematic selection would lead to a 'sorting society', to a society that lacks tolerance for difference, undermining the respect for human dignity. That is the effect built into the biological information. Therefore, as the Minister argued, such information (that early ultrasound may reveal) should be withheld.

The application of early ultrasound reveals information about the foetus. The mere existence of such potential information provokes a need or even an obligation to act. Thus it is the implications of knowing whether a foetus is in some way impaired that underpins the debate. The possibility of knowing activates a distinction between abortion on demand and selective abortion, disclosing a tension between the individual and society.[30] Whereas self-determined abortion is framed as an individual woman's right, selective abortion is framed in terms of society. To permit a practice that might potentially lead to systematic selection of a foetus with particular characteristics would be contrary to an idea of society that Norwegians should aspire to. The state acting on what it 'knows' deems it prudent to withhold information about the condition of a foetus. This is the effect that is built into the information. Therefore 'not-knowing' is proposed and accepted as the legal regulation irrespective of the fact that the woman may want to know (and may also choose alternative ways of accessing the information), and, paradoxically, with no regard for her common-sense judgement. Thus, and perhaps in contrast to the more immediate and concrete effects of kinship knowledge, the knowledge that PND (and more specifically early ultrasound) brings has mobilized a more abstract value, a more embracing relationality, namely that of a humane society, respect for human dignity and a tolerance for difference. It is in this sense, I suggest, that the legal regulation on early ultrasound privileges society over individual autonomy. Moreover, it might well be that refusing such information also avoids creating situations of choice that are difficult to handle. The value of not knowing may also be understood in these terms.

Conclusion

It is important to keep in mind that the issues I have discussed in this chapter are framed within a legislative process. In other words, we are dealing with phenomena and processes that the state finds necessary

to regulate. They concern developments in biotechnology, their potentialities and the possible implications of such developments for society.
Nevertheless, as I have indicated, this struggle over regulations is not
primarily about biotechnology. As elsewhere, the incorporation of
reproductive technologies in Norway has generated a moral dispute
where the practices these technologies potentially implicate were recognized as pertaining more widely to society. In other words, the legislative processes (and the ensuing legislation) both draw on and make
explicit some underlying cultural values; thus provoking an ethical
reflection. I have claimed that this regulatory regime is fuelled by an
imagination that translates biotechnology into a legal framework and
a precautionary mode. This imagination is tied to differing understandings of biotechnology and the potential risk they entail. On this
issue, there is – and has been – disagreement among politicians and
the public at large. Fundamentally, it seems that these disagreements
reflect a tension between individual autonomy and society. They also
reflect varying attitudes to science and scientific expertise, to technology and knowledge and the degree to which these can and should be
controlled.

The law has been based on a precautionary principle. Thus there is
an explicit recognition that the technologies may not only entail risk
but also that they contain ethical dilemmas. These dilemmas, moreover, reflect other values than those represented by expert knowledge.
These other values concern the nature of social relations and the
nature of society; in short, biological and social reproduction. They
are tied to kinship and kinship relations (such as marriage, maternity,
paternity and filiation); to the individual and his or her rights; and to
more abstract, diffuse values such as equality, tolerance for difference
and respect for human dignity. The meanings attached to these values
will obviously vary, as will their articulations. Hence, what constitutes
an ethical, correct position will necessarily be disputed. Moreover, a
central aspect of the ethical life of politics is sustained by 'being committed enough to that game to care how it turns out' (Keane 2015:
168).

I began this chapter with a reference to Dilley and will conclude
on the same note. Dilley argues that knowledge and ignorance must
be regarded as mutually constitutive 'not simply in terms of an opposition, but also in terms of how a dialectic between knowledge and
ignorance is played out in specific sets of social and political relations; indeed, how, too, moral value is placed upon knowledge and
ignorance in various ways' (Dilley 2010: 177–76). Although he sets
his argument within a broader perspective of an anthropology of

ignorance, and his empirical examples are very different from mine, he nevertheless draws attention to a tension between knowledge and ignorance that I find pertinent. My focus has been on policy and the role and implications of making certain information available – or not (and not on learning and skills). The question of availability is summoned in terms of a moral discourse and an ethical publicity. It is the moral value placed on knowledge and ignorance with regard to the two specific cases, sperm donation and early ultrasound, that has framed my discussion. In both cases, the state, through its legislators, has felt compelled to act on the availability of particular biological information.

In this regulatory regime, access to biological information plays a substantial role. Some kinds of biological information, it seems, are imbued with a certain sociocultural potency, with truth or imagination even. In the case of sperm donation, the rescinding of the anonymity clause rests on a perceived relation between a biological fact and identity. The moral value is placed on 'knowing' this relation. So much so that it is considered the child's best interest – even its right. The regulation, albeit uneasily, privileges biological over social relatedness; at the same time it reflects a shift in values with regard to certain kinship relations. The institution of marriage and the introduction of a third party, so significant in the 1950s, no longer guide the arguments as to what is the correct procedure. Secrecy with regard to paternity is no longer the norm; on the contrary, it is considered unethical. The argument that the prescription of known donor sperm might reduce the availability of sperm donation (in Norway), as it would be difficult to recruit donors, made no difference;[31] nor did the fact that Norwegians in want of anonymous sperm could obtain this treatment abroad.

The issue concerning early ultrasound sheds a different light, drawing other concerns to the fore. In this case, the value is placed on ignorance. More explicitly than in the case of sperm donation, this provision addresses the issue of risk – and hence also imagination. Permitting early ultrasound evokes the risk of potentially creating a sorting society. At the same time, not to permit the application of early ultrasound is to deny pregnant women access to knowledge about the condition of the foetus they are carrying. It is in fact to deny individual women a choice. The ethical positions are framed in these terms, pitting the individual (and her right to choose) against society. And so far, those insisting on the need for ignorance have won the moral high ground. Their claim, that prenatal diagnosis may result in the termination of pregnancy for immoral reasons and that such acts would threaten the very order of society, has, at least until now, found resonance. I believe that this can in part be explained by the way 'society' is contained in the technology and – in its imagined form – has been incorporated into the legislation (re reference to eugenics). It is perhaps an example of the way state and society become one. Thus, and seen from the point of view of the majority of the legislators, the provision concerning early ultrasound can be understood as avoiding a slippery slope in an attempt to pre-empt society's verdict.[32] That is their obligation to society; it is to act on behalf of society.

A regulation is brought into being to avoid and/or facilitate practices that science makes possible. In this process, biological information has been pivotal. It comes with certain effects depending on who is 'in the know'. The knowledge that this information entails, at the level of state and/or at individual level, has differing significance. This, of course, is not surprising – knowledge is managed and distributed unequally in any society. What is interesting is what knowledge the state recognizes as having value, how the state acts on what it knows, what is deemed morally acceptable to know – or not to know; and not least, how ethics is used to intervene in the space between politics and science and is mobilized to ground a morally correct position. The Norwegian Biotechnology Act and the debates surrounding sperm donation and early ultrasound provide rich food for thought on such issues, engaging a social imagination and an ethical publicity.

Marit Melhuus is Professor of Social Anthropology at the University of Oslo. She is a former Dean of the Faculty of Social Sciences and member of the Norwegian Academy of Science and Letters. Publications include *Problems of Conception: Issues of Law, Biotechnology, Individuals and Kinship* (Berghahn 2012); *Holding Worlds Together: Ethnographies of Knowing and Belonging* (co-editor) (Berghahn 2007); and *Machos, Mistresses, Madonnas* (co-editor) (Verso 1996).

Notes

1. See Act of 5 December 2003 No. 100 relating to the application of biotechnology in human medicine, etc. (cf. earlier Acts of 5 August 1994 No. 56 and 12 June 1989 No. 68).
2. See § 2–7 The child's right to information about the sperm donor and Chapter 4, Prenatal diagnosis, § 4–1 Definition. The term 'early ultrasound' refers to the application of ultrasound to pregnant women

before the twelfth week of pregnancy – that is, within the period of self-determined abortion. This will be discussed below.

3. Embryo research has been another controversial issue, implicating the moral status of the embryo. In contrast to the United Kingdom, for example, where the notion of 'pre-embryo' was introduced, this notion has not had any purchase in Norway (see Franklin 1999 [1993]; Melhuus 2015; Mulkay 1997; Sirnes 1997).

4. These comments are gleaned from my interviews with legislators who at some point had been involved in the legislative process (especially the process leading up to the 1994 law). These interviews were carried out before the last two revisions of the legislation – that is, before 2003. I also draw on pertinent public documents (including the period after 2003) related to the debates. See Melhuus 2005 and 2012a.

5. For example, in the earlier legislation, feminists aligned with Christians in arguing for a restrictive legislation. See Brekke (1995) for a detailed account of the various positions.

6. See also Nielsen, Monsen and Tenøe (2000) for a history of the developments of and attitudes to genetics and biotechnology in Norway.

7. For a comprehensive view on the Scandinavian welfare states, including notions of individual autonomy and freedom, see Sørensen and Stråth (1997), Kildal and Kuhnle (2005).

8. See also Strathern (2005b) where she discusses the problematic notion of society, with regard to policy recommendations made to the Canadian government, suggesting (among other things) that government and society become 'one' (Strathern 2005b: 472). See also Collier and Lakoff (2005).

9. The lack of knowledge (or shared ignorance) was solved in different ways: some members established permanent reference groups with relevant experts; others called on experts ad hoc, when necessary.

10. These points of view expressed in my interviews are also reflected in public documents and debates in Parliament.

11. 'Research' *(forskning)* is the term used to refer to developments in science.

12. The gloss 'expert knowledge' is in itself problematic. It is used as if the experts are all of one piece, or as a euphemism/cover-all for science or developments in science. Obviously 'experts' also disagree on the application of reproductive technologies. For example, the Christian Doctors' Association in Norway has had a restrictive attitude.

13. There is a history of ethics and biotechnology here that I am not able to cover. However, in the wake of the 1987 law, Parliament requested that the government submit a white paper on biotechnology that could form the basis for an informed ethical debate. The Ethics Committee was appointed in 1988 and submitted its report in 1990 (NOU 1991: 6 *Mennesker og bioteknologi*). This report laid the ground for the white paper that formed the basis of the 1994 law (Report nr 25 (1992–1993) *Om mennesker og bioteknologi*. An abbreviated English version exists:

Biotechnology related to human beings, issued by the Ministry of Health and Social Affairs, *Report No 25 (1992–1993)*. Meanwhile, in 1991, the Norwegian Biotechnology Advisory Board was appointed.

14. §2–7 The child's right to information about the sperm donor. Act of 5 December 2003 No. 100 relating to the application of biotechnology in human medicine, etc. With this new provision, Norway also had to create a sperm bank, as the sperm used in Norway for the purposes of donor insemination had until then been imported from Denmark, and Denmark still prescribed anonymous sperm.

15. *Innstilling fra Inseminasjonslovkomitéen* (1953).

16. For a detailed analysis, including the arguments related to adoption, see Melhuus (2012a, Chapter 3); Melhuus and Howell (2009). For further discussions on AID, see: Daniels and Haimes (1998), Blythe and Spiers (2004) and Hargreaves (2006).

17. To quote the minority: 'Our Christian culture rests on the home. Monogamous marriage is the very foundation of our culture. With insemination a third party is introduced to a relationship between those two, that should be one, and between parents and children' (*Inseminasjonslovkomitéens innstilling* 1953: 50).

18. This move must also be seen in relation to the revision of the Children's Act regarding new practices for ascertaining paternity, granting men the right unilaterally (within certain limits) to have paternity ascertained (through DNA tests). See Act pertaining to children and parents – the Children's Act: Act 1981 04-08-7; § 6 Change in paternity. Moreover, as I have argued, the insistence on the significance of biological related-ness can also be understood as a way of ensuring certainty in the face of uncertainties that reproductive technologies are seen to entail (Melhuus 2011, 2012a).

19. See Ot.prp nr 25 (1986–1987), page 15.

20. This is also an argument that supports the continual prohibition on egg donation. Moreover, and as a consequence of reproductive technologies, in 1997 Norway amended the Children's Act, including a clause defining motherhood (which had hitherto been considered unnecessary) as the state of the person who gives birth to a child (Act 1981-04- 08, nr 07 Lov om barn og foreldre).

21. In the Biotechnology Act, prenatal diagnosis is defined as 'an examina-tion of foetal cells, foetus or a pregnant woman with the aim of obtaining information about the genetic characteristics of the foetus or in order to detect or exclude illness or deviations in the development of the foetus. Ultrasound examination in the ordinary pregnancy control is not viewed as prenatal diagnosis ...' (§ 4–5).

22. See Kvande (2008a) for a detailed account and analysis of the develop-ment of ultrasound in Norway. My points in this section are drawn from her work (Kvande 2008a, 2008b). See Schwennesen et al. 2010 for a discussion of prenatal risk assessment in Denmark.

23. I do not have the space to pursue the notion of the 'sorting society' and its persuasive power in this context, but have done so elsewhere. See Melhuus 2009; 2012a, especially chapter 5; and 2012b.

24. His speech can be downloaded at http://www.regjeringen.no/en/archive/ Bondevik-2nd-Government/hd/265625/266491/ny_lov_om_biote- knologi.html?id=266994 (retrieved 2 December 2009). All translations are mine.

25. All quotes are taken from the debate in Odelstinget (one of the two cham- bers in Norwegian Parliament) Meeting 18 November 2003. https:// www.stortinget.no/globalassets/pdf/referater/odelstinget/2003-2004/ o031118.pdf (my translations). Retrieved 11 November 2016.

26. According to a report on late abortions (Mo et al. 2006) the number of such abortions in 2005 was forty-five. Figures released from the Medical Birth Register *(Medisinsk fødselsregister)* confirms that about 90 per cent of pregnant women who have had a PND and a foetus detected with Down's choose to abort. This number has been stable over the last ten years (Skodje 2011).

27. On 16 January, 2012, the Directorate of Health (on behalf of the Ministry of Health and Care) organized an open meeting about early ultrasound during pregnancy *(Åpent møte om tidlig ultralyd i svangerskapet)*. The agenda is an indication of the contested nature of these technologies. In addition to focusing on the medical and ethical issues, the meeting also focussed on priorities within the health care services. Six political parties were invited to present their positions.

28. For further arguments about the links between biotechnology and eugen- ics/racial hygiene, see Roll-Hansen 1999, 2005; Nielsen, Monsen and Tennøe 2000; also Melhuus 2012a.

29. As the legislation was passed in 2003, it is still too early to know whether children born of donor sperm will access the register on turning eigh- teen. I also do not have information about whether those who have made use of known donor sperm in fact have told the child about the conditions of its conception.

30. This distinction grows out of a particular historical context. Whereas self-determined abortion is the result of feminist struggle for reproduc- tive choice and a woman's control over her own body, selective abor- tion arises out of the potentials of biotechnology and has as its main site of contention the moral status of the embryo and/or foetus. Historically, the debate about selective abortion is linked to eugenics and the practice of racial hygiene (see Melhuus 2012a; also Giæver 2005).

31. In actual fact, this is precisely what has occurred. In 2011, the Norwegian Broadcasting Corporation (NRK) reported that there is a scarcity of donor sperm in Norway and that the two major fertility clinics offering sperm donation are not accepting new couples. http://www.nrk.no/ nyheter/1.7519093 (retrieved 15 March 2011).

32. See Strathern 2005b. Her argument relates to how 'science incorporates society into its aims and objectives in order to anticipate or pre-empt society's verdict' (2005b: 467). I am suggesting that legislation may work in the same way.

References

Blythe, E. and J. Spiers. 2004. 'Meeting the Rights and Needs of Donor Conceived People: The Contribution of a Voluntary Contact Register', *Nordisk sosialt arbeid* 4(24): 318–30.

Brekke, O.A. 1995. *Differensiering og integrasjon: Debatten om bioteknologi og etikk i Norge.* Rapport 9509. Bergen: LOS senteret.

Cadoret, A. 2009. 'The Contribution of Homoparental Families to the Current Debate on Kinship', in J. Edwards and C. Salazar (eds), *European Kinship in the Age of Biotechnology.* New York and Oxford: Berghahn, pp. 70–96.

Cohen, L. 1999. 'Where it Hurts: Indian Material for an Ethics of Organ Transplantation', *Daedalus* 128(4): 135–65.

Collier, S.J. and A. Lakoff. 2005. 'On Regimes of Living', in A. Ong and S. Collier (eds), *Global Assemblages: Technology, Politics, and Ethics as Anthropological Problems.* Wiley-Blackwell, pp. 22–39.

Daniels, K. and E. Haimes (eds). 1998. *Donor Insemination: International Social Science Perspectives.* Cambridge: Cambridge University Press.

Dilley, R. 2010. 'Reflections on Knowledge Practices and the Problem of Ignorance', *Journal of the Royal Anthropological Institute*, special issue, *Making Knowledge*, pp. 176–93.

Franklin, S. 1999 [1993]. 'Making Representations: The Parliamentary Debate on the Human Fertilisation and Embryology Act', in J. Edwards, S. Franklin, E. Hirsch, F. Price, M. Strathern, *Technologies of Procreation: Kinship in the Age of Assisted Conception.* London: Routledge, pp. 127–65.

Franklin, S. and M. Lock. 2005. 'Animation and Cessation: The Remaking of Life and Death', in S. Franklin and M. Lock (eds), *Remaking Life and Death. Toward an Anthropology of the Biosciences.* Oxford: James Currey, pp. 3–22.

Giæver, Ø. 2005. 'Eugenisk indikasjon for abort – en historisk oversikt', *Tidsskrift for Den norske legeforening* 24(125): 3472–76.

Haimes, E. 2002. 'What Can the Social Sciences Contribute to the Study of Ethics? Theoretical, Empirical and Substantive Considerations', *Bioethics* 16(2): 89–113.

Hargreaves, K. 2006. 'Constructing Families and Kinship through Donor Insemination', *Sociology of Health and Illness* 28(3): 261–83.

Howell, S. 2006. *The Kinning of Foreigners: Transnational Adoption in a Global Perspective.* New York and Oxford: Berghahn.

Keane, W. 2015. 'Varieties of Ethical Stance', in M. Lambek, V. Das, D. Fassin, W. Keane, *Four Lectures on Ethics: Anthropological Perspectives.* Chicago: Hau Books, pp. 127–73.

Kildal, N. and S. Kuhnle (eds). 2005. *Normative Foundations of the Welfare State: The Nordic Experience*. London: Routledge.

Kvande, L. 2008a. *Bilete av svangerskap – bilete av foster: Ultralyd-diagnostikk i norsk svangerskapsomsorg 1970–1995*. Ph.D. thesis. Trondheim: NTNU.

———. 2008b. 'Frå politikk til etikk – obstretisk ultralyd i 1980-og 90-åra', *Tidskrift for Den norske legeforening* 24(128): 2855–59, downloaded from www.tidsskriftet.no (retrieved 13 September 2011).

Lien, M.E. and M. Melhuus. 2009. 'Introduction', *Ethnologie francaise* 39(2): 197–207 (Special issue on Norway).

Løvset, J. 1951. 'Artificial Insemination: The Attitude of Patients in Norway', *Fertility and Sterility* 2(5): 414–29.

Melhuus, M. 2005. '"Better Safe than Sorry": Legislating Assisted Conception in Norway', in C. Krohn-Hansen and K. Nustad (eds), *State Formation: Anthropological Perspectives*. London: Pluto Press, pp. 212–33.

———. 2007. 'Imagining Society: When Experts Disagree on the Meanings of Kinship', in M. Lien and M. Melhuus (eds), *Holding Worlds Together: Ethnographies of Knowing and Belonging*. New York and Oxford: Berghahn, pp. 37–56.

———. 2009. 'Qui a peur de la 'sociéte´de tri'? Les biotechnologies, l'individu et l'État', *Ethnologie francaise* 39(2): 253–65.

———. 2011. 'Cyber-Stork Children and the Norwegian Biotechnology Act: Regulating Procreative Practice – Law and its Effects', in A. Hellum, S. Sardar Ali, and A. Griffiths (eds), *From Transnational Relations to Transnational Laws: Northern European Laws at the Crossroads*. Farnham, Surrey: Ashgate, pp. 51–70.

———. 2012a. *Problems of Conception: Individual and Society. Issues of Law, Biotechnology and Kinship*. New York and Oxford: Berghahn.

———. 2012b. 'Hva slags mening gir *sorteringssamfunnet*? En hendelse og noen refleksjoner omkring kunnskap, likhet, valg, individ og samfunn i Norge', *Norsk Antropologisk Tidsskrift* 23(1): 33–47.

———. 2015. 'The Embryo, Sacred and Profane', in C. Salazar and J. Bestard (eds), *Religion and Science as Forms of Life: Anthropological Insights into Reason and Unreason*. New York and Oxford: Berghahn, pp. 120–36.

Melhuus, M. and S. Howell. 2009. 'Adoption and Assisted Conception: One Universe of Unnatural Procreation', in J. Edwards and C. Salazar (eds), *European Cultures of Kinship in the Age of Biotechnology*. New York and Oxford: Berghahn, pp. 144–161.

Mo, E., I. Seliussen, M. Irgens and K. Gåsemyr. 2006. *Register over nemdbehandlede svangerskapsavbrudd: Rapport 2005*. Nasjonalt folkehelseinstitutt og Medisinsk fødselsregister.

Molne, K. 1976. 'Donorinseminasjon: En oversikt og et materiale', *Tidsskrift for Den norske lægeforening* 17–18: 982–86.

Mulkay, M. 1997. *The Embryo Research Debate: Science and the Politics of Reproduction*. Cambridge: Cambridge University Press.

Nielsen, T.H., A. Monsen and T. Tennøe. 2000. *Livets tre og kodenes Kode: Fra genetikk til bioteknologi. Norge 1900-2000.* Oslo: Gyldendal Akademiske.

Pottage, A. 2007 'The Socio-Legal Implications of the New Biotechnologies', *Annual Review of Law and Science* 3: 321–44.

Roll-Hansen, N. 1999. 'Eugenics in Scandinavia after 1945: Changes of Values and Growth of Knowledge', *Scandinavian Journal of History* 24(2): 199–213.

―――. 2005. 'Norwegian Eugenics: Sterilization as Social Reform', in G. Broberg and N. Roll-Hansen (eds), *Eugenics and the Welfare State: Sterilization Policy in Denmark, Sweden, Norway and Finland.* East Lansing, MI: Michigan University Press, pp. 151–94.

Saugstad, O.D. 2012. 'Livet i sorteringssamfunnet', *Aftenposten,* 10 January, pp. 4–5.

Scheper-Hughes, N. and M.M. Lock. 1987. 'The Mindful Body: A Prolegomenon to Future Work in Medical Anthropology', *Medical Anthropological Quarterly* 1(1): 6–41.

Schwennesen, N., M. Nordahl Svendsen and L. Koch. 2010. 'Beyond Informed Choice: Prenatal Risk Assessment, Decision-Making and Trust', *Etikk i praksis/Nordic Journal of Applied Ethics* 2. http://tapir.pdc.no/index. php?el=Kapittel&p=EIP&seks_id=24006&a=5&ids=ids24006# ids24006 (retrieved 13 September 2011).

Simpson, B. 2004. 'Impossible Gifts: Bodies, Buddhism and Bioethics in Contemporary Sri Lanka', in *Journal of the Royal Anthropological Institute* 10(4).

Sirnes, T. 1997. *Risiko og meining: Mentale brot og meiningsdimensjonar i industri og politikk. Bidrag til den sosiale stadietoerien.* Rapport nr 53; Ph.D. thesis, University of Bergen.

Skodje, H.T. 2011. '9 av 10 aborterer Downs', *Aftenposten* 18(3): 7.

Solberg, B. 2003. 'Den nye bioteknologiloven – ikke til barnets beste likevel?', *Nytt Norsk Tidsskrift* 20(3): 316–24.

Strathern, M. 1999. *Property, Substance, and Effect: Anthropological Essays on Persons and Things.* London: Athlone Press.

―――. 2005a. *Kinship, Law and the Unexpected: Relatives are Always a Surprise.* Cambridge: Cambridge University Press.

―――. 2005b. 'Robust Knowledge and Fragile Futures', in A. Ong and S. Collier (eds), *Global Assemblages: Technology, Politics, and Ethics as Anthropological Problems,* Wiley-Blackwell, pp. 464–81.

Sørensen, Ø. and B. Stråth. 1997. *The Cultural Construction of Norden.* Oslo: Scandinavian University Press.

Public Documents Consulted and/or Quoted

Act 1975-06-13, nr 50. Lov om svangerskapsavbrudd (abortloven) (The abortion law).

Act 1981-04-08, nr 7. Lov om barn og foreldre (barneloven) (The Children's Act) (amended in 1997, nr 39, defining who is the mother of the child).

Act 1987-06-12, nr 68. Lov om kunstig befruktning (Act relating to artificial procreation).

Act 1994-08-05, nr 56. Om medisinsk bruk av bioteknologi (bioteknologi-loven) (Act relating to the Application of Biotechnology in Medicine).

Act 2003-02- 05, nr 100. Act relating to the application of biotechnology in human medicine, etc. (The Biotechnology Act).

Act 2008-12-19, nr 112. Ekteskapsloven (The Marriage Act).

Innstilling fra Inseminasjonslovkomitéen (1953). Issued by the Ministry of Justice.

Innst. S. nr 238 (2001–2002). *Innstilling fra sosialkomitéen om evaluering av lov om medisinsk bruk av bioteknologi. St.meld. nr 14 (2001–2002)*.

Innst. O nr 60 (1986–1987). *Innstilling fra sosialkomitéen om lov om kunstig befruktning.*

Ot.prp. nr 25 (1986–1987).

Meeting in Odelstinget 18.11. 2003. http://www.stortinget.no/otid2003/o03118-01.html (Retrieved 20 May 2008).

NOU 1991: 6 *Mennesker og bioteknologi.*

NOU 2009: 5 *Farskap og annen morskap. Fastsettelse og endring av foreldreskap.*

Report nr 25 (1992–1993) *Om mennesker og bioteknologi.*

Report nr 25 (1992–1993) *Biotechnology related to human beings.*

Chapter 8

TOWARDS AN EPISTEMOLOGY OF ETHICAL KNOWLEDGE

Lisette Josephides

'Why Does an Epistemology Need an Ethics?'

Daston and Galison (2010: 39) pose this question at the beginning of their study on the emergence of objectivity as a scientific concept. Their answer immediately links the knower and that which is known: to pursue objectivity, they argue, is simultaneously to cultivate a distinctive scientific self in whom knowing and knower converge. It is conceivable that an epistemology without ethics may exist, they muse, but they have not encountered it (ibid.: 40). This chapter is offered as a contribution to the enquiry about the cultivation of the kind of selves required for knowledge. It draws on an eclectic assortment of philosophers and anthropologists.

In anthropology, the relationship between the knower and knowing has been understood in different ways since the inception of the discipline. At the risk of simplifying, I describe the currently prevailing view as follows: 'the relationship between ethics and anthropological knowledge creation is grounded in an ethnographic encounter that is shaped by cultural and contextual determinants'. Yet in today's world, what does it mean to make distinctions between local and non-local knowledge and to see the relationship between the two in terms of an ethical attitude or a sort of methodology of understanding? In my usage, the term 'knowing' encompasses the act or process of acquiring and shaping knowledge, and the content of that knowledge as a building block of a shared reality. Though my topic is not about 'a theory of our knowledge of other selves' (Schutz 1967 [1932]: 139), it does concern the understanding of other persons' experience, based on our own subjective experience, and experienced as a 'social world'. We become aware that we are experiencing a world shared by others. In the three paragraphs below I identify three key terms ('Relations', 'Knowledge', 'Persons') and outline three sets of questions concerning knowledge about human beings and their lives. Among the terms, 'relations' is both a linking word (between knowledge and persons) and a substantive entity. In subsequent paragraphs I take up in more detail the substantive themes of knowledge, the creation of the knower, and ethics as a linking relationship.

Relations

What kinds of relations are required for knowledge about human beings and their lives to become possible? What makes such relations ethical, and thus the creation of knowledge itself an ethical project? Do the value and efficacy of knowledge depend on the relations established in the course of its creation? What are the personal negotiations, investments and transformations, both ethical and epistemological, of those involved in knowledge transactions? Lorraine Daston and Peter Galison (2010) engage some of these points in their opus on the history of objectivity, and their careful delineations inform much of my discussion. Writing from an anthropological perspective, Marilyn Strathern questions whether human subjects are necessarily the subject of the research, suggesting instead that the subject of the research is 'the manifold products of people's interactions' (2000: 294). But since these products include knowledge and transformed persons and relations, it is clear that whatever the subject of research its results will always illuminate the human condition. The stress on relations is underlined in Strathern's observation that institutional ethics, as manifested in the audit, 'belittles the creative power of social relations' (ibid.: 295).

Knowledge (Content, Creation, Ownership)

Given that extensive negotiations are engaged in the process of knowledge creation, during which understandings on both sides become expanded, to what extent can it be argued that the knowledge thus gained remains exclusively, intrinsically and inherently the property, and/or description, of those who are the ostensible subjects of study? It seems rather that these ethnographic case studies described in monographs and articles (e.g., Jenkins 1994) give access to otherwise unavailable meanings and values, now assigned to the other, but made available only in the encounter. A question here is how the content and ownership of knowledge can be linked to the conditions of its creation, thus expanding Strathern's point in the preceding paragraph.

Persons

Is the creation of a particular kind of ethical and epistemic person required for knowledge? And does the creation of this person parallel the way in which local knowledge can be transmuted into knowledge whose local moorings have been loosened, such that it is no longer possible to attribute it solely to specific localities and ways of being? This knowledge, to which the attribution of the term 'local' becomes misleading and unhelpful, can be understood by the phenomenological term 'epoche' or bracketing, or by Michael Jackson's (2005: xxix) use of 'the event'. Jackson explores these critical moments of being (events) that go beyond the local when local persons transform events that befall them into scenarios of their own choosing (ibid.: xxii), thus '[allegorizing] the precariousness of all human existence' (ibid.: xx). Since knowledge is entangled in relations and engagements between people, I emphasize how such relations and commitments are part of philosophical debates about the person. Questions about the place of the ethical in human life (Lambek 2010), how an ethical life is lived, and how one constructs oneself through ethical practices (Rabinow 2003) are implicit in these debates, but will be given only glancing attention. Instead, more attention will be given to the 'epistemic virtues' of the scientist as knower, examined by Daston and Galison (2010).

Knowledge, persons: the relations between these terms are ethical relations. Below I discuss them further under three subheadings: knowledge, the creation of the knower, and ethics.

Knowledge

Philosophical debates on knowledge invariably link knowledge with value, virtue and goodness. In the *Meno*, one of Plato's dialogues, virtue is at first investigated as knowledge that can be learned; but this understanding is abandoned on the grounds that there is no empirical evidence that virtue is knowledge that can be taught, but rather is more akin to 'correct opinion' that is possessed as a gift from the gods (Plato 1997: 888–97). From a different perspective, Duncan Pritchard argues that 'Knowledge is non-lucky true belief that is the product of the agent's reliable cognitive abilities' (Pritchard 2009: 24–37). The relationship between knowledge and virtue, or virtue ethics, has been increasingly debated by anthropologists. In his book on the subject of virtue, James Laidlaw (2014: 52) outlines the various relevant concepts. Deontological, consequentialist and virtue ethics pit phronesis (prudence) against sophia (wisdom), and judgement or practical reason combine the capability of rational thinking with a type of knowledge that is not just skill but the ability to reflect about living well. Thus knowledge and ethics or virtue appear as subsets of each other and are impossible to separate either methodologically or substantively.

Similar to Laidlaw but from a philosophical perspective, Timothy Chappell (2014: 271) lays out the variety of forms of knowledge: propositional knowledge (knowing-that, factual or descriptive knowledge), experiential knowledge, and knowledge-how (practical knowledge). All three types of knowledge bring with them 'epistemic credit', which can be claimed only with the relevant knowledge-how, experimental knowledge, or propositional knowledge (2014: 265). According to this classification, moral knowledge may be understood as knowing-how; aesthetic knowledge as experiential knowledge; and folk-psychological knowledge as a mixture of the two, making it less vulnerable to the kinds of challenges that ethics, aesthetics and religion pose to propositional knowledge (2014: 270). Chappell (2014: 263) distinguishes between the kinds of knowledge that might be involved in 'moral awareness' ('knowing why things have their particular moral values') and in 'practical awareness' ('knowing what to do'). When Aristotle (in Nicomachean Ethics) outlined the five intellectual virtues that can be called knowledge (techne, episteme, phronesis, sophia and nous), he insisted that they were powers of the mind that are 'truth-apt' (Chappell 2014: 271). Aristotle rejected the intellectual approach to ethics through *theoria*, insisting that his enquiry 'is not in order to know what excellence [virtue] is, but in order to become good [virtuous]' (Chappell 2014: 24). Chappell (2014: 269) reminds us of two points that are relevant to the current enquiry. First, that even scientific knowledge is not exclusively propositional (that is, factual or descriptive knowledge; Daston and Galison 2010 also underline this point). Second, any argument to the effect that systematic moral thinking must be based on knowledge of the good makes ethics propositional knowledge (2014: 277) – that is, factual or descriptive. Yet, Chappell continues, the 'capacity to feel ourselves into things' 'is the basis of our understanding of and connectedness to the world' (2014: 289). Through our imagination, we project our life into other forms.

These discussions of scientific and moral knowledge provide a minimal contextualization of the topic into broader debates. But they do not address the precise question of the ethics of knowledge acquisition, which implicates relations with others and the together-building-something question (see below) that is of interest to the current enquiry and generally to anthropologists. Chappell moves towards this approach in his definition of 'objectual knowledge' (Kvanvig 2003: 189 may have coined the term 'objectual understand-ing' as opposed to propositional understanding). Objectual knowledge is defined as knowledge of objects, where objects are particular things, such as 'molecules, mathematical structures, philosophical theories, musical symphonies, novels, poems, persons, and dispositions such as virtues, alongside perhaps more obvious cases of objects such as tables, houses, bicycles, and laptops' (Chappell 2014: 284). Whereas the ideal for propositional knowledge and its theorizing seems to be 'definitive control and domination', by contrast, 'the ideal for objec-tual knowledge is something more like humble and unending pilgrim-age towards the demands set by an external reality'. This trajectory makes objectual knowledge 'more value-loaded than propositional knowledge' (2014: 288–89).

The mention of 'humble and unending pilgrimage' recalls the description of fieldwork given by the anthropologist Timothy Jenkins (1994: 442, citing Bloch 1991): 'fieldwork, like indigenous life, is characterized by a series of apprenticeships'. Jenkins argues that we understand others by engaging with them in practical activities, and that knowledge itself is created in those interactions. There is no inde-pendently existing knowledge prior to these interactions, thus no such thing exists as objective, uninvolved knowledge. Chappell, a philos-opher, reasons (from fellow philosopher Iris Murdoch) in terms that appear to describe the anthropologist's craft:

> The point [as Murdoch outlines] is to approach something outside oneself, something indefinitely demanding and in some ways myste-rious, and to try to be both truthful and illuminating in one's under-standing of it. This exercise – the exercise of study or contemplation – is something that requires humility, patience, persistence, imagination, and resourcefulness from the inquirer. And notably, it is part of the way things are that the seeker after objectual knowledge *never* completes his

quest; there is always more to know about any object, especially about any complex and interesting object.

Another writer, a novelist this time, outlines the difference between knowledge and judgement. In his epistolary novel on the Roman Emperor Augustus, John Williams (2003 [1971]: 128) has Maecenas (a supporter of Augustus and a patron of literature) write the following chastisement in a letter to Livy (Titus Livius, Roman historian):

> [It] seems to me that the moralist is the most useless and contemptible of creatures. He is useless in that he would expend his energies upon making judgments rather than upon gaining knowledge, for the reason that judgment is easy and knowledge is difficult. He is contemptible in that his judgments reflect a vision of himself which in his ignorance and pride he would impose upon the world.

As John McGahern elaborates in his introduction to the novel, 'Knowledge, since it involves an act of the imagination on behalf of others and their situations in the exigencies of the world, is difficult' (Williams 2003: xi). Judgement is easy, but ethnographers 'defer' it during their fieldwork, in the manner that phenomenologist philosophers 'bracket' or suspend judgement to focus on the analysis of experience. The moralist's judgement is clearly not what is meant by ethics in this enquiry. Rather, the 'capacity to feel ourselves into things' 'is the basis of our understanding of and connectedness to the world' (Chappell 2014: 289). Through our imagination, we project our life into other forms. But what is missing in all this debate for anthropologists is the relationship and the together-building-something (Ingold 2013). Since knowledge is entangled in relations and engagements between people, I emphasize how such relations and commitments are part of philosophical debates about common humanity (Gaita 2002; Josephides 2008b). These debates include questions such as: What is the place of the ethical in human life (Lambek 2010)? How is an ethical life lived? How does one construct oneself through ethical practices (Rabinow 2003)?

The person and ethics meet most productively in the creation of the knower. Four kinds of knowers are described below, in broad historical and philosophical strokes. Subsequent discussion will refer to (or slot into) these categories, which are not always clear-cut: the pure observer, the thinking man/woman, the same captured by apparatuses, and the researcher tackling the obligations and requirements of knowledge.

Creation of the Knower

One: The Pure Observer

The philosopher Peter Sloterdijk (2012 [2010]) outlines the 'near-death' conditions for creating the historical agent of a particular kind of knowing: the 'pure observer'. This observer practises a profession dedicated to theory (Socrates' contemplative life or 'bios theoretikos') in a life that must be seen as ascetic. This kind of knowledge requires 'bracketing', a sort of suspended animation (hence 'near-death') defined as abstention from judgement but also real life. By 'stepping back' from existential involvement, the pure observer allows the 'phenomenalization' of things in a process that invests the objects of consciousness with meaning, making phenomena present in the sphere of understanding. Consciousness, having thus given active if not material life to its internalized observations, becomes imbued with theory. In an exercise of 'not taking up a position' by abstaining from judgement ('bracketing'), consciousness could then temporarily keep real existence at bay. The term 'epoche', borrowed from the Greek sceptics, denotes this 'bracketing'.

How can the bracketing of objects arising from life, and their replacement by stable logical objects (that is, ideas) in consciousness, be plausible? Sloterdijk proffers an explanation that encompasses political and epistemic developments. After the ancient Greek polis collapsed, the brilliant individual no longer needed a political afterworld to live on in the memory. Knowledge, gathered from the external world, became internalized and then transcendent, entailing a retreat from profane (or external) life. Knowledge became the noetic (knowing) soul's memory of itself and its transcendent origin. This 'beautiful death' exchanged a small subjectivity for the 'great soul'. Sloterdijk sees the idea of cosmopolitanism, arising with the Cynics and proclaiming that thinkers were citizens of the universe, as part of this sort of transcendence. But later, 'cognitive modernism' brought about the assassination of the neutral observer. As a result of the secularization of cognitive processes, the 'pure observer' is dead (2012: 4–5).

Two: The Thinking Man/Woman

In a very short introduction to *The Accompaniment*, the anthropologist Paul Rabinow describes the creation of Herr Keuner. The scant two pages draw on a collection of very short stories, some of them mere aphorisms, by the German poet and dramatist Bertolt Brecht and interpreted by Brecht's philosopher friend, Walter Benjamin. Herr Keuner, the etymology of whose name may be 'everyone', 'everyday speech', or 'political community', is nicknamed by Brecht 'the thinking man' – pointing 'to what is shared or understood by people in common' (Rabinow 2011: 1). But Benjamin, who provided the etymologies above, also linked Keuner to *keiner* – 'no one' in German (2011: 2). Rabinow cites two of these very short stories:

> "We can't go on talking to each other," said Mr K. to a man. "Why not?" asked the latter, taken aback. "In your presence I am incapable of saying anything intelligent," complained Mr. K. "But I really don't mind," the other comforted him. "That I can believe," said Mr. K. angrily, "but I mind."

> "He who bears knowledge has only one virtue: that he bears knowledge," said Mr. Keuner. (Bertolt Brecht, cited in Rabinow 2011: 1)

The moral point made in the second Keuner story is what interests Rabinow: that 'He who bears knowledge has the virtue of bearing it as well as having the obligation to care for the knowledge and the bearing of it' (2011: 3). The thinking man is justly angry, comments Rabinow, when the virtue of knowledge is devalued through indifference.

In an earlier version of this chapter, I wrote that Rabinow described the creation of the 'thinking man', an individual with a tangled pedigree, whose convoluted genealogy Rabinow traced, beginning with Socrates and the care of the self (*melete* and the creation of the historical agent of knowledge) through to a minor work by Bertolt Brecht. When I went back to Rabinow's text for the correct references, I found that I had read into the text a more complete portrait than was there. I realized then that I had made the connections from other works of Rabinow (e.g., *Anthropos today*, 2003), the writings of Foucault and Greek philosophy. The thinking man, even if not quite Herr Keuner, is nevertheless a worthy kind of knower who is bound to exist. He exemplifies the virtues of holding knowledge in respect and recognizing its obligations; he is serious, precise and meticulous, and practices care of the self. He demonstrates that ethics is not just a matter of attentiveness to others, but also attentiveness to the self.

Three: The Thinking Man Captured by an Apparatus

The philosopher Giorgio Agamben considers living beings as being partitioned into two classes: living beings and apparatuses (what Foucault calls 'dispositif'). Continuing the theme of the thinking man/woman, Agamben asks: 'What is an Apparatus?' Answer: it is a 'heterogeneous set consisting of discourses, institutions, architectural forms, regulatory decisions, laws, administrative measures, scientific statements, moral and philanthropic propositions'; in other words, a set of strategies of the relations of forces supporting, and supported by, certain types of knowledge (2009: 2). Being itself a network, the apparatus has a concrete strategic function and is located 'at the intersection of power relations and relations of knowledge' (2009: 3). Living beings are 'incessantly captured' in these apparatuses that 'seek to govern and guide them toward the good' (2009: 13). Yet when Agamben then describes the current 'extreme phase' of capitalism as a 'massive accumulation of apparatuses' (2009: 15), one might ask, whose good?

Agamben's discussion captures the idea of the knower as shaped simultaneously by what is known and the context of knowing. As every apparatus implies a process of subjectification, the operation of the apparatuses as a network of discourses goes towards clarifying how the conditions of knowing in different social, cultural, epistemic and political milieus at different historical times can create different kinds of knowers, thus linking this paragraph to the two above. Only the paragraph below, on obligations and requirements, describes conditions of knowing that are shared by all knowers at all times.

Four: Between Obligations and Requirements

In her extensive opus on cosmopolitics, the philosopher Isabelle Stengers considers the mechanics of knowledge practices along two types of exchange: a circulating one (the obligations of ethics, which acknowledge the ethical moment of their formation) and one leading to closure (the requirements of knowledge, which seek recognition for their achievements). This divergent pull leads to an asymmetric relationship, which is felt particularly in anthropology in the different stages of fieldwork and writing up; the ethnography provides 'us' with a knowledge of others, yet the relationship with those others 'appears only in the service of the science that produces it' (Stengers 2011: 305). Thus such knowledge practices assume a difference in kind between 'us' and the 'others' 'as expressed in the possibility "we" claim of judging "others" in terms of beliefs without ever encountering them' (2011: 305). Ethnographers clearly do 'encounter' the 'others', so the reference here is to the further dissemination of that knowledge, as for instance described by Rabinow following the exit from the field (see next section below). While obligations refer to relations in the field, requirements relate to the knowledge questions themselves: whether they answer or tackle the research question, use appropriate forms of evidence, and can be broadened beyond the field situation.

The figure of the diplomat is a good one for elucidating these contrasts.

> Like the diplomat, the practitioner of a science for which "the conditions of the production of knowledge for one are, inevitably, also the conditions for the production of existence for the other" should situate herself at the intersection of two regimes of obligation: the obligation to acknowledge that the dreams of those she studies, their fears, their doubts, and their hopes, pass through her, and the obligation to "report" what she has learned from them to others, to transform it into an ingredient in the construction of knowledge. (Stengers 2011: 377)

A fieldworker must connect with the people in the field, but as an ethnographer she must 'bring into existence' what she has learned, and transmit it effectively (2011: 377). In continuing to translate, the anthropologist, like the diplomat, risks betraying (ibid.). This is why anthropological knowledge creation cannot be seen as produced exclusively in the local encounter.

Kirsten Hastrup (1995) makes a suggestive point in her discussion of the difference between written ethnography and ethnographic film. She argues that text articulates the thick description of an event; film the thin description. Authenticity and concern with audience understanding are counterposed in her argument: authenticity demands loyalty to source –that is, the people who are the object of the film or study – whereas a concern with audience understanding requires that audiences are co-builders of meaning. Does written text (more than film) betray those studied by colluding with the audience, inviting viewers in confidentially? The suggestion is that it is impossible to be true both to the source and the audience.

The four figures of knowers discussed above give a picture of the knower as shaped simultaneously by the knowledge and the context of knowing, thus suggesting how different conditions of knowing can create different kinds of knowers. The last figure only, caught between obligations and requirements, is enmeshed in conditions of knowing that are shared by all knowers and at all times. Ethnographers in particular must deal with the ethical problems of such a quandary. The greater the distance from the field, the more peremptory and insidious is the pressure to loosen old obligations, especially when new obligations sprout up with their own 'demands of the day', as we shall see below.

Knowledge as Demands of the Day

In their quest for a way forward for anthropology, Rabinow and Stavrianakis take up Max Weber's notion of the 'demands of the day'. These demands, they argue, are no longer primarily about the relations of fieldwork and the knowledge produced there, but 'how one *exits* from the field and what one engages in during the subsequent period' (Rabinow and Stavrianakis 2013: 32). They describe this exit as also a 'gathering' (2013: 33), when they 'recuperate and curate' (2013: 47) by taking up the objects from the fieldwork and working through them, '[disarticulating] them from the direct experiences of participant observation and creating a narrative by turning objects into artifacts and artifacts into terms' (2013: 49, 51).

This process is far more radical than 'virtual returns', which I describe as the impact of fieldwork 'recollected in tranquillity' on what is considered to be ethnographic evidence (Josephides 2008a; the method was used by William Wordsworth in his poetry). Rabinow and Stavrianakis describe the trajectory of the process of recuperation and curation as follows: 'field, exit, publicity, actual – narrated from the mode of observation of the contemporary' (2013: 98). Following the relationships and obligations as they are transferred from the field, they argue, is a kind of 'phenomenology of the logic of anthropological inquiry' (2013: 98). This being collaborative work, loyalties and communities were of a different kind from those of the 'lone ethnographer'. In a suggestive table that invites reflection (2013: 102), the authors set out the differences between 'Research' and 'Work' as a way to examine how *logos* and *ethos*, standing for knowledge and ethics, might be compounded (2013: 101). The two-column chart aligns/opposes two sets of descriptions, not unlike Agamben's apparatuses (above) in their heterogeneity. One set represents current anthropological practices; the other outlines the requirements of an anthropology of the contemporary, towards which anthropology must move if it is to keep up with the demands of the day.

Here is the information in the table in slightly modified form, with the terms of each column given on different sides of the solidus and each opposed pair separated by a semi-colon: Timeliness/Untimeliness; Morality, procedure/Equipment; Networks/Venues; Trained incapacities/Vocational imperative; Projects/Shared problems; Passion-Affect/Affect-Passion; Method/Meditation (care); Individualism/Collaboration; Ethnography/Second-Order Participant Observation; Performative/*Parrhesia*; *Stultitia*/Restive; Connected/Adjacent;

Reconstruction/Narrative modes (*Metalepsis*); Research/Work (2013: 102).

Though not all the terms above are taken up in my discussion, they are all important and I include them here for the sake of presenting a complete picture (I discuss other aspects of this picture in Josephides 2015). The pairs that are directly relevant to the current argument are: morality and procedure versus equipment; method versus meditation (care); individualism versus collaboration; ethnography versus second-order participant observation; and reconstruction versus narrative modes. In the first column, morality, method, individualism, ethnography and reconstruction describe 'research' or fieldwork in its 'traditional' form. In the second column, equipment, meditation (care), collaboration, second-order participant observation and narrative modes describe 'work' in the anthropology of the contemporary. Most importantly, morality and method give way to equipment and meditation (care) in the move from 'research' to the 'work' of the anthropology of the contemporary. Morality is the sort of 'ethics' discussed in this volume as being part of knowledge creation, and 'method' is part of the relations mediating between fieldwork and the hard-copy knowledge resulting from it.

In the second-order anthropology of the contemporary, what does it mean to replace morality with equipment, and method with meditation (care)? In the first case, it would bode well if Enlightenment had been achieved, and human beings had reached their seniority and were responsible (Kant [1784] 1983; Nietzsche, various; Foucault 1984). 'Equipment' is not the same as the apparatuses described by Agamben, which are largely enforced from the outside, but a set of ethical practices developed and designed according to the needs of the work (Rabinow and Stavrianakis 2013: 17). An additional distinction that may notionally be added to the table (ibid.: 102) is 'bricolage' on the side of 'research', and 'engineering' on the side of 'work'. Research is cold; work is hot. The second case (replacing method with meditation (care)) also points to such Enlightenment seniority having been achieved.

But the exit from the field is at the same time an entry into a different field, another milieu with its network of obligations. Here we have colleagues – fellow anthropologists or at least scholars – engaged in the creation of a mutually constitutive world. The contemporary is said to be anthropological and not ethnographic, 'in that it attends not directly to the present' but rather only to the 'doubly curated objects and artifacts originally taken from the present' (2013: 104). This is not the place for a discussion of sedimented alienation in Marxist terms, but it should be noted that layers of relations are congealed in any knowledge and do not all necessarily have to sink Lethe-wards (in Greek mythology Lethe was a river in Hades that caused forgetfulness; wine performed that function in Keats's poem 'Ode to a Nightingale', from where 'Lethe-wards' is taken). For the authors, it is now a question of curated elements. What is neglected is a discussion of how the curated objects parallel a transformed self (2013: 105), an operation described in the case of the traditional ethnographic self. But the authors are aware of the need to specify a mode of subjectivation for the anthropologist, who becomes the 'thinking man/woman'.

The setting out of this new field of the anthropology of the contemporary answering to the demands of the day is necessary, exciting, and to be applauded. It should be assumed that anthropological 'research' and 'work' will be carried out in tandem. The latter may be a second research for a more seasoned researcher and the two neat columns in the table may sometimes become blurred. Ethical aspects, especially as outlined in Stengers' distinction between obligations and requirements, may need more attention. There is much to consult in recent research on ethics and anthropology, as the section below demonstrates.

Ethics and Anthropology

'The argument … is simply that the ethical dimension of social life – the fact that everyday conduct is constitutively pervaded by reflective evaluation – is irreducible, and that social theory needs to be reformulated to make our analysis of diverse phenomena and states of affairs cognizant of this'. Thus reasons James Laidlaw in his discussion of virtue, ethics and freedom (2014: 44–45). Ethics here is reflective evaluation.

To understand – gain knowledge – from others and the lives of others, Laidlaw continues, a person must gain 'an imaginative understanding from the inside of a set of ethical concepts and the form of life, and … learn to use and think with those concepts and participate in the form of life, without, as a prerequisite for doing so, having to adopt its concepts and values as his or her own' (2014: 45). Laidlaw cites the philosopher Bernard Williams, who observed that 'capturing the way in which ethical concepts cannot exist other than as woven into a way of life' (ibid.), but also points to the fact of ethical diversity and the need to keep hold of both together. This is the ethnographic stance, which requires that we take seriously the forms of life we describe, learning from them in such a way that they become 'resources in our own critical reflection and self-constitution' (2014: 46). This, for Laidlaw (and I agree), is a precondition for anthropology as ethical practice (see also Kresse 2007). This is another reason for being concerned with the person in any discussion of knowledge, as outlined in the four figures of the knower.

Pradeep Jeganathan provides a thoughtful discussion of the 'episte-mological ethics' of a disciplinary anthropologist, arguing that secur-ing anthropological knowledge 'requires an epistemological ethic of *disciplined affect*' (2005: 150–51). In his attempt to steer a path between this and 'militant political arguments within Tamil nation-alism', Jeganathan argues that epistemology and politics have always been conjoined in the anthropological craft, and many anthropolo-gists will insist that they are 'always already' political (2005: 150). As this view glosses over the location of the political, such a location 'does not sit easily with the epistemological ethics of disciplinary anthropol-ogy' (2005: 151). It is here that he insists on the epistemological ethic of disciplined affect. Citing David Scott's *Formation of Ritual*, he argues that so long as anthropology assumes its objects are self-evident, it remains both ideologically and theoretically colonial (2005: 155). This is part of the internal logic of anthropology, which is not just a form of writing (ethnography).

An important aspect of anthropological ethics is access to ethno-graphic field sites that are the homes of those studied, or sometimes their dystopias. From ethnographic research on torture, Pradeep Jeganathan concludes that anthropological objects 'do not autho-rize transparent access to the world', but 'thinking them through an archive [of post-Enlightenment thought] leads to theoretical gain' (2005: 159). What Jeganathan takes away from this realization con-nects to the insights from Daston (2005) on moral economies: 'the anthropology of the tortured person may hinge on the intelligibility of the pain of the tortured to the investigator, taken as an anthropol-ogist' (2005: 159). That is, ethical practices constitute the person of the anthropologist, who becomes a particular kind of knower because of this ethical construction. Thus, modes of knowing, such as quan-tification and empiricism, 'are secured by *moral economies*'; these are 'particular relations of affect between investigator and field ... and investigator and critical audience' (2005: 160). There is an ethical and epistemological link here with Stengers' (2011) discussion of 'obligations and requirements'.

But Jeganathan turns to Lorraine Daston's argument, in which the empirical is secured by three modes of knowing, or three moral economies: testimony, facticity and novelty; 'testimony works through trust, facticity through civility, and novelty through transformation of curiosity into a virtue' (2005: 160). In this way, the 'investigative self' develops the knowledge through 'disciplined curiosity', in a process that Jeganathan identifies as a moral economy (2005: 161). The category of disciplinary experience is worth pursuing here, especially the suggestive comments on the transactions between personal and disciplinary experience, where personal experience is seen as disciplinary experience's excess (2005: 163): 'These double invocations of experience are perhaps also transacted', he suggests, in a way that produces anthropological knowledge (2005: 163). Jeganathan extends Daston's argument to a moral economy of anthropological knowledge that doubles the personal and the disciplinary, through trust (2005: 164). The anthropologist Veena Das, by bringing in an investigative self, is seen by Jeganathan as doing crucial work in this economy (2005: 160). Trust as part of a moral economy links to the relationship between ethics and knowledge (2005: 164). Most importantly, Jeganathan points to the difference between experimental and experiential, the differences in imagination and interpretation between the sciences and ethnography. Anthropological truth combines a sense of 'moral' as 'certain, well-known, and well-accepted' with the more seventeenth-century idea of 'moral' 'as "sentiment," as disciplined affect' (2005: 165).

In their introduction to their edited volume *Embedding Ethics*, in which Jeganathan's chapter appears, Lynn Meskel and Peter Pels emphasize the need for negotiation between experts and their diverse audiences and question 'the artifice of abstracting ethics from scholarly practice' (2005: 3). They argue against a conception that 'turns the ethical code into a kind of "constitution" for the profession', adjudication rather than negotiation, and requiring a redefinition of the location of anthropological expertise itself (2005: 3, 7). They reject the reliance of symbols of 'expert' and 'ethics' on 'dichotomous purifications of knowledge and morals that customarily dismiss large parts of its everyday workings' (ibid.). They also reject the 'autonomous self' in favour of embedded setting, rethinking expertise and bringing us, via Joel Kahn, to listening to Malaysian voices because 'only they [in Kahn's case] are capable of really shifting us away from the particularistic presuppositions that inform existing cosmopolitan practices' (2005: 8). Yet one might reasonably posit that Malaysians too have 'particularistic presuppositions' and might be giving their point of view from their perspective. As anthropologists we should not fall into the trap of assuming that the people we study always speak with the authority conferred by their community. But Meskel and Pels are surely right to caution against 'disembedding ethics' through various forms of 'professionalist ideology', which results in the neglect of the guiding anthropological debate about the link between theory and method, with a deleterious effect on how anthropologists relate to people during research (2005: 23).

Elsewhere, Pels identifies the ethics concerned in the trickster's dilemma as part of a 'specific technology of the (professional) self' (Pels 2000: 136). The trickster's quandary in audit cultures is peculiar to the constitution of the liberal self and in particular the anthropologist's 'duplex' position (or 'duplicitous' self), one that discovers the difficulties 'of maintaining the liberal desire for individual autonomy of choice and opinion at a distance from political struggle over existing inequalities in the world' (2000: 135–36). In Pels's account, the term 'technologies' suggests the possibility of subterfuge rather than a developmental practice or a more general part of being a person or a self, as in the ancient Greek practices of care of the self. Pels's uncomfortable conclusion encourages this reading: 'owing public allegiance to both research sponsors and research subjects', he argues, anthropologists can show neither of them a 'true' face (2000: 137). While it is true that dilemmas and quandaries are legion, they are not confined to anthropologists; as Stengers tells us, this is the fate of the practitioners of the sciences of contemporaneity, who share the same temporality as those about whom they produce knowledge (Stengers 2011: 378). Nonetheless, the rise of audit means that we must distinguish between ethics 'as a set of quasi-legal principles', the 'ethic' in which a set of principles is deployed, and 'the technologies of self that make both "ethics" and "ethic" operative' (Pels 2000: 146).

Elsewhere in the same volume, Strathern refers to audit's 'rituals of verification' (2000: 283), in which professional protocols have replaced anthropological models of society and culture as providing a cue to the conduct of encounters (2000: 280; a point also taken up in Pels above). Instead, audit and ethics enforce new principles of organization (2000: 281), with codes and practices designed to protect the interests of third parties (2000: 292–3). 'Accountability' is used to refer to this new ethical attitude. For all its merits, the term does not (and was not intended to) go to the heart of the inextricable connection between the knower and the manner in which knowledge must be approached. The following sections go into these questions.

Persons, Knowledge and Ethics:
From Objectivity to Nanomanipulation

In their endlessly fascinating book on objectivity (2010), Daston and Galison posit that epistemology and ethics are intertwined, since a way of being is at the same time a way of knowing (2010: 4). They identify three distinct codes of epistemic virtue occurring in a historical series: 'truth-to-nature, mechanical objectivity, and trained judgment' (2010: 18). The history of scientific objectivity, they contend, is to be understood as part and parcel of the history of the scientific self (2010: 37–39), which is thus linked to epistemic virtues:

> If knowledge were independent of the knower, then it would indeed be puzzling to encounter admonitions, reproaches, and confessions pertaining to the character of the investigator strewn among descriptions of the character of the investigation. Why does an epistemology need an ethics? But if objectivity and other epistemic virtues were intertwined with the historically conditioned person of the inquirer, shaped by scientific practices that blurred into techniques of the self, moralized epistemology was just what one would expect. Epistemic virtues would turn out to be literal, not just metaphorical, virtues. (2010: 39)

In this understanding, techniques of the self concern epistemic virtues, which in science go beyond directives to 'know thyself' but 'are preached and practiced in order to know the world, not the self' (2010: 39). At the time of the Scientific Revolution key epistemological claims about the character of science depended on 'the schism between knower and knowledge', such that the alchemist's failure, for instance, could no longer be blamed on an impure soul. Personal qualities required of the scientist (or knower) were seen as 'matters of competence, not ethics' (ibid.).

While objectivism split knower and knowledge, there remained a core ethical imperative on how to do science and become a scientist: 'the humility of the seeker, the wonder of the psalmist who praises creation, the asceticism of the saint' (ibid.: 40). The mastery of scientific practices was linked to self-mastery; as long as knowledge posits a knower, Daston and Galison argue, 'the self of the knower will be at epistemological issue' (ibid.). Virtues may differ over time, but they continue to appeal to techniques of the self that are interwoven with scientific practices (2010: 41). Nineteenth-century objectivity preached asceticism, grounding morality in science, but its requirements were more modest than previously. The 'ways of being in the world' at issue included 'training the senses in scientific observation, keeping lab notebooks, drawing specimens, habitually monitoring one's own beliefs and hypotheses, quieting the will, and channeling the attention'. Thus, more than merely expressing the self, these 'technologies of the self' forge and constitute it (2010: 199). What grew in significance was the view of subjectivity, more and more feared as 'the enemy within', the 'untrustworthy scientific self' (2010: 197–98).

Daston and Galison outline two visions of the self at that time: the passive self, where the origin of the network (interpreted as a spider) dominates in a unity of the self with all its networks, and the active self, Henry James's 'assertive subject of subjectivity', who meets experience with outstretched hand, receiving thought and feeling and 'presiding over' the clamour of perception (2010: 200–1). The 'passive and permeable self, shaped by its environment', is fragmented, 'fragile as a cobweb' and 'guaranteed only by memory and the continuity of consciousness', always under threat both from within and without. By contrast, the Jamesian assertive self was active and integrated, possessing autonomous will, 'fusing raw sensations into coherent experience', acting on the world and projecting itself outward (2010: 201).

In their investigation of the kinds of selves that meet the demands of epistemic virtues, such as truth-to-nature and objectivity, Daston and Galison observe that 'prototypical knowers of nature', such as the 'insightful sage' and the 'diligent worker', can be reconstructed from the biographical literature. They take this as evidence of 'how an ethos must be grafted onto a scientific persona, [and] an ethical and epistemological code imagined as a self'. This supports their argument 'about how epistemology and ethos fuse' (2010: 204). *Doing* science moulded the scientist; may we say likewise that doing ethnography moulded the anthropologist? Biographies of Newton exemplify how 'a specific historical individual is turned into a model of the prevailing scientific persona' (2010: 216), until in the mid-nineteenth century a new type of intellectual emerged, who needed a coherent, well-ordered self: the scientist (2010: 217). In the 1860s, when 'passive observation' came to be opposed to 'active experimentation', the scientist had to be both 'speculative and bold' *and* a passive observer (2010: 243); thus the personality of the scientific knower became split. But no theory lasts forever. 'Only relations endure', and for Poincaré they 'constituted objectivity' (2010: 288–89).

As mentioned, Daston and Galison identify three historical codes of epistemic virtue: truth-to-nature, mechanical objectivity and trained judgement (2010: 19). They now move to their third avatar of scientific self: trained judgement (ibid.: 309), experienced, trained eye/observer (2010: 330, 333, 338). They identify four features of judgement (from Morgan, Keenan and Kellman): classification involving similar relations not specified in terms of a fixed set of standard criteria; an evaluative process that is not necessarily a conscious one; a cognitive process represented as holistic; and finally, precision: 'nothing in the process of judgment is necessarily vague or indefinite' (2010: 335). Early twentieth-century scientists 'reframed the scientific self', making room 'for an unconscious, subjective element' (2010: 361), but by the mid-twentieth century, 'objectivity and subjectivity no longer appeared like opposite poles; rather, like a strand of DNA, they executed the complementary pairing that underlay understanding of the working objects of science' (2010: 361). As will be seen, these codes of epistemic virtue form part of the maker of scientific knowers.

Having made their case about the history of objectivity, Daston and Galison now reach some bold and superb conclusions. All epistemology begins in fear, they write, and seeks reasons. Objectivity fears subjectivity, but subjectivity is the core self, 'the root of both knowledge and error' (2010: 374). It is not 'a weakness of the self to be corrected or controlled ... It *is* the self' (ibid.). Objectivity, on the other hand, 'is not just one intellectual discipline among many. It is a sacrifice' (ibid.). All epistemological approaches identify some individuating features as detrimental and harmful, but what makes objectivity different is 'the conviction that *all* such individuating features interfere with knowledge' (ibid.: 380). Yet, as the authors have demonstrated, scientific objectivity, 'like all techniques of the self, cultivated certain aspects of the self at the expense of others' (2010: 381).

Something seismic seems to have happened in the move from representation to presentation (2010: 363), radically altering the tone of the authors' narrative. In all forms of representation, they observe, 'fidelity to nature was always a triple obligation: visual, epistemological, ethical' (2010: 382). But what happens when fidelity is abandoned and nature merges with artifact? These are images used to alter the physical world: haptic images, enabling manipulation of objects using the senses of touch and proprioception, replace virtual images. The latter function for representation; the former for presentation, 'presented like wares in a shop' (2010: 383). ('Haptic' refers to the sense of touch, and the perception and manipulation of objects using the senses of touch and proprioception, thus receiving stimuli produced within the organism.)

Haptic images are part and parcel of the fabrication process itself, and positioned as art as well as science (2010: 384). To extrapolate: how would ethnographies-as-tools be, rather than ethnographies-as-evidence? (2010: 385). Ethnography as actual, as interpretation, as tool, meshing with a new kind of knower: the engineering self. 'In the realm of nanomanipulation, images are examples of right depiction – but of objects that are being made, not found' (2010: 391). With nanomanipulable images, then, scientists as knowers move from the contemplative life to the active life of science, no longer 'under the heading of representation' but 'under the heading of intervention' (2010: 392). This is a move away from the field, to theory (see Rabinow above). Ontology is not of much interest to engineers-as-knowers, who just want to know what will work; efficacy trumps explanations (2010: 303).

In the move from representation to presentation, anthropologists might consider the periodization table on p. 371. Where would they see themselves fitting under the three categories of 'scientific self' identified as available to scientists at different times?

Twentieth Century:	Trained Judgment (scientific self: trained expert; interpreted image; pattern depiction; families of objects)
Nineteenth Century:	Mechanical Objectivity (scientific self: will-abnegating worker; mechanical image; procedural depiction; particular objects)
Eighteenth Century:	Truth-to-Nature (scientific self: sage; reasoned image; idealized depiction; universal objects). (modified from Daston and Galison 2010: 371)

Compare the table above with the table on p. 413 on right depiction ('image-as-tool'). Here, object manipulation is coupled with aesthetics in a presentation that fuses artifactual and natural (as opposed to the fidelity to nature in representation). Is there a place there for anthropology? Have anthropologists moved from four-eyed sight to blind sight to physiognomic sight to haptic sight? (2010: 413). The presentational table on p. 414, in which a scientist's ethos is combined with the device orientation of the industrial engineer and the authorial ambition of the artist, produces a hybrid image of simulation, mimesis and manipulation. Daston and Galison ask whether we have now moved to a 'simultaneity of making and seeing', with '"nanofactured" goods straddling the divide between natural and artifactual' (compare Bruno Latour's reported quip: 'It's true, I made it in the laboratory'). Nanotechnology is a clear intervention by the scientist that brings about the deepest change at the level of the engineering-scientific self, from fidelity to right manufacture, calling for an examination of the development of scientific virtues (ibid.: 414–45).

The final paragraph of *Objectivity* invites a comparison with anthropology. Are images of truth-to-nature/idealized world equivalent to perceptions of the 'noble savage' (though not anthropologists' depictions)? Is their 'vaunted objectivity, all nature and none of us' equivalent to cultural relativism? Is 'trained judgement', images as bridges, 'part us, part not-us' the postmodernist 1980s turn of fieldwork as creating something new? And what corresponds to the latest phase of images as part tool kit and part art, nanomanufacturers' aesthetic objects and marketing tags, through which 'to create and manipulate a brave new world of atom-sized objects'? (2010: 415). The scientific image 'begins to shed its representational aspect altogether as it takes on its power to build'. Once again, Daston and Galison tell us, the scientific self is in flux (ibid.).

Daston and Galison's history of knowledge links epistemic virtues with distinctive selves of the knower and thus 'traces a trajectory of a different shape from familiar histories of philosophy and science' (2010: 375). Though there are different models of knowers and knowing, a certain kind of knower is always 'the precondition for knowledge' (2010: 376). In the historical examination of the three types of epistemic virtue (truth-to-nature, objectivity and trained judgement) the authors wanted to show that epistemology is 'less about trailblazing than about path clearing'; removing sources of error, epistemology is a route to truth (2010: 19, 377). It can be seen, as Chappell outlined, that types of knowledge bring with them 'epistemic credit', which can be claimed only with the relevant knowledge-how (Chappell 2014: 265). It would be easy but unnecessary to slot the four 'figures of knowers' and their experiences into the three distinct historical codes of epistemic virtue. There is room for the terminal pure observer, the thinking man/woman attending to the self and ferociously championing the virtues of knowledge, the knower shaped simultaneously by the content and the context of knowing, and the researcher placed between obligations and requirements; the latter being, so far, a constant.

But with the haptic move and nanomanipulable images, Daston and Galison find themselves quite literally out of their depth; there is no depth of history to enable a comforting narrative, in the sense that any history, since we have survived it, is comforting. But to end with the beginning, while we remain human, an epistemology without ethics is unlikely. We are just not sure what form it will take.

Conclusion

This meditation on knowledge, ethics and the person as knower has attempted to cut through, but without ignoring (perhaps 'bracketing') the constraints enforced by 'rehearsed talk' (Josephides 2008b) about such relations. Instead I considered, historically and in terms of professional, social, personal and human relations, how knowers and knowledge developed in tandem with the current 'demands of the day', understood as the undeniable calls issuing from the practical, physical, intellectual and epistemological contexts of those knowledge-creation relations. At all times, no matter how changed the context, such calls were grounded in/imposed by/arose from the conditions of what was being studied, and through relations with that object of study that, in the process, became a subject that blurred the object/subject lines in some respects. 'Some respects' is a loaded phrase and should not remain a vague, 'get-out-of-ethics' card. The seekers after knowledge cannot be shriven by professional ethics codes or audits, which mostly succeed in transforming anthropological knowledge by adding a 'player' with an unclear role in knowledge creation (Pels, Strathern); a player, in effect, with stakes in quite a different pot.

While the meditation/study/investigation found that all knowledge creation was linked through the knower to certain expectations about what was proper and demanded by the exigencies of the content of that knowledge, it also found that the ethics concerned in each case changed and expanded, without implying betrayal of the persons and things involved at different stages of knowledge-building. In the case of anthropology, while in the field, the ethnographer proceeded as in Stengers' description of the primatologist, attentive to the questions posed by those they were observing, 'because [they] demanded it of them in order to be well-studied' (Stengers et al. 2014: 37). It was 'the exigencies of the profession' that made good scientific practice (2014: 38). But after exiting from the field, as Rabinow describes, and entering into new alliances, whether intellectual, epistemological, professional, pedagogical or social, in short a different milieu of networks and obligations, common purpose is made with others beyond the field, without thereby betraying the subjects of the original study. As mentioned earlier, the thinking man/woman bore 'the obligation to care for the knowledge and the bearing of it' (Rabinow 2011: 3).

This chapter started by questioning the prevailing view of the relationship between ethics and anthropological knowledge creation, seen as an ethnographic encounter shaped by cultural and

contextual determinants. Part of my disquietude was about the legitimacy, especially in today's world, of making a distinction between
local and non-local knowledge, and seeing the relationship between
the two in terms of an ethical attitude or a sort of methodology of
understanding. This is not to posit a dichotomy between fieldwork
and theory-making; theories take shape in the field and are grounded
in local observation, experience and relations, then take flight into
wider knowledge worlds. But it is to insist that the many layers result
in plural obligations, imposed by what is being studied, by those participating in the study at all levels and stages and by the complex
responses called forth from our own humanity. The tension between
ethics and knowledge cannot be resolved while the requirement of
knowledge entails closure and distancing. Thus being ethical is always
a struggle (and an ongoing project), and the degree of success can
never be known in advance.

Lisette Josephides is Professor of Anthropology at Queen's University
Belfast. Previously she has taught at the University of Papua New
Guinea, the London School of Economics and the University of
Minnesota. She trained in anthropology and philosophy and con-
ducted lengthy fieldwork in Papua New Guinea. Major books include
The Production of Inequality (1984) *Melanesian Odysseys* (2008) *We the
Cosmopolitans: Moral and Existential Conditions of Being Human* (2014,
co-editor A. Hall) and *Knowledge and Ethics in Anthropology: Obligations
and Requirements* (2015).

References

Agamben, G. 2009. *What is an Apparatus?* Stanford: Stanford University Press.
Aristotle. 1984. *The Complete Works*, Volume Two, edited by J. Barnes.
    Princeton, NJ: Princeton University Press.
Chappell, T. 2014. *Knowing What to Do: Imagination, Virtue and Platonism in
    Ethics.* Oxford: Oxford University Press.
Daston, L. and P. Galison. 2010. *Objectivity.* Brooklyn: Zone Books.
Foucault, M. 1984. 'What is Enlightenment?' in P. Rabinow (ed.), *The Foucault
    Reader.* New York: Pantheon Books, pp. 32–50.
Gaita, R. 2002. *A Common Humanity: Thinking about Truth, Love and Justice.*
    London: Routledge.
Hastrup, K. 1995. 'Prologue: The Itinerary and the Ethnographic Present',
    in K. Hastrup, *A Passage to Anthropology: Between Experience and Theory.*
    London: Routledge.

Ingold, T. 2013. *Making: Anthropology, Archaeology, Art and Architecture.* London: Routledge.

Jackson, M. 2005. *Existential Anthropology: Events, Exigencies and Effects.* New York and Oxford: Berghahn.

Jeganathan, P. 2005. 'Pain, Politics, and the Epistemological Ethics of Anthropological Disciplinarity', in L. Meskell and P. Pels (eds), *Embedding Ethics.* Oxford: Berg, pp. 147–67.

Jenkins, T. 1994. 'Fieldwork and the Perception of Everyday Life', *MAN* 29(2): 433–56.

Josephides, L. 2008a. 'Virtual Returns: Fieldwork Recollected in Tranquillity', in T. Lau, C. High and L. Chua (eds), *How Do We Know? Evidence, Ethnography, and the Making of Anthropological Knowledge.* Cambridge Scholars Publishing, pp. 179–200.

———. 2008b. *Melanesian Odysseys: Negotiating the Self, Narrative and Modernity.* New York and Oxford: Berghahn.

———. 2014. 'Imagining the Future: An Existential and Practical Activity', in W. Rollason (ed.), *Future Selves in the Pacific – Projects, Politics and Interests.* New York and Oxford: Berghahn, pp. 28–47.

———. 2015. 'Obligations and Requirements: The Contexts of Knowledge', in L. Josephides (ed.), *Knowledge and Ethics in Anthropology: Obligations and Requirements.* London: Bloomsbury Academic, pp. 1–27.

Kant, I. 1983 [1784]. 'An Answer to the Question: What is Enlightenment?', in *Perpetual Peace and Other Essays.* Indianapolis and Cambridge: Hackett.

Kresse, K. 2007. 'Practising an Anthropology of Philosophy: General Reflections and the Swahili Context', in M. Harris (ed.), *Ways of Knowing: New Approaches in the Anthropology of Experience and Learning.* New York and Oxford: Berghahn, pp. 42–63.

Kvanvig, J. 2003. *The Value of Knowledge and the Pursuit of Understanding.* Cambridge University Press.

Laidlaw, J. 2014. *The Subject of Virtue: An Anthropology of Ethics and Freedom.* Cambridge: Cambridge University Press.

Lambek, M. 2010. *Ordinary Ethics: Anthropology, Language, and Action.* New York: Fordham University Press.

McGahern, J. 2003. 'Introduction' to J. Williams' *Augustus: A Novel.* London: Vintage.

Meskel, L. and P. Pels (eds). 2005. *Embedding Ethic.* Oxford: Berg, pp. 1–26.

Pels, P. 2000. 'The Trickster's Dilemma: Ethics and the Technologies of the Anthropological Self', in M. Strathern (ed.) *Audit Cultures.* London: Routledge, pp. 135–72.

Plato. 1997. *Complete Works*, edited by J.M. Cooper. Indianapolis, ID: Hackett.

Pritchard, D. 2009. 'Knowledge', in J. Shand (ed.) *Central Issues of Philosophy.* Wiley-Blackwell, pp. 24–36 (p. 13 of online article).

Rabinow, P. 2003. *Anthropos Today: Reflections on Modern Equipment.* Princeton, NJ: Princeton University Press.

————. 2011. *The Accompaniment: Assembling the Contemporary.* Chicago University Press.

Rabinow, P. and A. Stavrianakis. 2013. *Demands of the Day.* Chicago University Press.

Schutz, A. 1967 [1932]. *The Phenomenology of the Social World.* Evanston: Northwestern University Press.

Sloterdijk, P. 2010 [2006]. *Rage and Time: A Psychopolitical Investigation.* New York: Columbia University Press.

————. 2012 [2010]. *The Art of Philosophy: Wisdom as a Practice* [*Scheintod im Denken*]. New York: Columbia University Press.

Stengers, I. 2011. *Cosmopolitics II.* Minneapolis and London: University of Minnesota Press (French version 2003).

Stengers, I. and V. Despre et al. 2014 [2011]. *Women who Make a Fuss: The Unfaithful Daughters of Virginia Woolf.* Minneapolis, MN: Univocal.

Strathern, M. 2000. *Audit Cultures.* London: Routledge.

Williams, J. 2003 [1971]. *Augustus: A Novel.* London: Vintage.

AFTERWORD

Marilyn Strathern

'The interview is saturated with ethical concerns'. An early impetus for this volume lay in a conference on the interview,[1] and this was the original opening line to a panel rubric, the panel being convened as 'the ethics of (relations of) knowledge creation'. That starting point – though by no means the only one – illuminates a central concern of this volume. It is with knowledge understood as an attribution of persons; whether or not it is directly about them and their lives, it is part of them and their lives. Regardless of the kind of information or data it may also be, this origin is routinely acknowledged in the protocols of interviewing. Yet the interview is itself only a starting point for the challenge that this book takes up. In the human and social sciences, insofar as activities that create knowledge for the person of the investigator are activities involving other persons, there is an ethical dimension to the very definition of what 'knowledge' becomes. As we shall see, the relations turn out to be a bit more complicated than a matter of interpersonal interaction; the original bracketing pointed to relations whose objects are as yet to be specified.

There are other sources of impetus, not least the very lively interest currently shown in the anthropology of ethics, with its own diverse relations to the anthropology of moralities as well as engagement with diverse philosophies. Here reflections on the conditions for human flourishing are sometimes held to reflect (positively) back on the enquirer, but invariably require assembling knowledge about other lives. An enquirer's relations with the object of enquiry, in these circumstances, entail understanding such lives as the lives of persons who are also enquirers. This serves as a refreshing divergence from the current and equally present understanding of ethics as protocol or code, especially in the form of institutional ethics, whose paramount concern with protection makes the object of its relations not persons but human subjects. The arena, familiar to medical science, is manifested in ethics review boards and bioethics committees, as well as in ethical guidelines and research clearance procedures for the prospective fieldworker. Here standard processes that define an ethical approach to knowledge creation may well circumscribe in advance any proposal to interview anyone.

The volume is at an intriguing point between these two positions. First, it addresses understandings of ethical action across diverse social and cultural fields. However, its particular focus is on understanding what it means for persons to acquire 'knowledge' of one another when the question has already been accented by foregrounding the investigator as a kind of person who acquires knowledge (that is, knowledge for the investigator's self) from another. This foregrounding of the 'interviewer' (aka investigator, fieldworker) is most apparent in the first part of the book, but it has a ripple effect as the book moves through what it calls indirect or mediated ethnography to, in the third part, more general concerns about ethical practice in acquiring knowledge from and about persons. Second, these final chapters touch directly on issues in institutional ethics. Here, however, apparently familiar examples from bioethics (concerning genetic and reproductive information) yield questions about the nature of personal knowledge – obtained or withheld – that are not reducible to guides for action. Indeed they presage a concluding chapter that takes knowledge not just as a means to reflection but, in and of itself, as an object of reflection. What relations must be mobilized to create this knowledge about knowledge?

There is a sense in which the discussions in between, presented in part two, pinpoint an enquiry that the concerns of the first and last parts, each in their own way, occlude. What do we learn when we learn about the ethical constraints on knowledge gathering under conditions where there is a specific investigator (interviewer) yet where this investigator is a kind of third party, one whose own capacity for an ethical response is rendered – and this is observed with sympathy – momentarily nugatory or after the event? Let us reflect further on the movement of the book.

Encounters

The opening chapters ask us specifically to think about the ethics of knowledge creation as evinced through interpersonal encounters, for which the interview might stand as a metonym. For a fieldworker who assumes he/she is going to collect a range of information on various topics by manifold means, there is an arresting conjuncture here. On the one hand, 'informants' appear not just as people with information but as people with knowledge. To consider the way they work out for themselves their purposes, aspirations and estimations of worth focuses attention on persons caught up in their own circumstances, with their own trajectories of reflection and judgement in the company of others. Such knowledge may then become visible as part of an ethical life. On the other hand, encounters sought out by the anthropologist – whether or not there is a specific question and answer format – points to a form of interaction that cuts across the comings and goings of ordinary social intercourse. To be conscious of that form may well make interviewers conscious of themselves as ethical persons, insofar as it is their reflections, reasons and aspirations for the encounter, the kind of knowledge they hope to acquire, which seemingly frame it. There is nothing new here. But if this conjuncture repeats in microcosm the two positions sketched above, these chapters thicken them in interesting ways.

Just as thinking about ethics, then, singles out one dimension of the relational toing and froing of interactions, the interpersonal encounter (the 'interview') is cut out from all the lines of investigation open to the fieldworker. Yet what happens, we may ask, when the only possibility for conversation is the interview in the strict sense, when one can only talk to people by paying them visits, whose lives permit no other kind of interaction? This was Grønseth's situation (Chapter One): her interaction with Papushpa was circumscribed because Papushpa was circumscribed, unable to leave the house. While the fieldworker could put her encounter into the context of a wider study of Tamil refugees in Norway, as far as that person was concerned it seemed that the only resources that could be brought to the encounter lay between them. Grønseth describes how the situation at once elicited her empathy and challenged it. She had theorized 'empathy' as her own ethical stance. But Papushpa required her to accept the conditions of confinement (if not of suffering) that she (Papushpa) had accepted. Behind every person are other people, and whether she wanted to or not, the fieldworker had to bring into the picture other members of the family. Now Grønseth presents the visits she made as different from the other kinds of interviews she conducted through an interpreter, and different from the sharing of experience that she calls 'embodying the other'. She was taught a lesson about power that she might otherwise have been reluctant to accept; the reader, in turn, is shown a triangulation of relations that seemingly exceeds the particular way in which a self-other paradigm otherwise does so much work in this chapter.

But suppose, again, that anything like an interview as a form of interpersonal encounter is almost a practical impossibility. The inhabitants of the Chilean island of Apiao (Chapter Two) would not extend empathy, and with that the possibility of open conversation, to strangers. Bacchiddu understood this as a treatment of her 'difference', although, as she explains, people were also reserved among themselves. It was only by learning to relate Apiao-style that Bacchiddu learnt anything. This was the beginning of an enquiry that was also to illuminate a later study of potential strangers, Chilean adoptees in Sardinian families. As far as Apiao was concerned, in order to do anything she had to know for herself what knowledge meant to the islanders. Local, shared, relational knowledge was not objectified in the same way as the 'knowledge' that strangers and witches brought with them, a danger to everyone else: an instrument of discrimination where there should be none, non-encompassable. This she came to know. Bacchiddu's own possibilities for acquiring information were thus pre-empted by conventions about knowledge (knowledge essential to social life was not readily turned into 'information' – there was, to take an example, no interest in gossip). For much of what might have been its relational potential was, so to speak, closed to the fieldworker (she could not experience her strangeness as they did), and in a manner that bore an uncanny comparison with a realm of dangerous knowledge on Sardinia. Indeed the relational implications of information about birth and adoption, the knowledge it creates for people, gives an insight in turn as to how the reader might think of local knowledge in Apiao.

Chapter Three addresses four different styles of knowledge creation, in order to put into a comparative frame a discussion of institutional ethics that in some senses anticipates concerns raised in the last part of the book. Kohn moves from the Scottish islands – where her direct enquiries ('interviews') were seen as dabbling in local history and elicited answers that parroted it, so that she had to try informal techniques – to surreptitious participation (risk-taking) in Nepal, to the martial arts master who took control of her questions and orchestrated their encounter. Importantly, the formality of the interview here allowed things to be said that would not be said otherwise; but, in an echo of Papushpa's control of the ethnographer, Kohn makes clear the considerations of power that lay behind the master's insistence on form. In another echo of Chapter One, she then turns to prison inmates, only to find that they were in one sense not imprisoned; that revelation had to come through an indirect encounter, the correspondence by letter-writing that mostly avoided asking questions. Kohn might be summing up this set of chapters when she says that the ethicality of field-based research must lie in the practice itself. Serendipity and flexibility are not the prerogative of one fieldwork style alone, and the reader has been introduced to several different framings of relations. Kohn thus comes to ethical review boards with a complex appreciation of what needs defending and what might be open to scrutiny. Ethical oversight, as much as response, is damaged if it is imagined that everything is predictable in advance. In effect, where others might see politics, she lays out an ethical position: one should not shut down the potential in any kind of encounter and this applies to anthropological dealings with review boards too.

Layers

If keeping alive the capacity for ethical response is to be cherished by the investigator, what of those situations where the investigator is a kind of third party, one whose own capacity for ethical response is challenged? Such moments may emerge in any context, including some of those already brought to the reader's attention. In part two of the book they move into focus. And what comes into focus with these moments are worlds of reference at once beyond and within the interpersonal encounter.

There seems a double triangulation of relations in Huttunen's account of the request that Mustafa makes of her (Chapter Four). The first triangulation, conceptually understood, was embodied in different social personas. Mustafa telling his story to a psychotherapist also wanted to bring in an anthropologist, a witness to those parts of his account concerning what had happened in Bosnia that he regarded as – or that he created as – extending beyond his relations with the therapist. (These relations may have been crucial to his making the request, as Huttunen's comparison with the public telling of truth commissions suggests.) The story was, as it were, no longer being told in Finland. Rather like the appearance of the prisoners' letters in Chapter Three, the reader is told that Mustafa produces a written statement, a list of atrocities as they were once told in Bosnia, and then duplicates it for events to which he was himself a more immediate witness. The second triangulation, for which the anthropologist's receipt of the lists was a hinge, established the speaker along with those to whom he was speaking – and an audience that the anthropologist cognized as the world – as the generators of 'global opinion', the witnesses from afar forever missing from the events when they occurred. It is as though the ethnographer were being treated at once as a kind of screen and as a kind of channel, both reflecting back the layerings of the patient's own social persona and affording him the possibility of translating his knowledge into the kind of information that the world should have. Huttunen's hesitations capture the (ethical) reality of the situation: there was no simple sense in which she could act as an intermediary on his behalf.

What in several of the accounts has made the ethnographer 'open' to learning has been the capacity, or freedom, to draw in personal resources pertinent to the moment. There seems a potential shift of viewpoints on this in Chapter Five, depending on whether one considers Bradley's perspective or that of the local researchers, whose dilemmas she documents. However, the ethnographer as research coordinator appeared caught in the same multilayered situation as the locally recruited fieldworkers. It is not just that the latter were carrying out interviews according to the dictates of a research programme designed by others far away; they were reduced in the eyes of those who saw them simply as extractors of information, and certainly not allowed to analyse the data.[2] (What makes an anthropologist of a fieldworker, among other things, is that data collection is followed by knowledge-making.) Then, on top of this, they were asked to do 'ethnography'. Another world of reference! It was assumed that their being 'local' would offer the best chances of high quality information. Instead this became a source of ethical dilemma. Might a distant research programme have been better tolerated alongside distancing interviews of the structured kind, which they obviously preferred? (The interviewers would at least have been able to borrow some authority for themselves). But being required to conduct informal conversations set up problems in all kinds of relations. As Bradley implies, retrospectively, if at the outset the fieldworkers had been asked, maybe they could have brought to the study their own reflections on knowledge practices. It is not often that a researcher in her position spells out such unease, including some awkward consequences of trying to be true to ethnographic methods.

Horizons

Yet another world of reference seems ushered in by the first two chapters of the last section. Until now, attention to 'ethics' has assumed an interplay of interpretations or understandings between writer and reader prompted by the circumstances presented for consideration. What might be recognized as an ethical orientation on the part of an investigator is conveyed as reflection on the part of an author.

Such orientations are variously attached to, among other things, the conduct of encounters (the limits of the interview), self-governance (nurturing the imagination, extending empathy), translation (how intimate knowledge morphs into general information), and – ever present in the background – practices of description. Together these slide into expectations surrounding interpersonal relations, including the parameters of trust, mistrust and the 'complexities and contradictions' (Chapter Five) of interaction. It is a sine qua non for anthropologists that something of their interlocutors' own (multiple) worlds of reference are in the picture, and in terms of the interests of this volume the implications of speaking about knowledge. We now jump into another world. It is signalled by the repositioning of the author, who is an investigator with a different range of relations: with published texts, circulated reports and media communications. While the other chapters have at times moved in and out of such authorial relations, for these it is a primary source of creativity. And the 'ethics' has shifted to what is – or is made to be – audible in public discussion, when a public is imagined as a population that looks to the state for well-being or appeals to society for an endorsement of values.

While Finkler (Chapter Six) raises several questions of her own from an examination of the rise of personalized genetic testing in the United States, she also gives us the terms of the accompanying debates. These include issues that are recognizably ethical in the wider medical field, for instance privacy and confidentiality, as well as matters that, depending on context, may or may not signal ethical concerns, such as property and ownership. It is the relations between such terms that seem the first step to determining ethicality. Thus a central concern of the chapter is with what has been rendered contradictory about heredity: appropriate to the autonomy of individuals, persons may bypass any dealings with those to whom they are related, yet in gaining information about themselves also gain information about them. Here come in terms already ethically loaded (responsibility) or that acquire ethical resonance (concealment). This ready play between terms, the chapter shows, cannot cover up an ongoing ideational and potentially powerful shift consonant with the very idea of the new genetics as 'information processing', namely the eclipse of what anthropologists might call social knowledge. It is encapsulated in the ancestry analyses that obviate the need to know one's ancestors. As an amalgam of health indicators, diagnostic markers, genetic predispositions and, as Finkler observes, the biotechnology industry, the assemblage that is self-knowledge assumes, like psychotherapy (Chapter Four), a global form. Dangerous knowledge (Chapter Two), it generates its counterpart in risk control. But the chapter also raises a question that escapes ready formulation in ethical terms: does people's ignorance about the implications and imperfections of so-called genetic knowledge, as gleaned from personalized testing, matter?

The question is echoed in Chapter Seven. It is one that can only be asked from a third party position, that is, from those who have more information at their disposal than the protagonists, which Melhuus suggests is the case with the Norwegian state. The question, philosophically speaking, is whether a child ignorant of its genetic origin does not really know who it is. This arises in a context where the resolution of ethical issues is seen as a prelude to regulation, and where the state is charged with acting in the best interests of 'society'. Society's 'core values' are codified in ethical precepts that may apply to individuals (self-determination) or to itself – society – at large (respect for human dignity). The prominence given to knowledge, made evident in the two spheres of reproductive medicine discussed here, entails an evaluation of not-knowing as well as knowing, and the possibility of an ethically sustained ignorance. Yet who should have access to information, who should hold it or withhold it, and as Melhuus puts it, the whole critical matter of who is the 'knower', are issues that seem, in the moulding of public debate, to spill over the handful of recurring precepts that signal an 'ethical' response. The institutionalization of ethics, ideologically aligned with the common sense of the people or not, recalls the review boards mentioned in Chapter Three, which make it unethical to acquire information outside what has already received clearance. What spills over there is everything entailed in acquiring knowledge through relations with persons. Here, through Melhuus's account of changing political preoccupations, we see how particular social values acquire ethical correctness. A parallel spillover for states, societies and their publics is the issue of how ethical an 'ethically correct' position can (ever) be.

Josephides reminds us of the rationale of the volume as a whole, that knowledge is an attribute of persons, thus always implying a knower, with all the implications this has for the enquirer's quest for knowledge through the knowledge of others (Chapter Eight). At the same time, the preceding chapters indicate that when we think of knowledge as acquired or held by persons, we are probably thinking of knowledge as we might think of information or data. Apiao local knowledge (Chapter Two) is not the only insight into an a-informational world, but presents a stark case of a very different relation between 'it' and the knower – in truth, it is probably not that order of relation at all. In other words, the kind of Euro-American 'knowledge' that is itself the object of enquiry is subject to the same epistemic practices of objectification as other such objects. (The tautology is unavoidable.) Enlarging on the need for historicization (in Chapter Six, concerning probability and risk; in Chapter Seven, the waxing and waning of certain public virtues), Josephides' turn to the history of objectivity illuminates just why it is (culturally, socially) appropriate for a present-day human, or social-science investigator to be aware of 'the person'. Knowing and knower may be more or less distinctive or convergent, but exist for each other. Perhaps it is not surprising that in a collection written by anthropologists such a coexistence surfaces most readily for the persona of the investigator. The different types of persons (knowers) outlined here are observers and thinkers pondering on the responsibilities they acquire with the knowledge they acquire. Do they invite comparison with other 'third party' knowledge-holders, as we have encountered in bioethical contexts?

Looking back from this chapter over the earlier contributions to this volume is to appreciate the obvious, but needing to be spoken, premise that the authorial reflections derived not from the encounters with their specific (local) conditions but rather from the 'virtual returns' these encounters stimulated. Differing fields of relations have come into view. Together these accounts compose a portrait, indeed a portfolio, of considerable and very timely worth: captured here are diverse conditions under which one may discern just how, in constituting 'the person of the anthropologist', ethical practices produce 'a particular kind of knower'.

Marilyn Strathern is Emeritus Professor of Social Anthropology, Cambridge, and Life President of the Association of Social Anthropologists. Her research is divided between Papua New Guinean and British ethnography. She has written on reproductive technologies, intellectual and cultural property, and 'critique of good practice', an umbrella for reflections on audit and accountability, and has served with the Nuffield Council on Bioethics.

Notes

1. See ASA Monographs 49, *The Interview: An Ethnographic Approach*, ed. J Skinner, London: Berg.
2. I take the liberty of drawing on an observation made in an earlier draft of this chapter, which seems pertinent to the discussion here.

INDEX